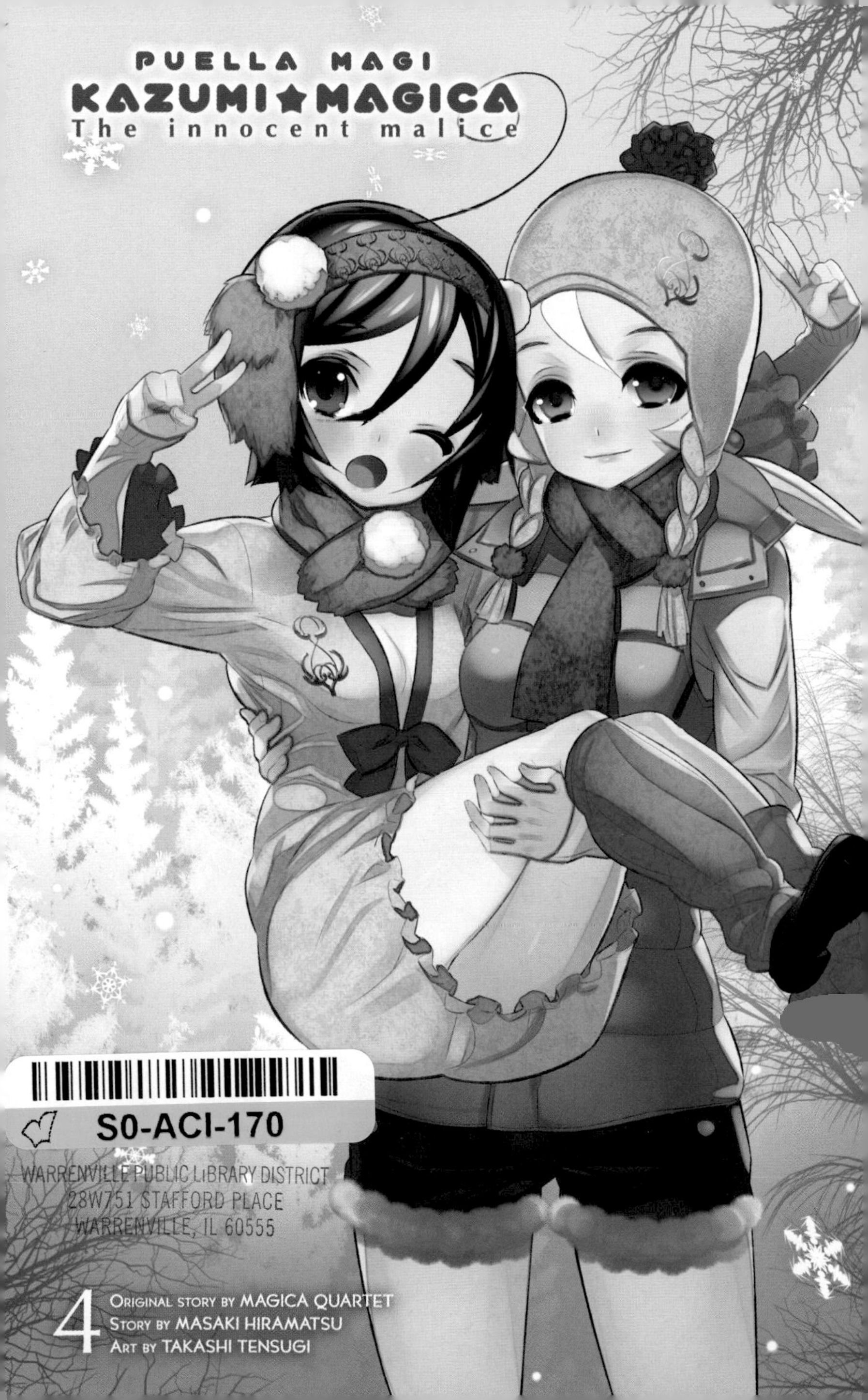
PUELLA MAGI
KAZUMI MAGICA
The innocent malice
4
Original story by MAGICA QUARTET
Story by MASAKI HIRAMATSU
Art by TAKASHI TENSUGI

4

PUELLA MAGI KAZUMI MAGICA
The innocent malice

Original story by Magica Quartet / Story by Masaki Hiramatsu / Art by Takashi Tensugi

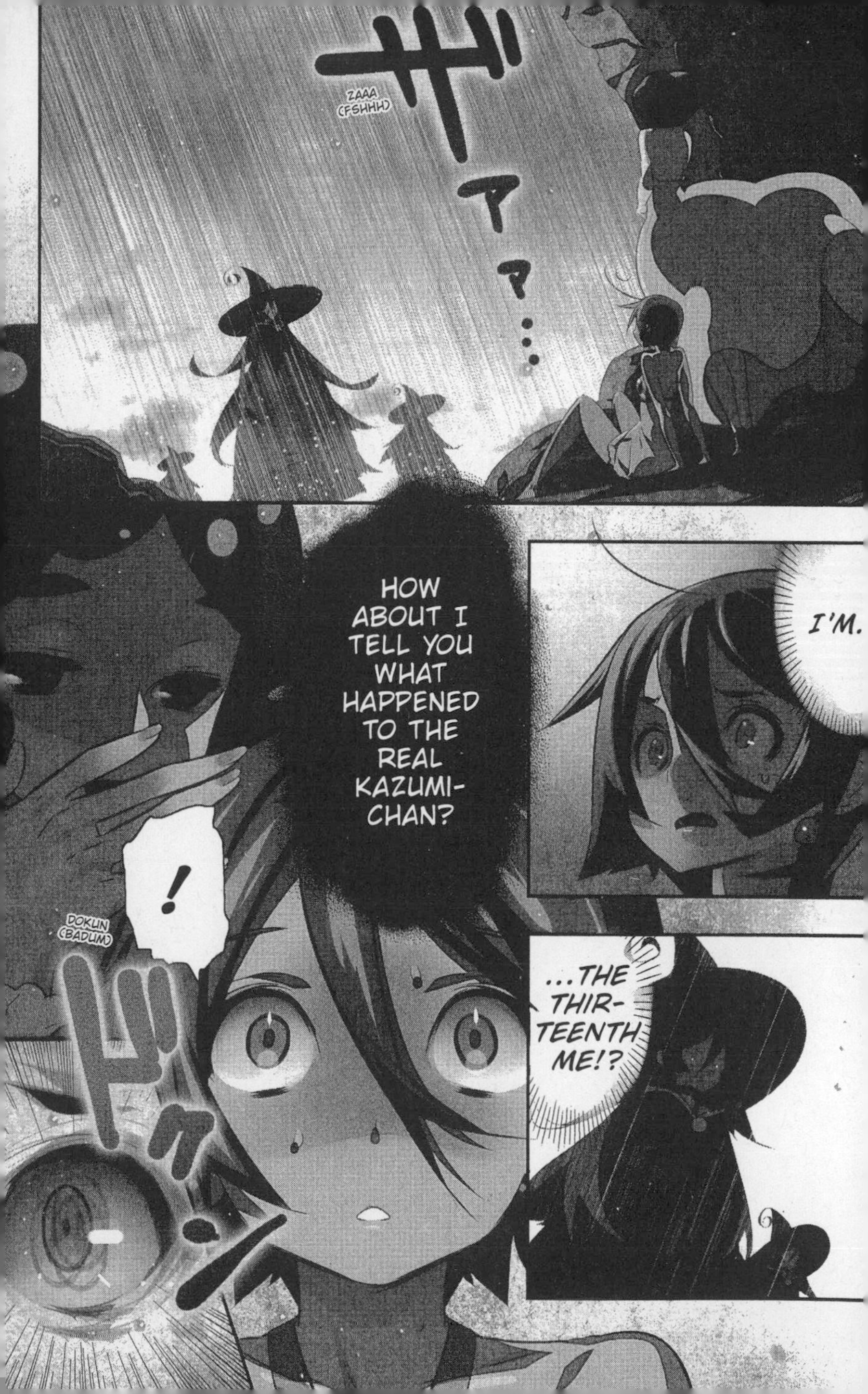
ZAAA (FSHHH)
I'M.
...THE THIRTEENTH ME!?
HOW ABOUT I TELL YOU WHAT HAPPENED TO THE REAL KAZUMI-CHAN?
!
DOKUN (BADUM)

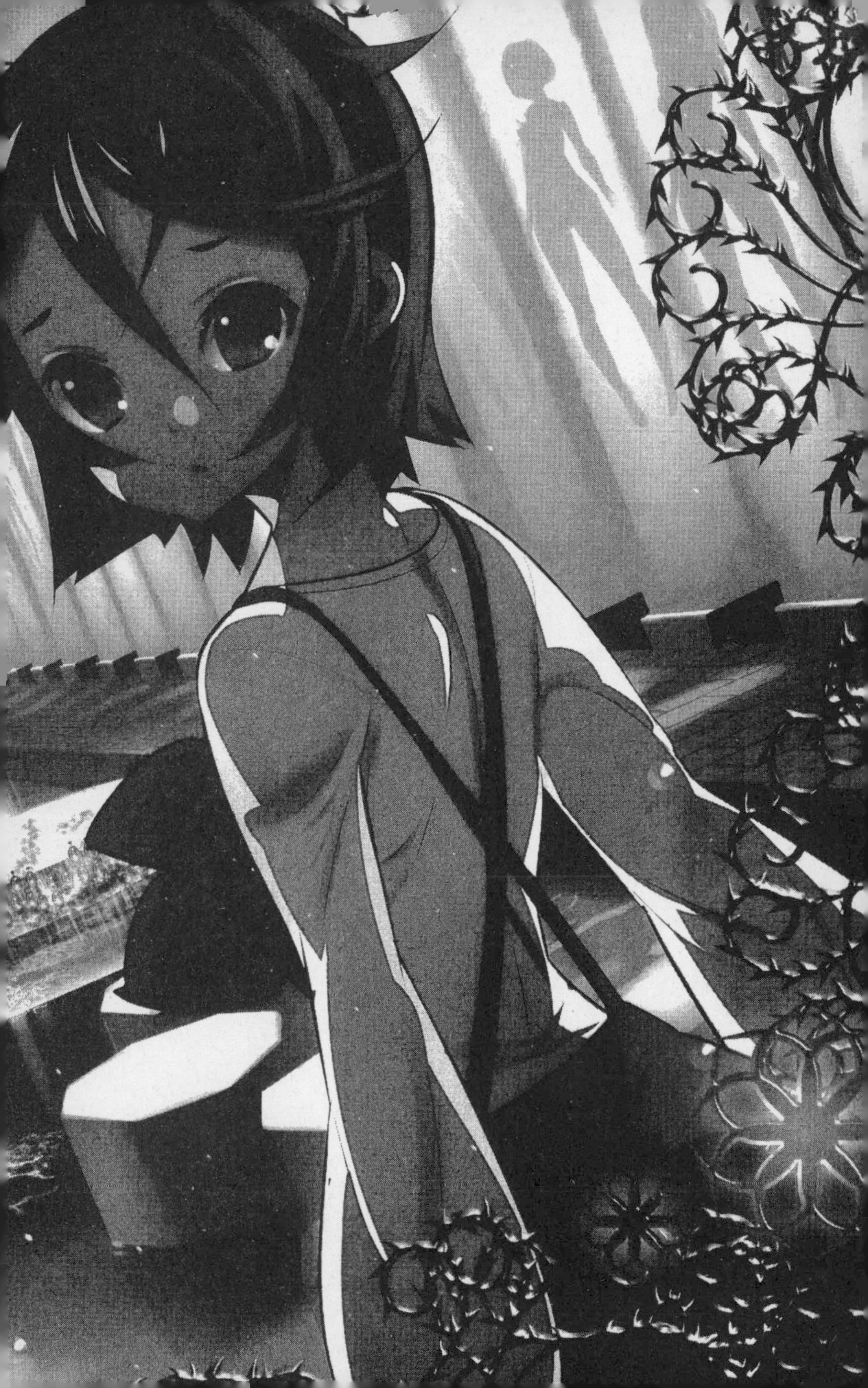

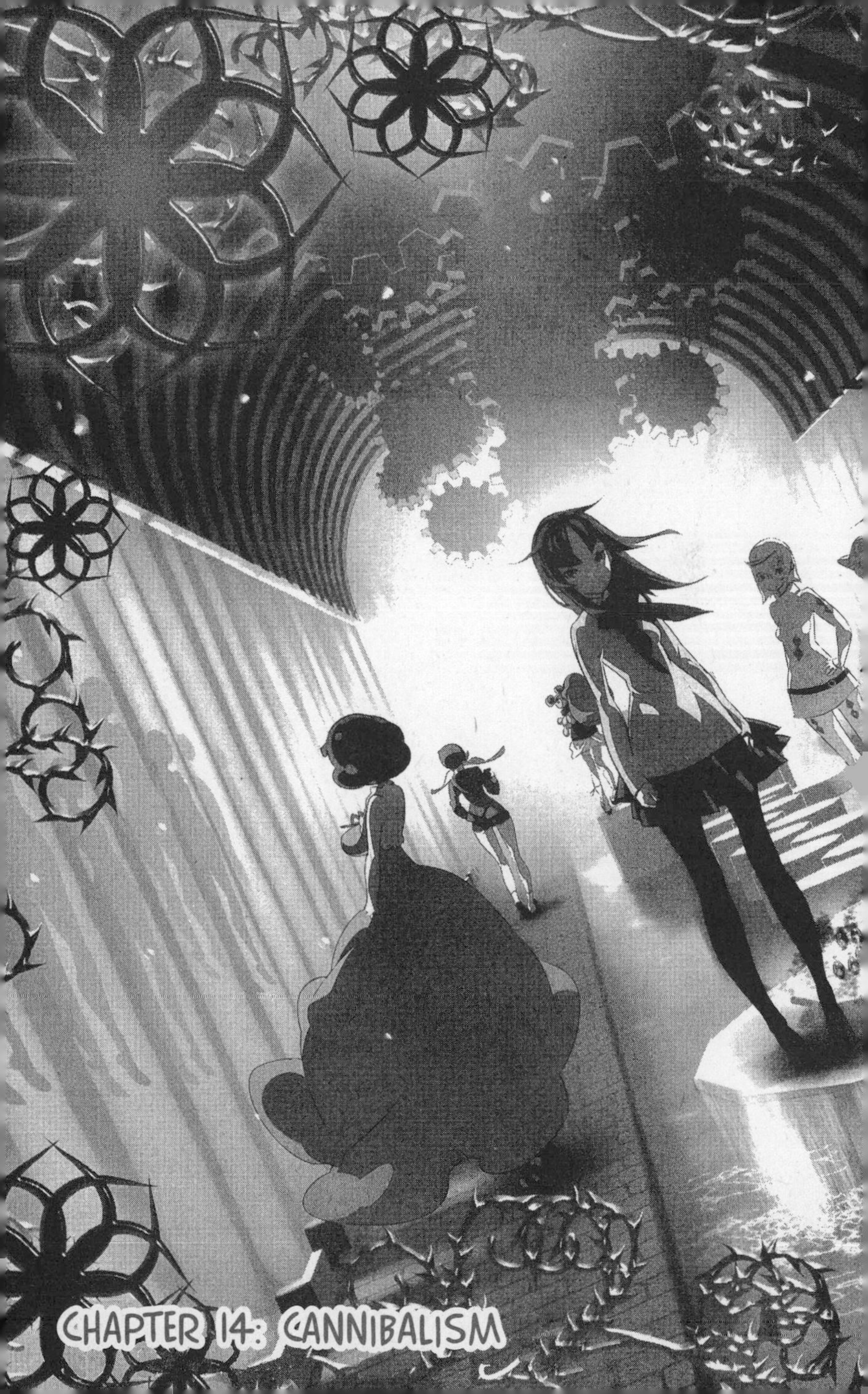
CHAPTER 14: CANNIBALISM

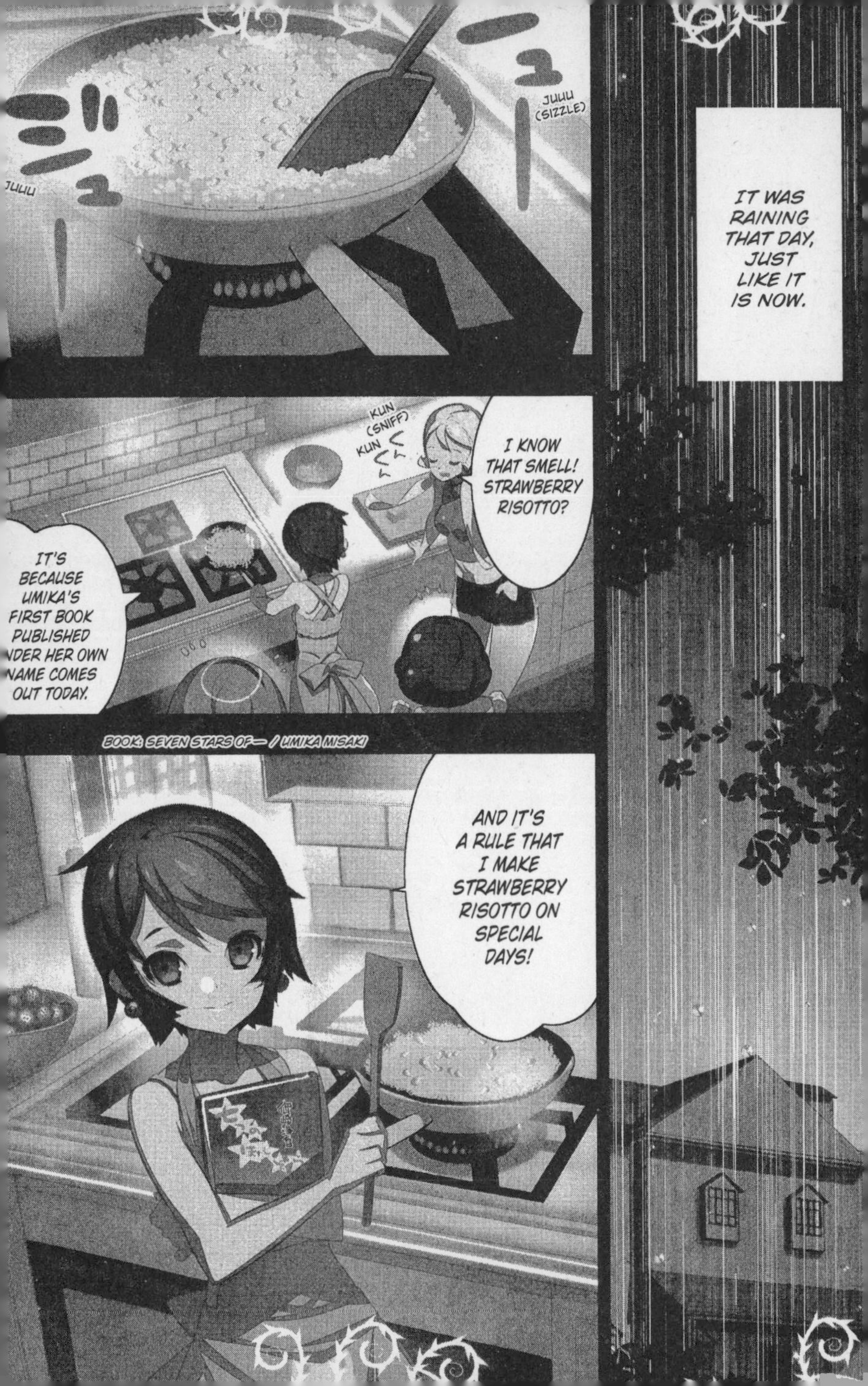
IT WAS RAINING THAT DAY, JUST LIKE IT IS NOW.
JUUU (SIZZLE)
JUUU
I KNOW THAT SMELL! STRAWBERRY RISOTTO?
KUN (SNIFF) KUN
IT'S BECAUSE UMIKA'S FIRST BOOK PUBLISHED NDER HER OWN NAME COMES OUT TODAY.
BOOK: SEVEN STARS OF— / UMIKA MISAKI
AND IT'S A RULE THAT I MAKE STRAWBERRY RISOTTO ON SPECIAL DAYS!

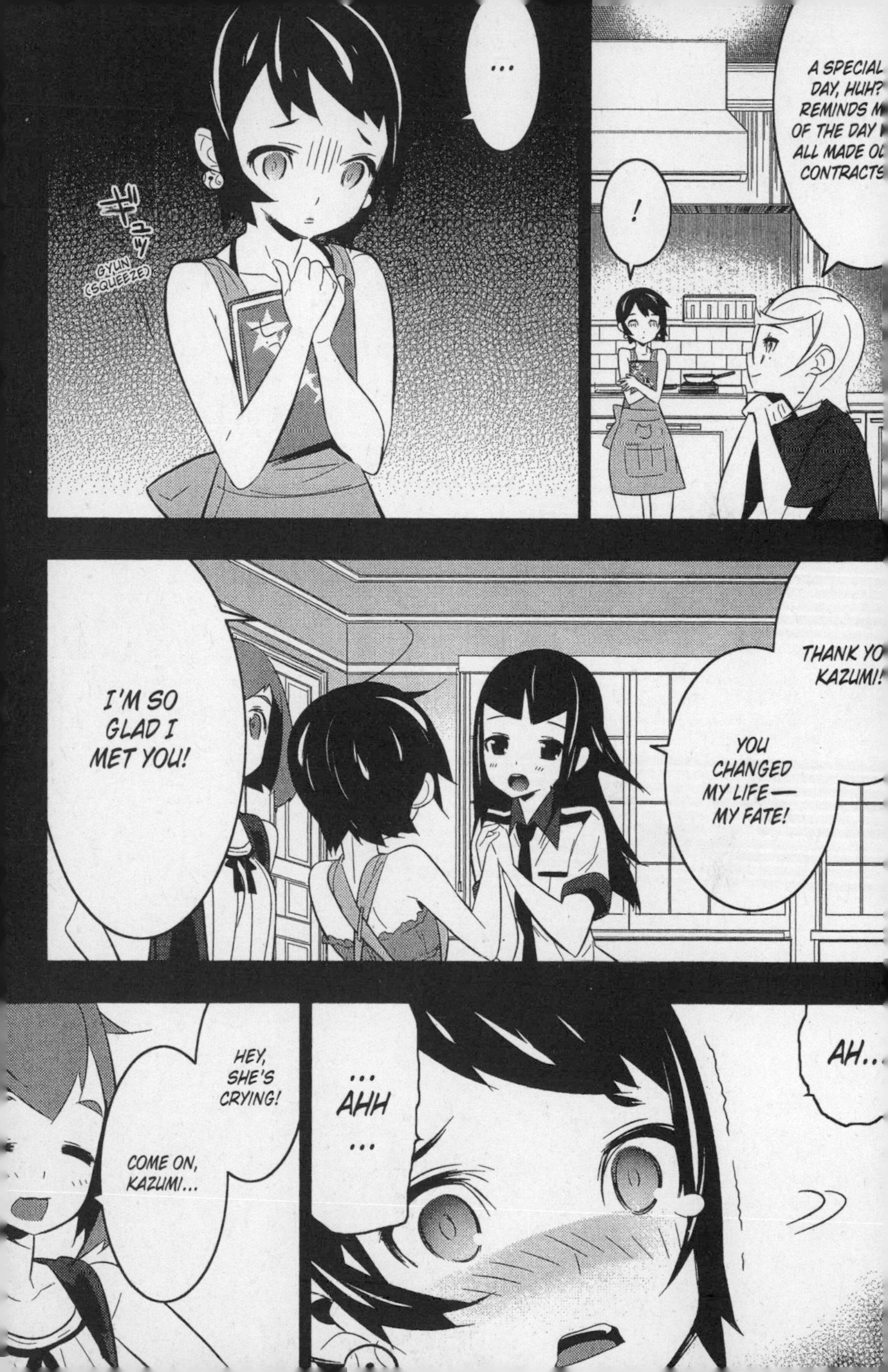

A SPECIAL DAY, HUH? REMINDS M OF THE DAY ALL MADE OU CONTRACTS
!
...
ギュッ
GYUN (SQUEEZE)
THANK YO KAZUMI!
YOU CHANGED MY LIFE— MY FATE!
I'M SO GLAD I MET YOU!
AH...
...AHH...
HEY, SHE'S CRYING!
COME ON, KAZUMI...

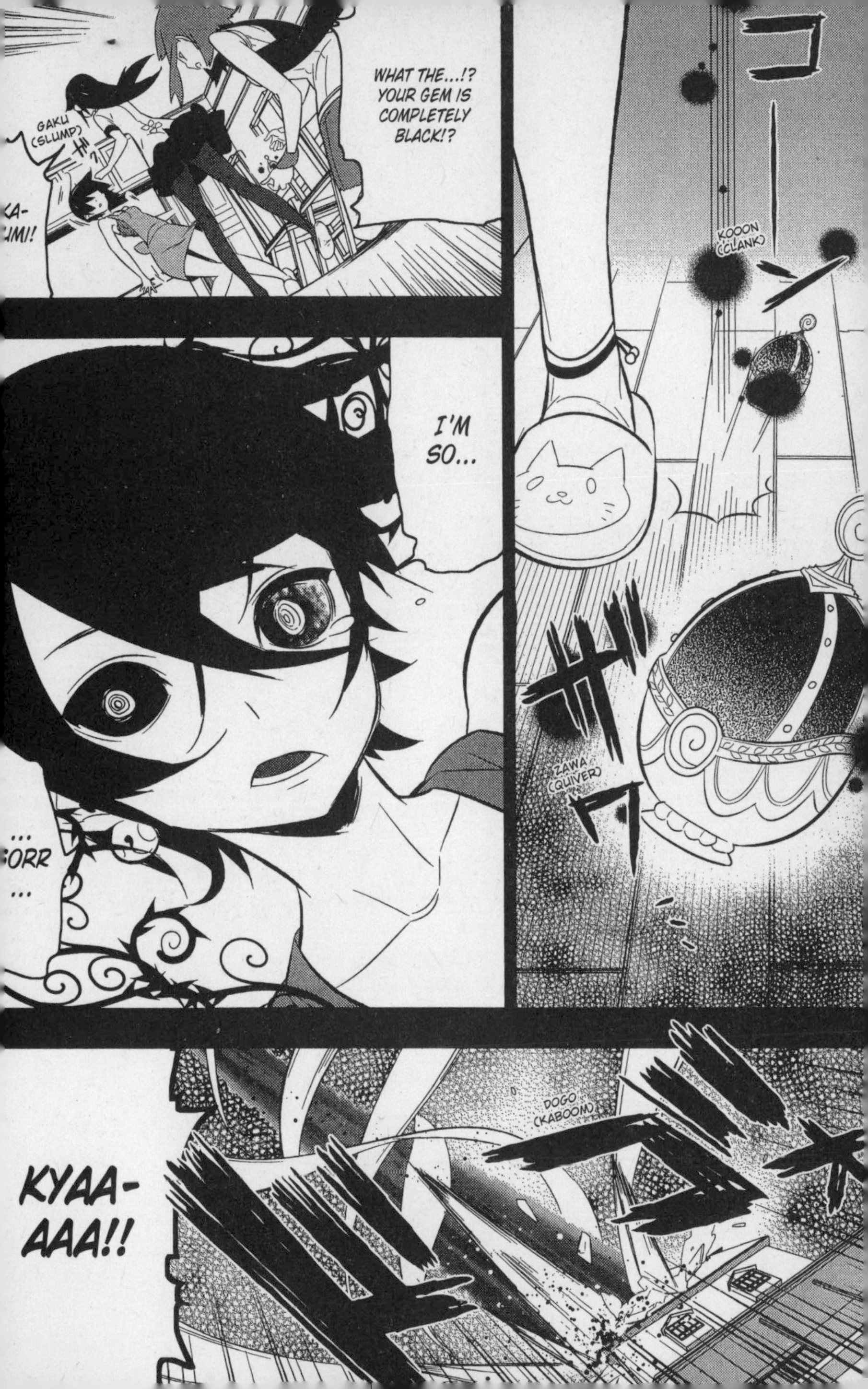
KOOON (CLANK)
ZAWA (QUIVER)
WHAT THE...!? YOUR GEM IS COMPLETELY BLACK!?
GAKU (SLUMP)
KA-
MI!
I'M SO...
...
SORR
...
DOGO (KABOOM)
KYAA-AAA!!

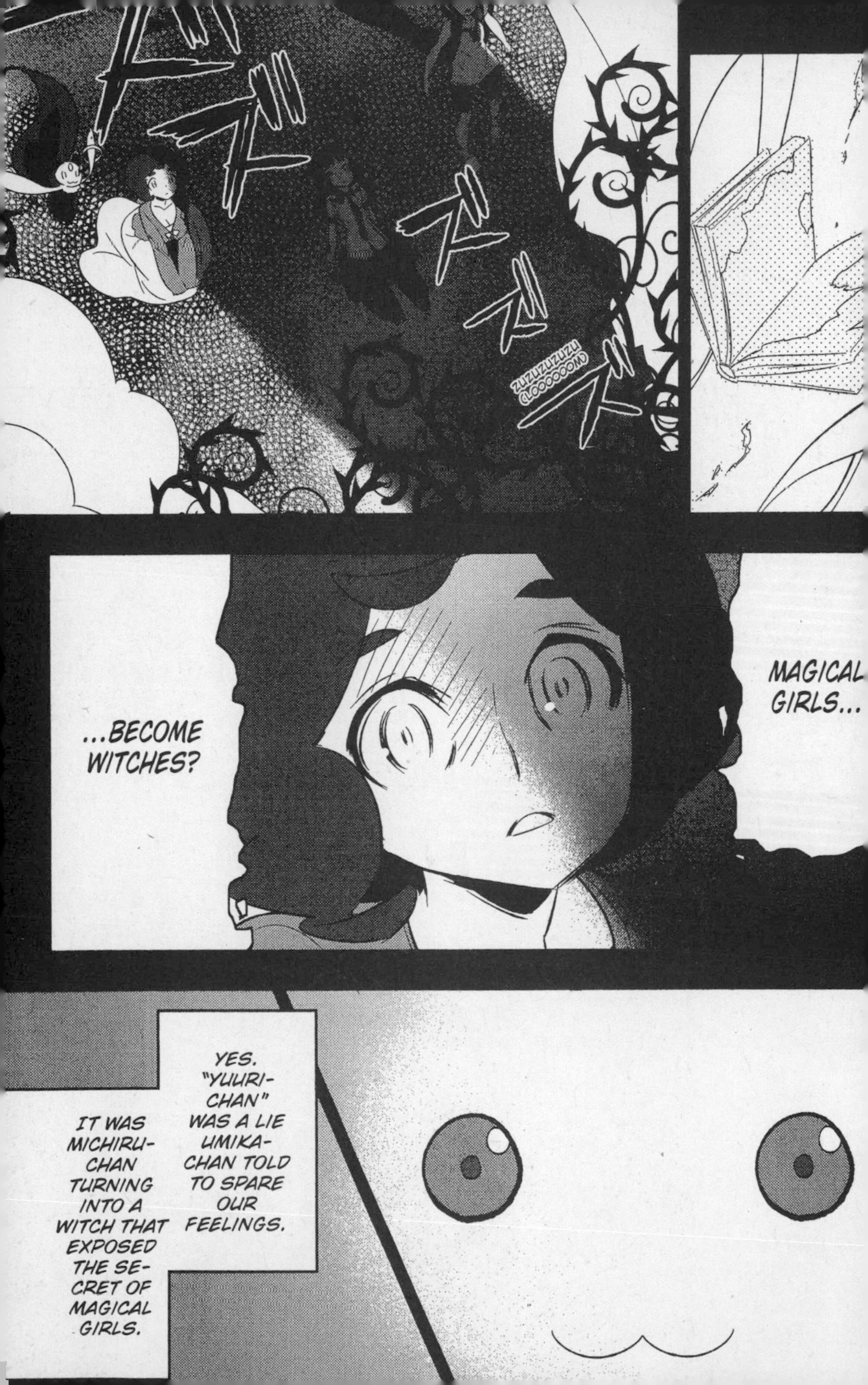
ZUZUZUZUZU
(LOOOOOOOM)
MAGICAL GIRLS...
...BECOME WITCHES?
YES. "YUURI-CHAN" WAS A LIE UMIKA-CHAN TOLD TO SPARE OUR FEELINGS.
IT WAS MICHIRU-CHAN TURNING INTO A WITCH THAT EXPOSED THE SE-CRET OF MAGICAL GIRLS.

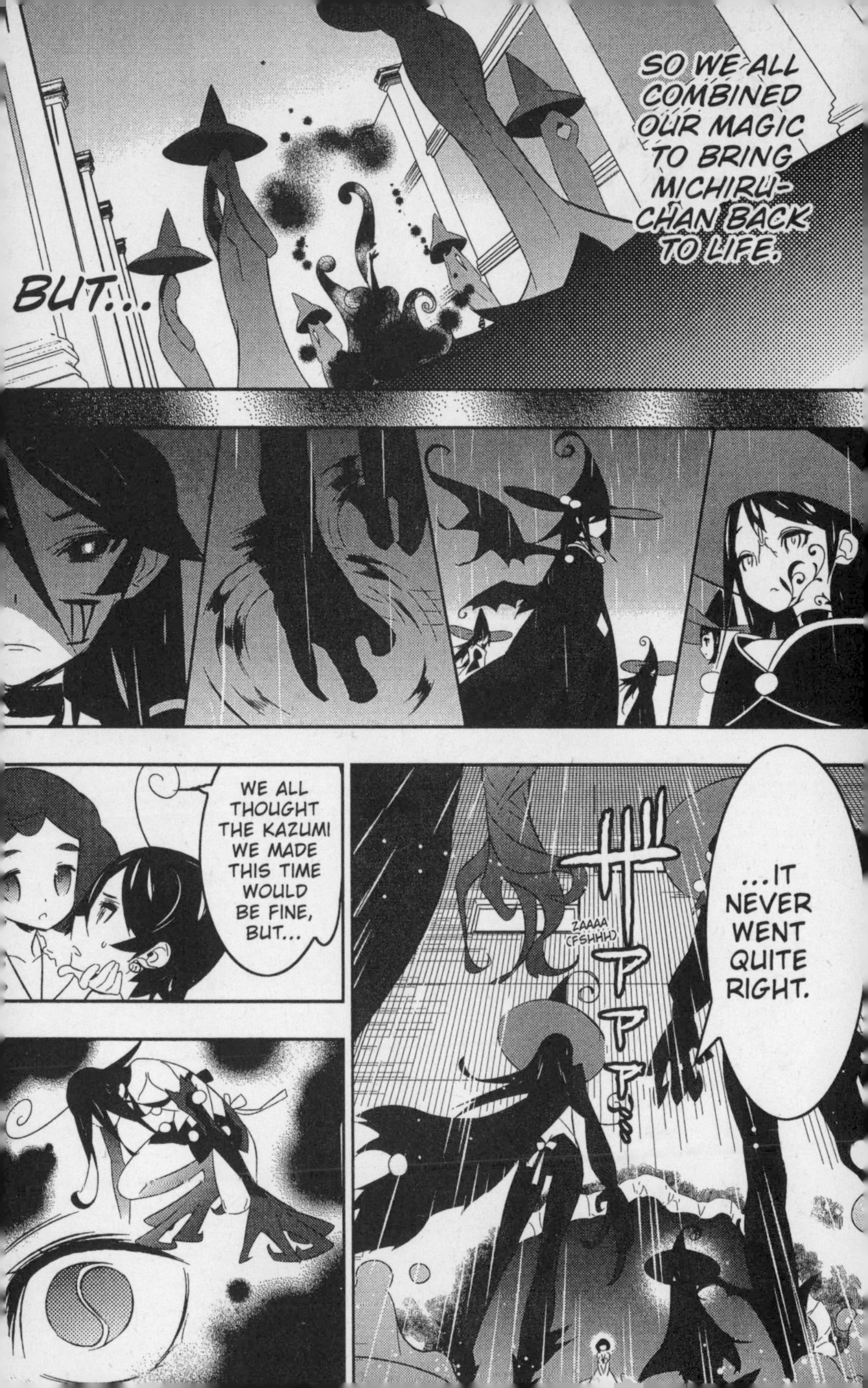
SO WE ALL COMBINED OUR MAGIC TO BRING MICHIRU-CHAN BACK TO LIFE.
BUT...
...IT NEVER WENT QUITE RIGHT.
ZAAAA (FSHHH)
WE ALL THOUGHT THE KAZUMI WE MADE THIS TIME WOULD BE FINE, BUT...

...WE HAVE TO ADMIT THAT EVEN THIS KAZUMI-CHAN ISN'T REALLY HUMAN.

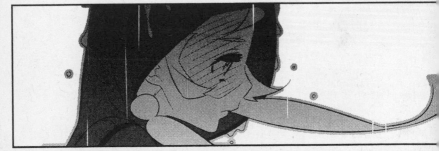

YOU HAD TO GO AND SAY IT...

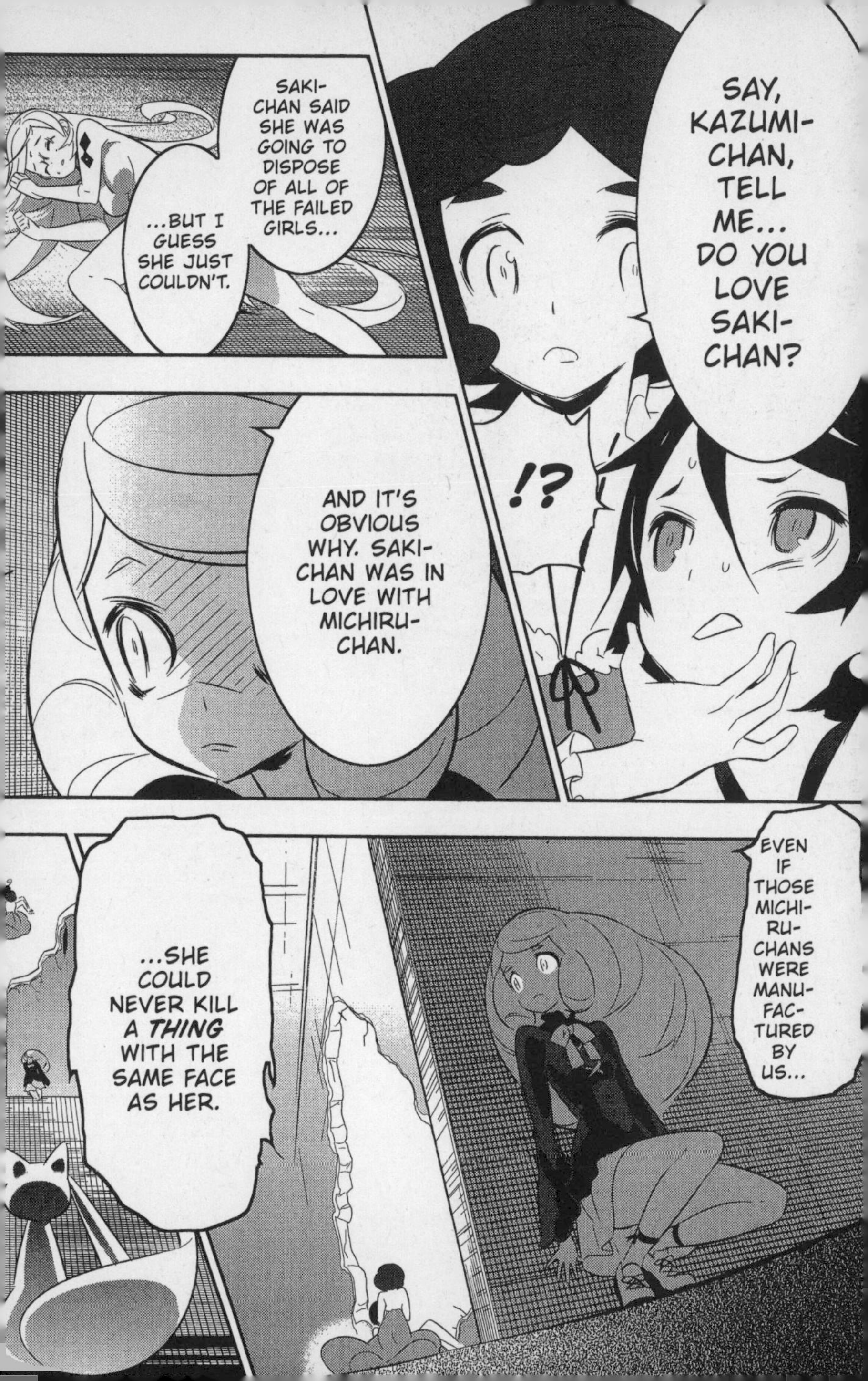
SAY, KAZUMI-CHAN, TELL ME... DO YOU LOVE SAKI-CHAN?
!?
SAKI-CHAN SAID SHE WAS GOING TO DISPOSE OF ALL OF THE FAILED GIRLS...
...BUT I GUESS SHE JUST COULDN'T.
AND IT'S OBVIOUS WHY. SAKI-CHAN WAS IN LOVE WITH MICHIRU-CHAN.
EVEN IF THOSE MICHIRU-CHANS WERE MANUFACTURED BY US...
...SHE COULD NEVER KILL A *THING* WITH THE SAME FACE AS HER.

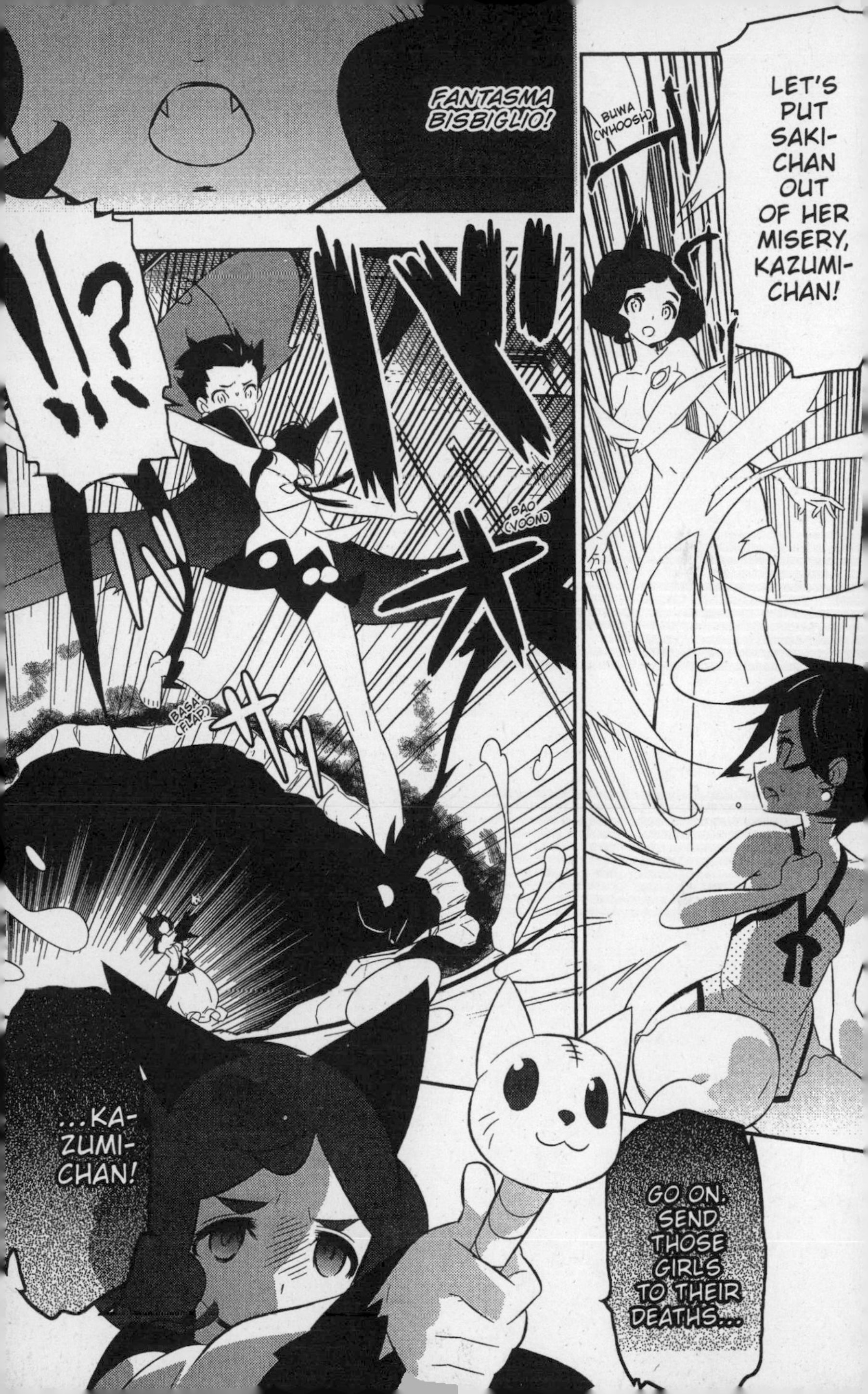
LET'S PUT SAKI-CHAN OUT OF HER MISERY, KAZUMI-CHAN!
BUWA (WHOOSH)
FANTASMA BISBIGLIO!
!!?
BAO (VOOM)
BASA (FLAP)
GO ON. SEND THOSE GIRLS TO THEIR DEATHS...
...KA-ZUMI-CHAN!

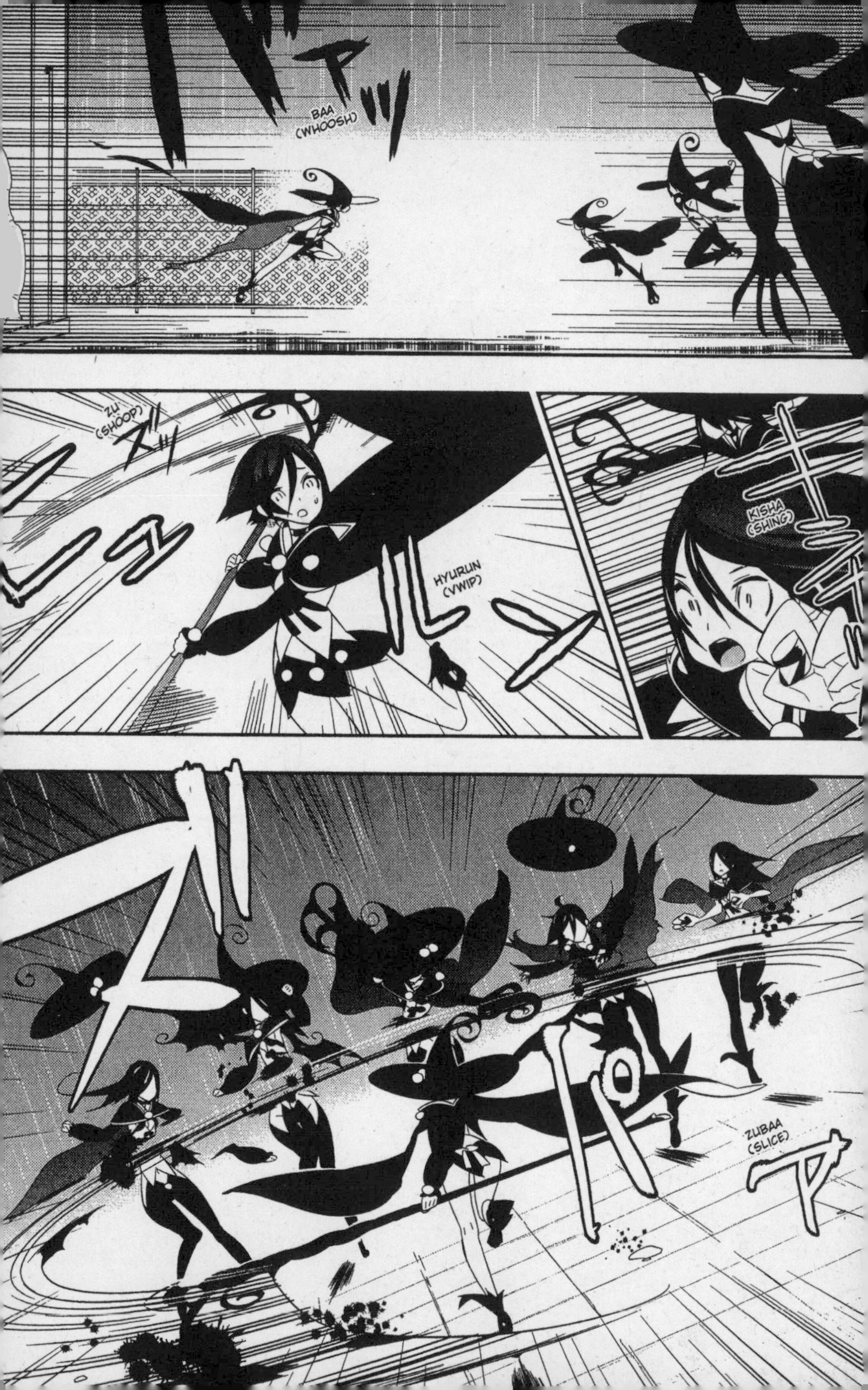
BAA (WHOOSH)
KISHA (SHING)
ZU (SHOOP)
HYURUN (VWIP)
ZUBAA (SLICE)

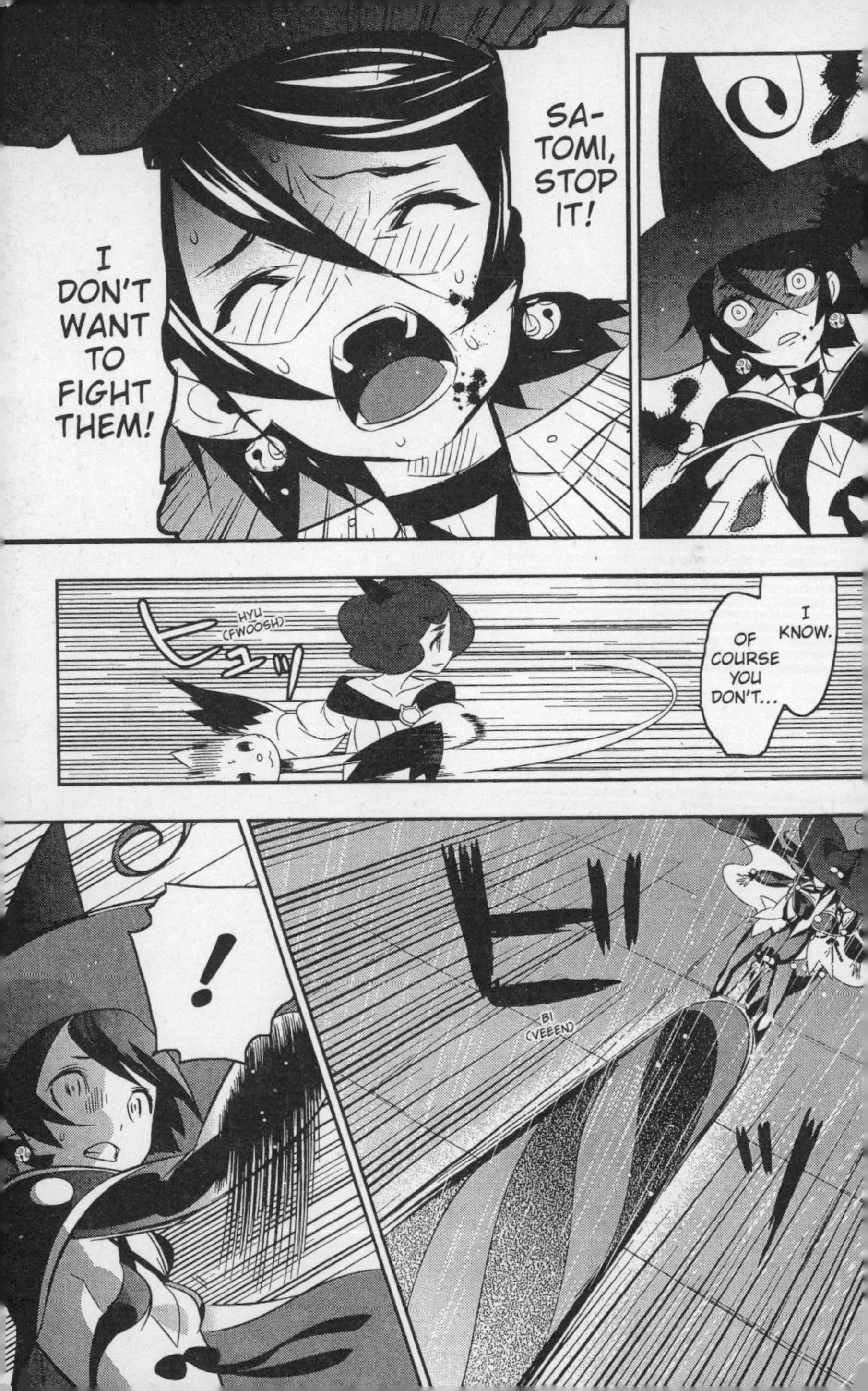
SA-TOMI, STOP IT!
I DON'T WANT TO FIGHT THEM!
I KNOW. OF COURSE YOU DON'T...
HYU (FWOOSH)
BI (VEEEN)
!

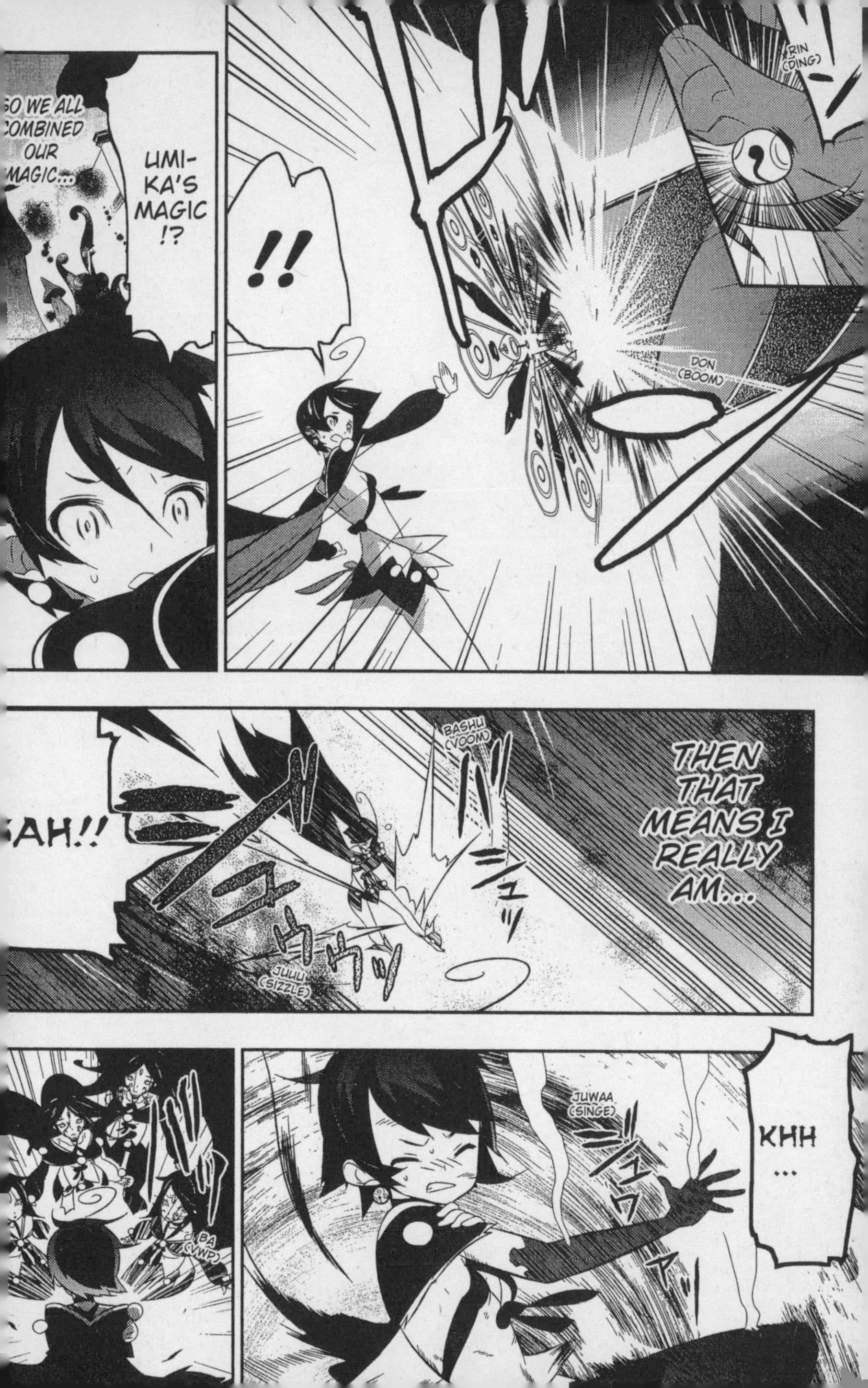
RIN (DING)
DON (BOOM)
!!
UMI-KA'S MAGIC !?
SO WE ALL COMBINED OUR MAGIC...
THEN THAT MEANS I REALLY AM...
BASHU (VOOM)
JUUU (SIZZLE)
AH!!
KHH ...
JUWAA (SINGE)
BA (VWP)

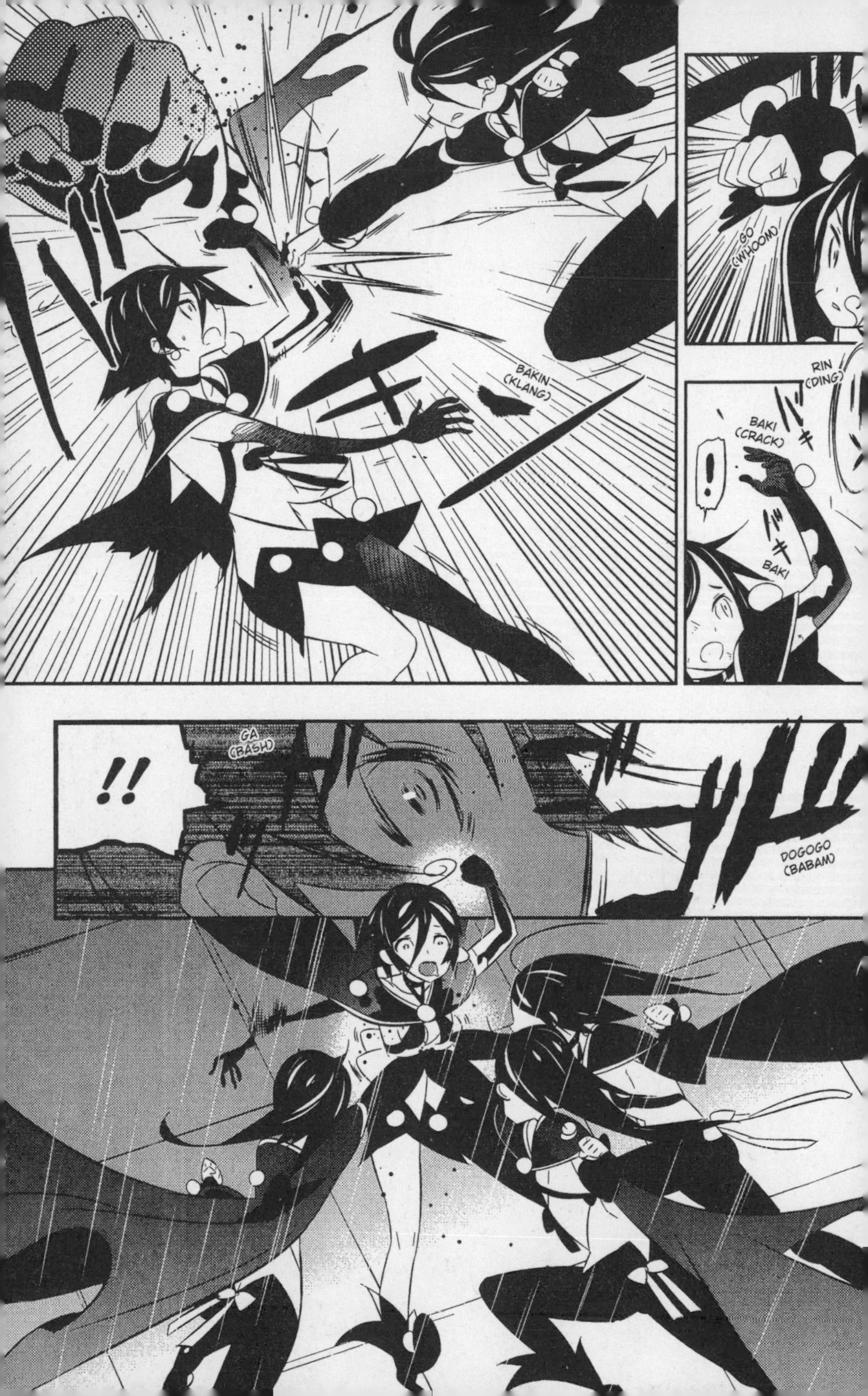
GO (WHOOM)
RIN (DING)
BAKI (CRACK)
!
BAKI
BAKIN (KLANG)
GA (BASH)
!!
DOGOGO (BABAM)

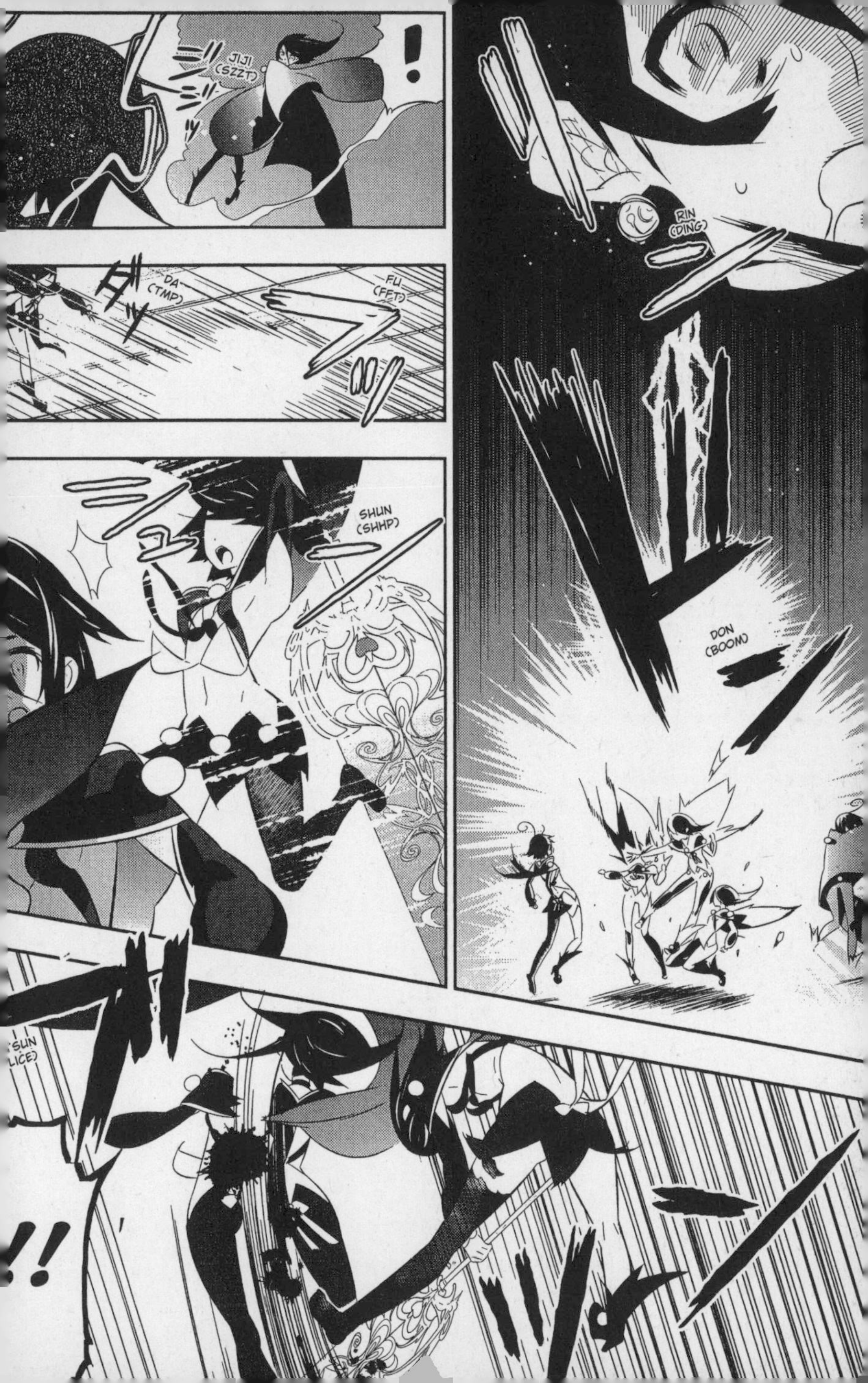
RIN (DING)
DON (BOOM)
JIJI (SZZT)
FU (FFT)
DA (TMP)
SHUN (SHHP)

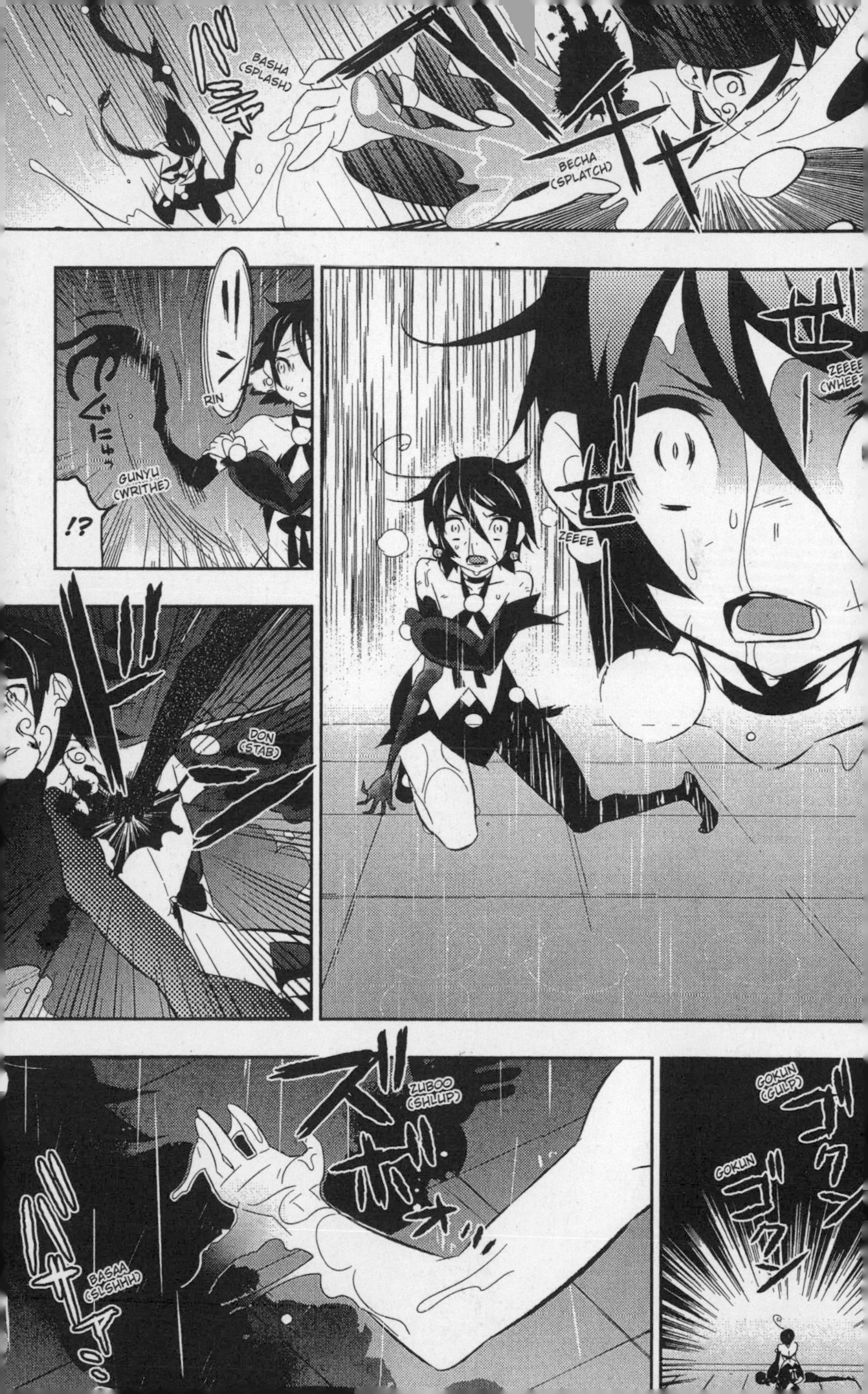
BECHA (SPLATCH)
BASHA (SPLASH)
ZEEEE (WHEE
ZEEEE
RIN
GUNYU (WRITHE)
!?
DON (STAB)
GOKUN (GULP)
GOKUN
ZUBOO (SHLUP)
BASAA (SLSHHH)

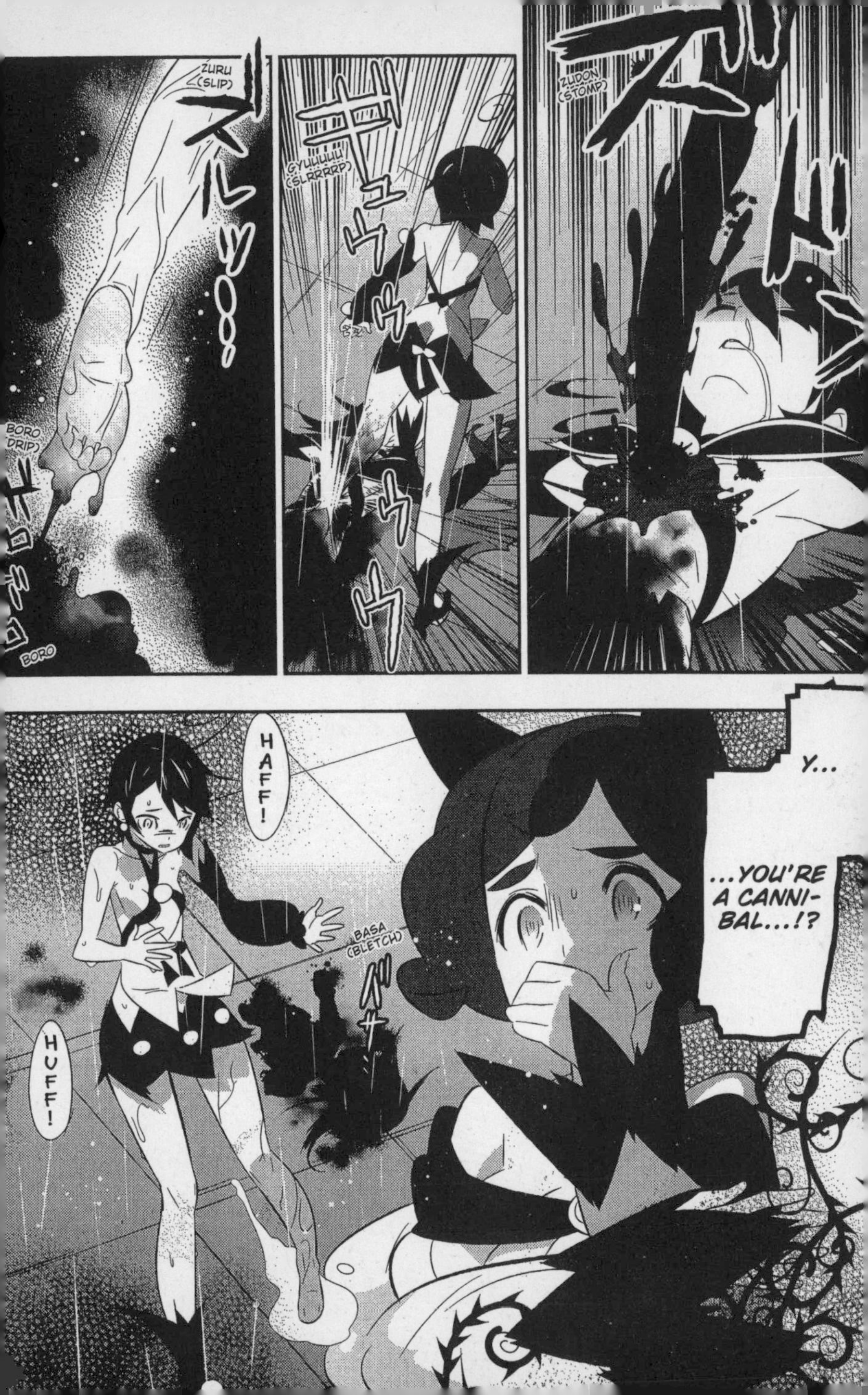
ZUDON
(STOMP)
GYUUUUU
(SLRRRRP)
ZURU
(SLIP)
BORO
DRIP)
BORO
Y...
...YOU'RE A CANNI-BAL...!?
HAFF!
BASA
(BLETCH)
HUFF!

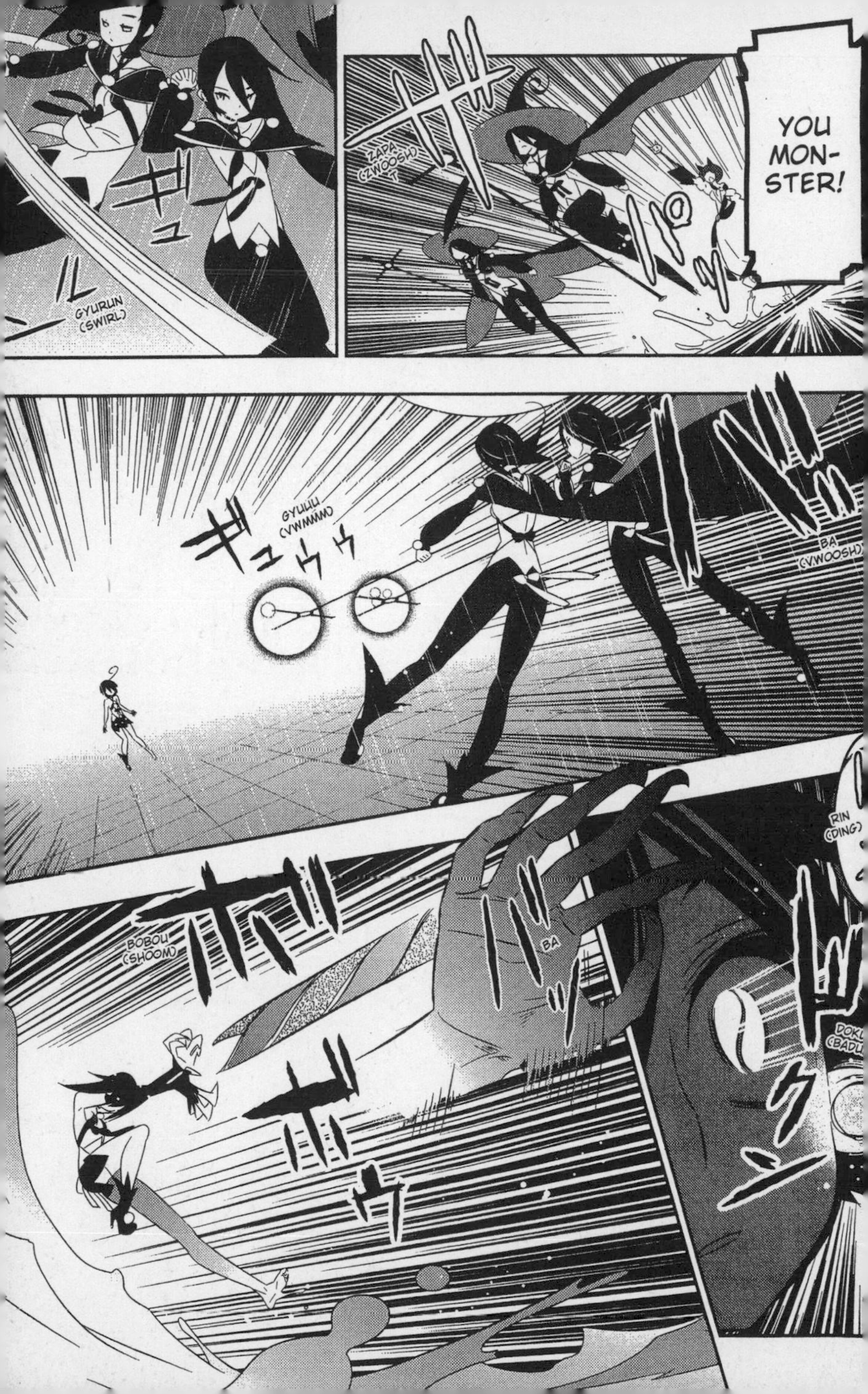
YOU MONSTER!
ZAPA (ZWOOSH)
GYURUN (SWIRL)
BA (VWOOSH)
GYUUU (VWMMM)
RIN (DING)
BA
BOBOU (SHOOM)

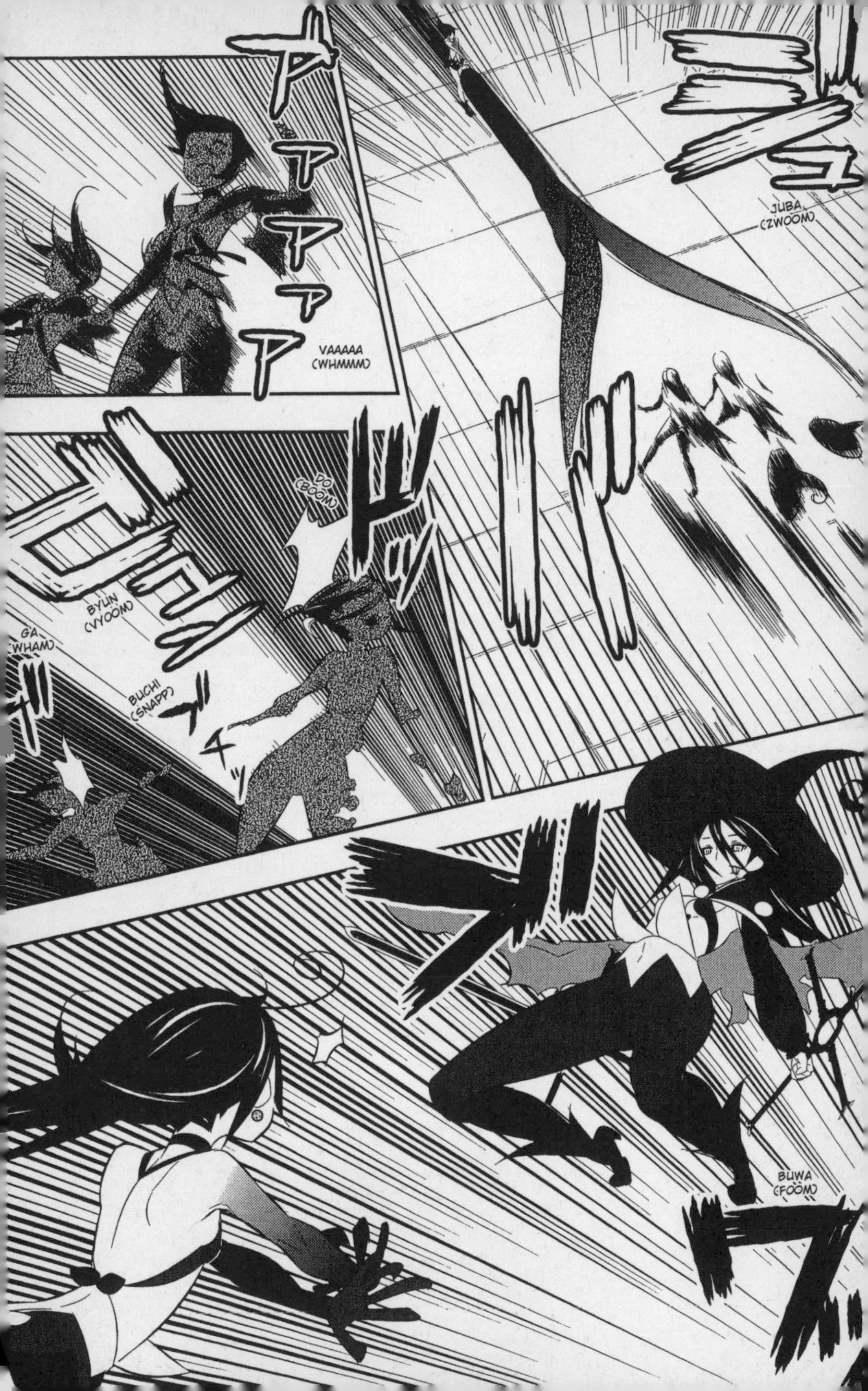
JUBA (ZWOOM)
VAAAAA (WHMMM)
DO (BOOM)
BYUN (VYOOM)
GA (WHAM)
BUCHI (SNAPP)
BUWA (FOOM)

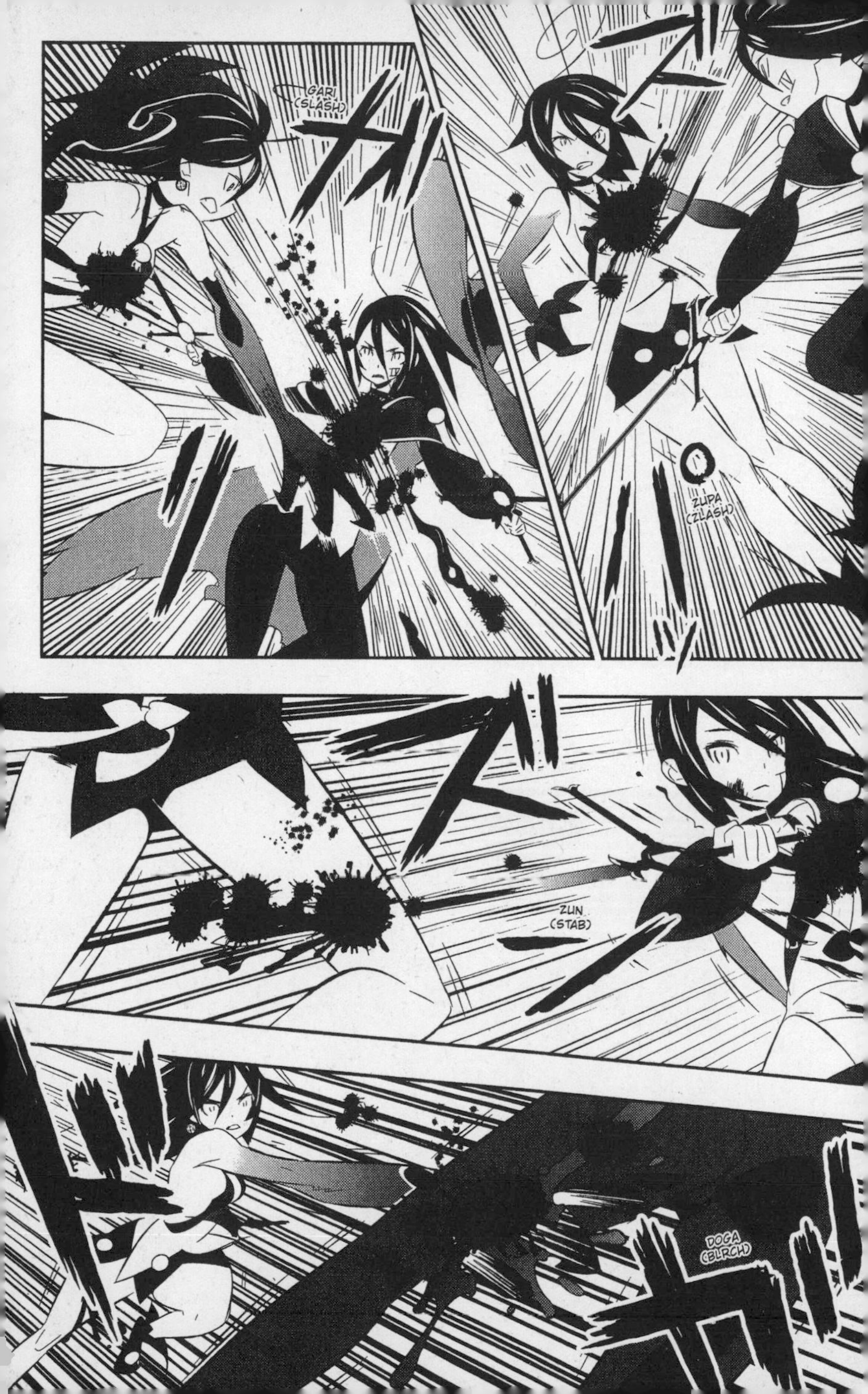
ZUPA (ZLASH)
GARI (SLASH)
ZUN (STAB)
DOGA (BLRCH)

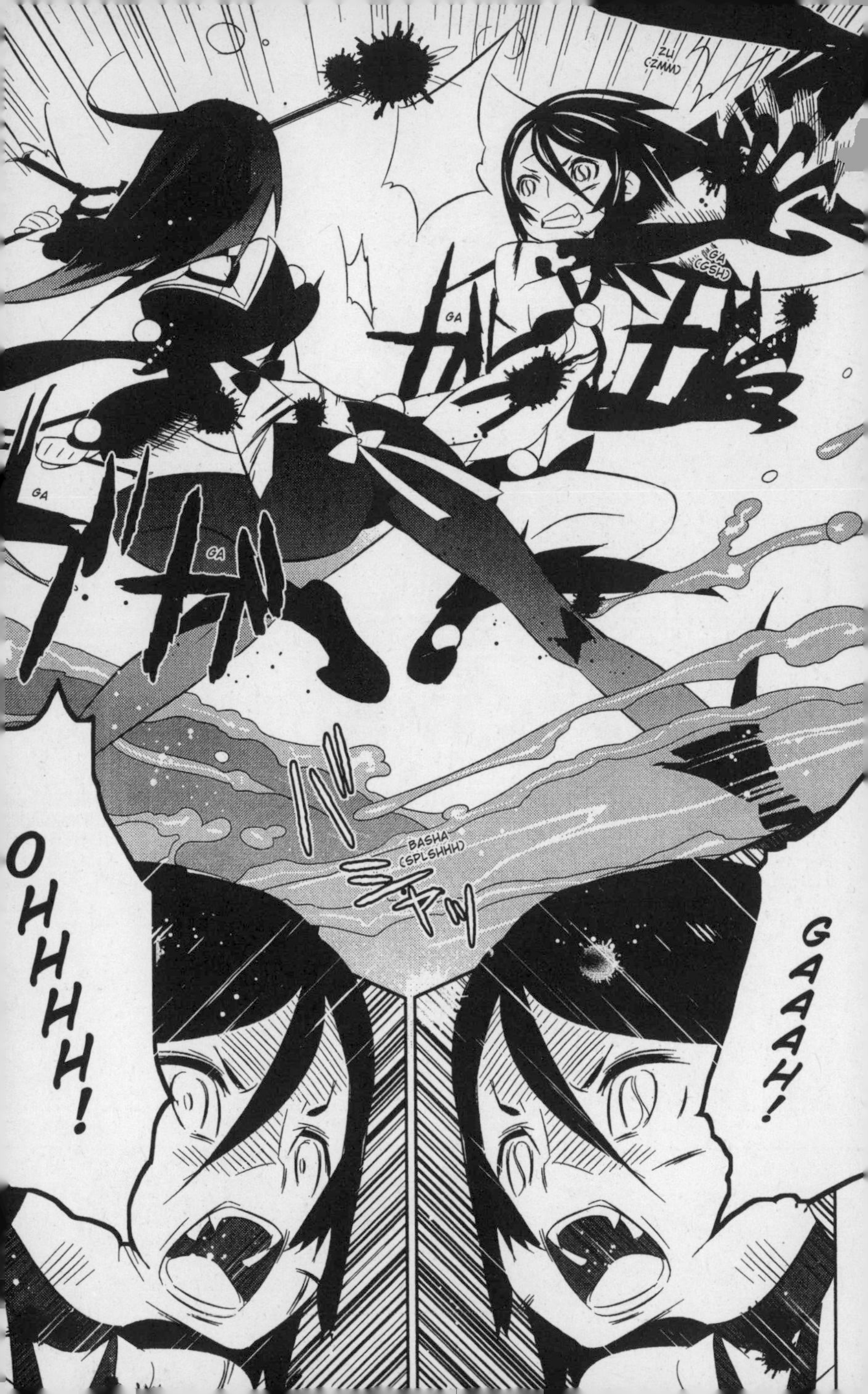
ZU (ZMM)
GA (GSH)
GA
GA
GA
BASHA (SPLSHHH)
GAAAH!
OHHHH!

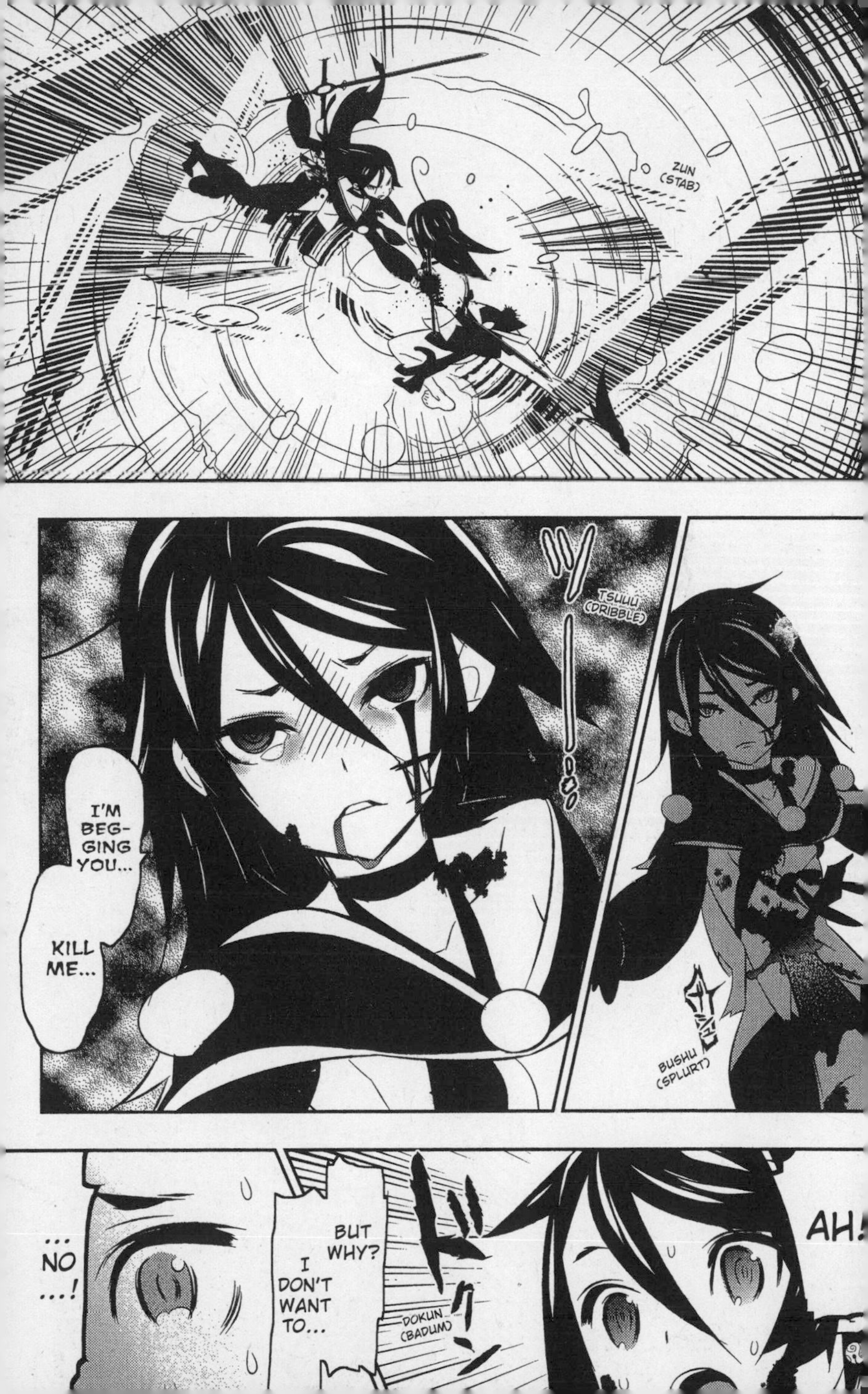
ZUN (STAB)
BUSHU (SPLURT)
TSUUU (DRIBBLE)
I'M BEG-GING YOU...
KILL ME...
AH!
DOKUN (BADUMP)
BUT WHY?
I DON'T WANT TO...
...NO...!

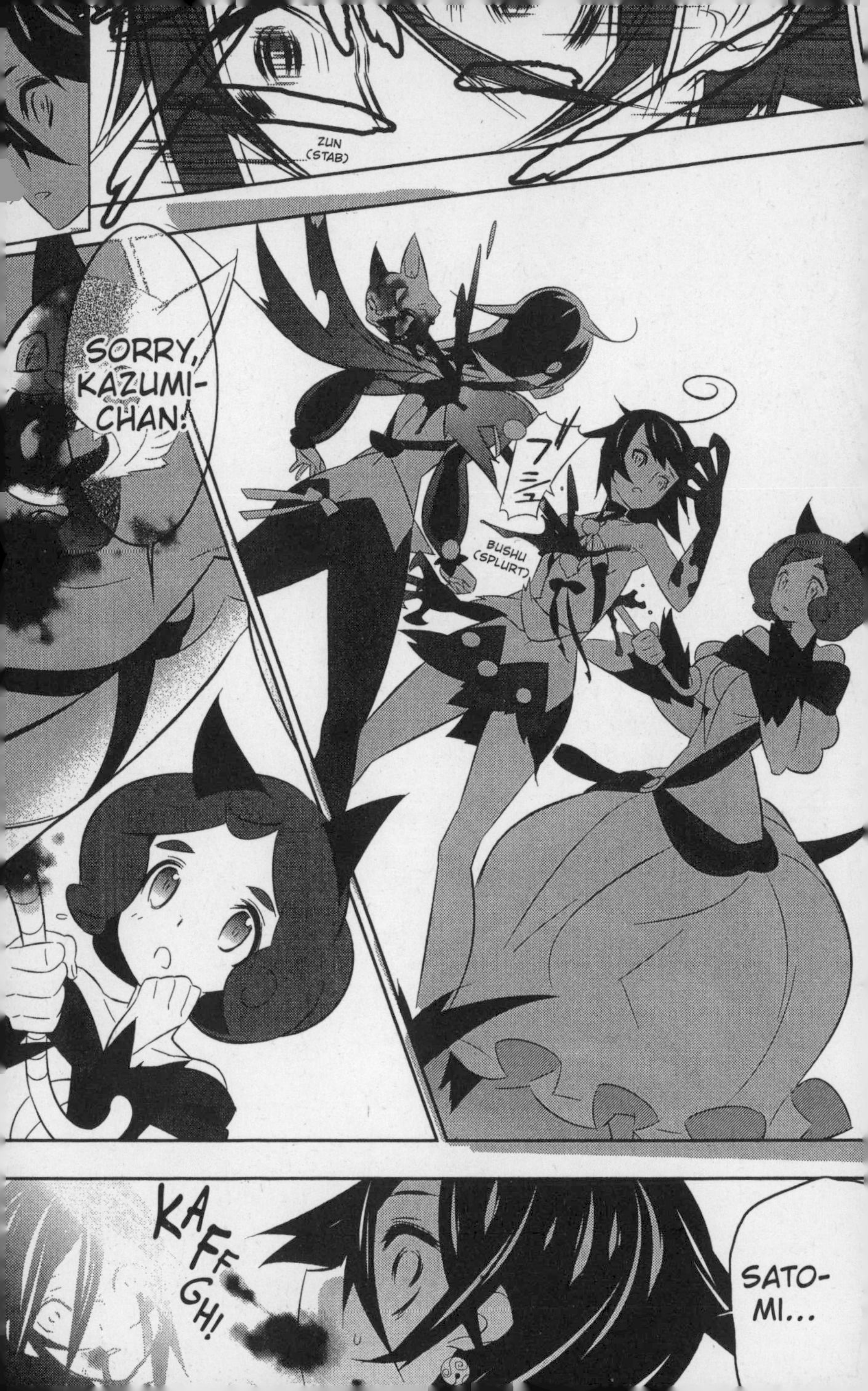
ZUN
(STAB)
SORRY, KAZUMI-CHAN!
BUSHU
(SPLURT)
SATO-MI...
KAFFGH!

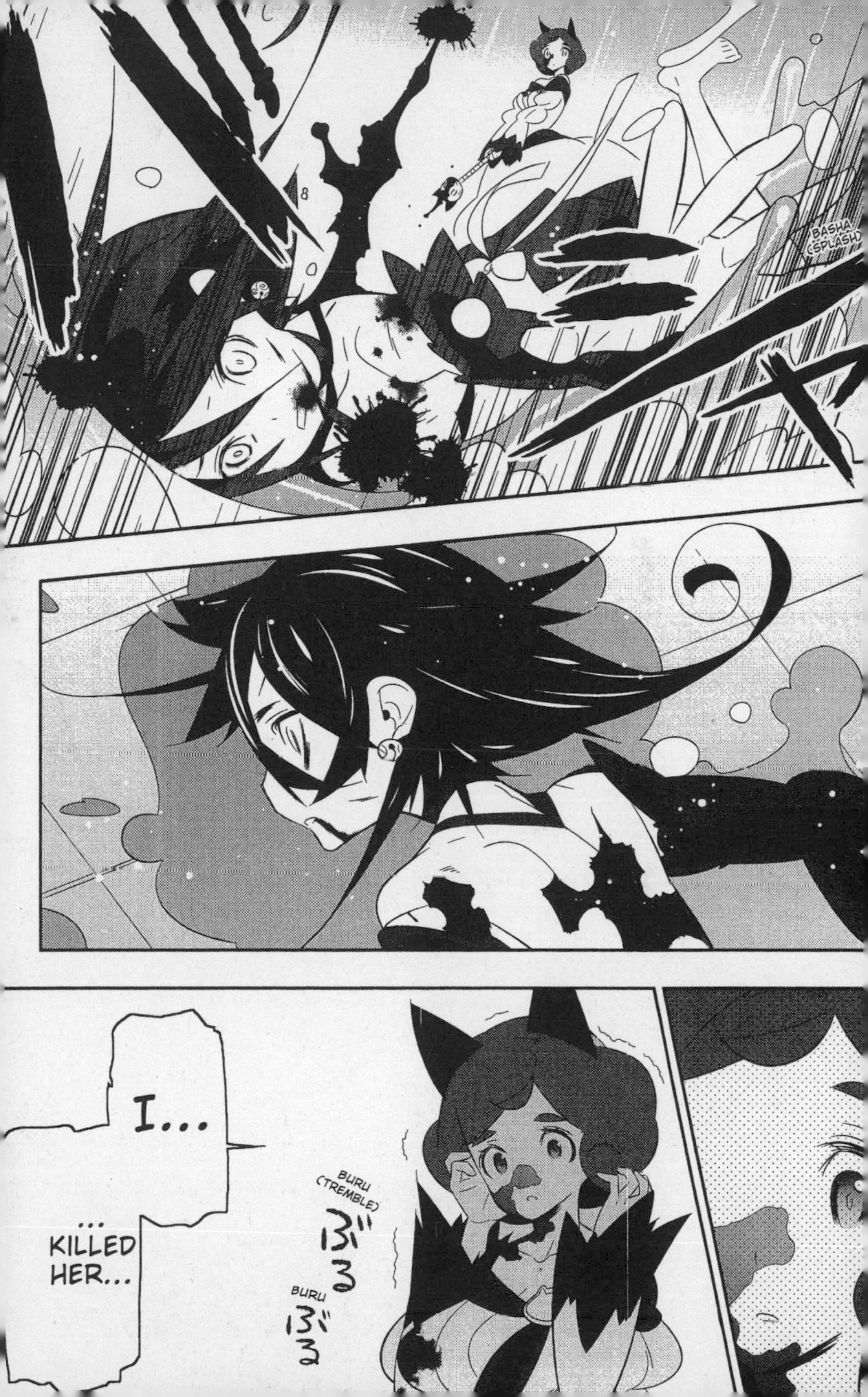
BASHA
(SPLASH)
BURU
(TREMBLE)
ぶる
BURU
ぶる
I...
...
KILLED
HER...

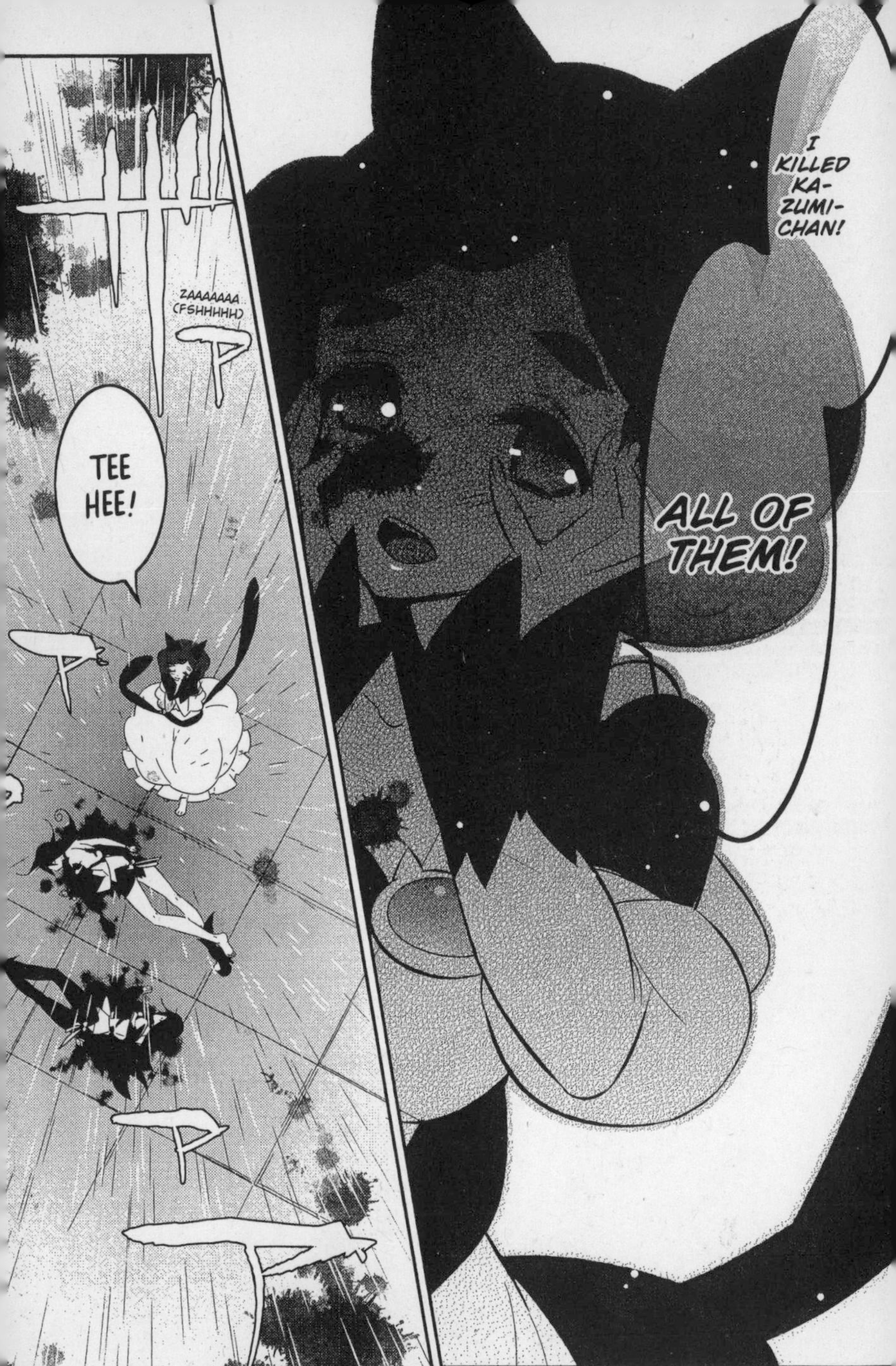
I KILLED KA-ZUMI-CHAN!
ALL OF THEM!
ZAAAAAAA (FSHHHHH)
TEE HEE!

Kazumi Series

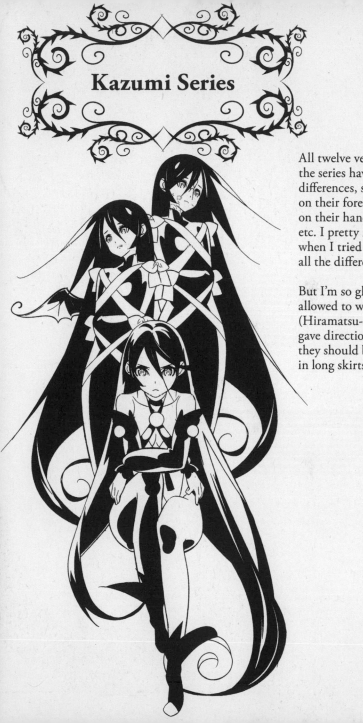

All twelve versions in the series have individual differences, such as stones on their foreheads, talons on their hands and feet, etc. I pretty much cried when I tried to draw all the differences.

But I'm so glad they were allowed to wear tights! (Hiramatsu-san initially gave directions that they should be dressed in long skirts.)

PUELLA MAGI
KAZUMI ★ MAGICA
The innocent malice

CHAPTER 15: ESSENCE OF SATOMI

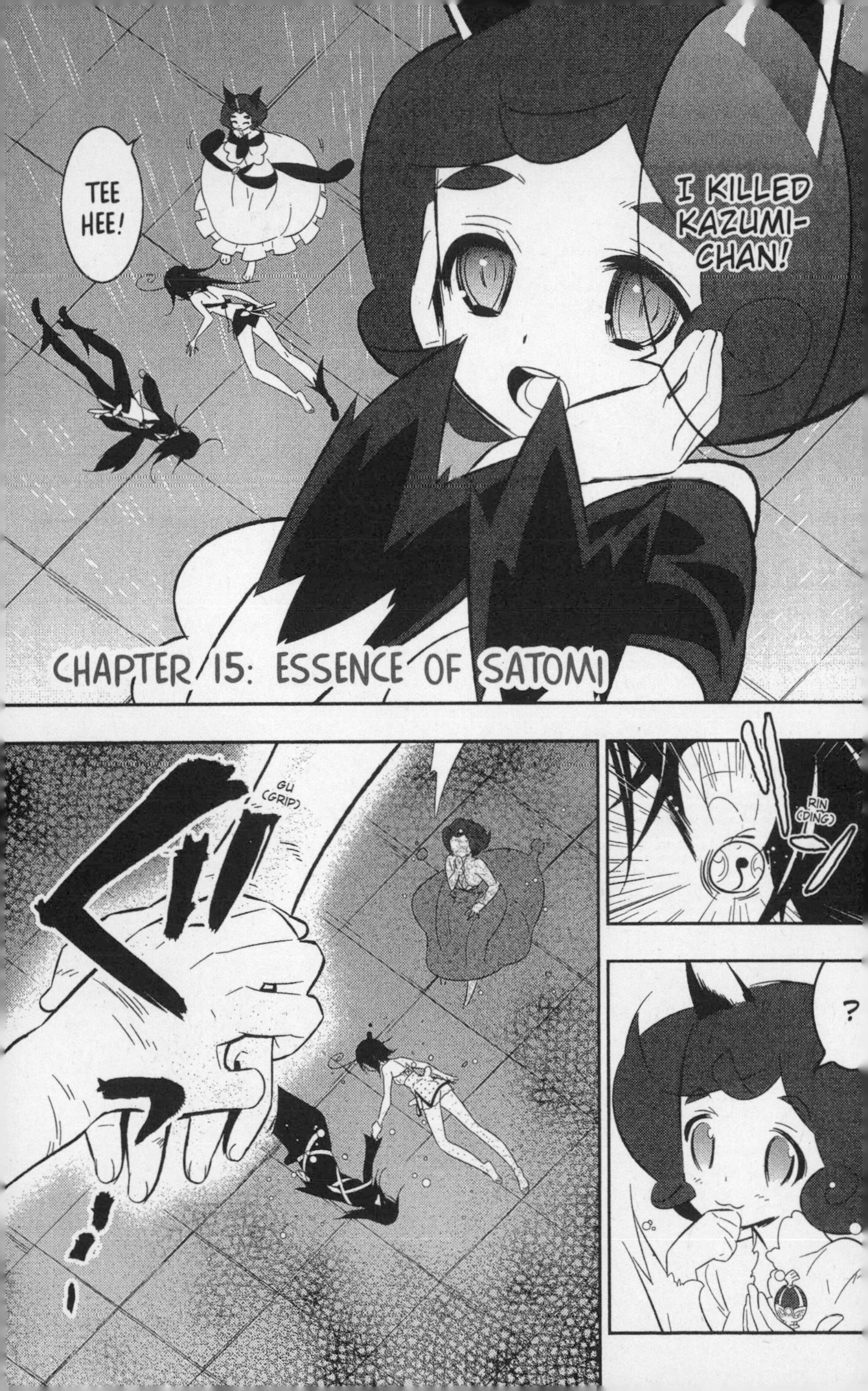
I KILLED KAZUMI-CHAN!
TEE HEE!
RIN (DING)
?
GU (GRIP)
!

GYUUUU
(SLRRRRP)

HEE-HEE...
WITCHES
ARE
REALLY...

...REALLY
TOUGH,
AREN'T
THEY...?
TEE-HEE...

ZAWA
(SHUDDER)

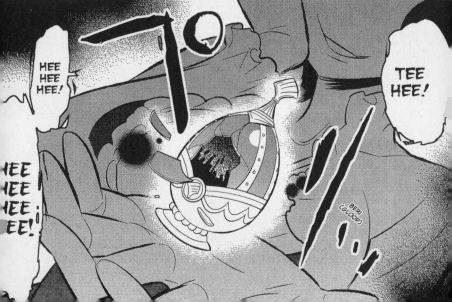

HEE
HEE
HEE!

HEE
HEE
HEE!

TEE
HEE!

BERI
(GLOOP)

PAN
(SLAP)

SA-
TOMI
...?

YORO
(WOBBLE)

HFF!

HFF!

HEE
HEE
HEE!

BAS

...BY A
WITCH
!!

PAKI
(CRACK)

I CAN'T
LET
MYSELF
BE DE-
FILED...

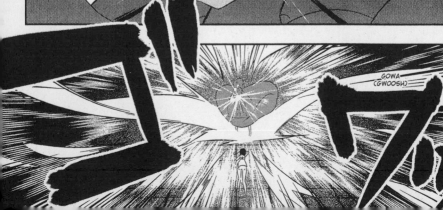

GOWA
(GWOOSH)

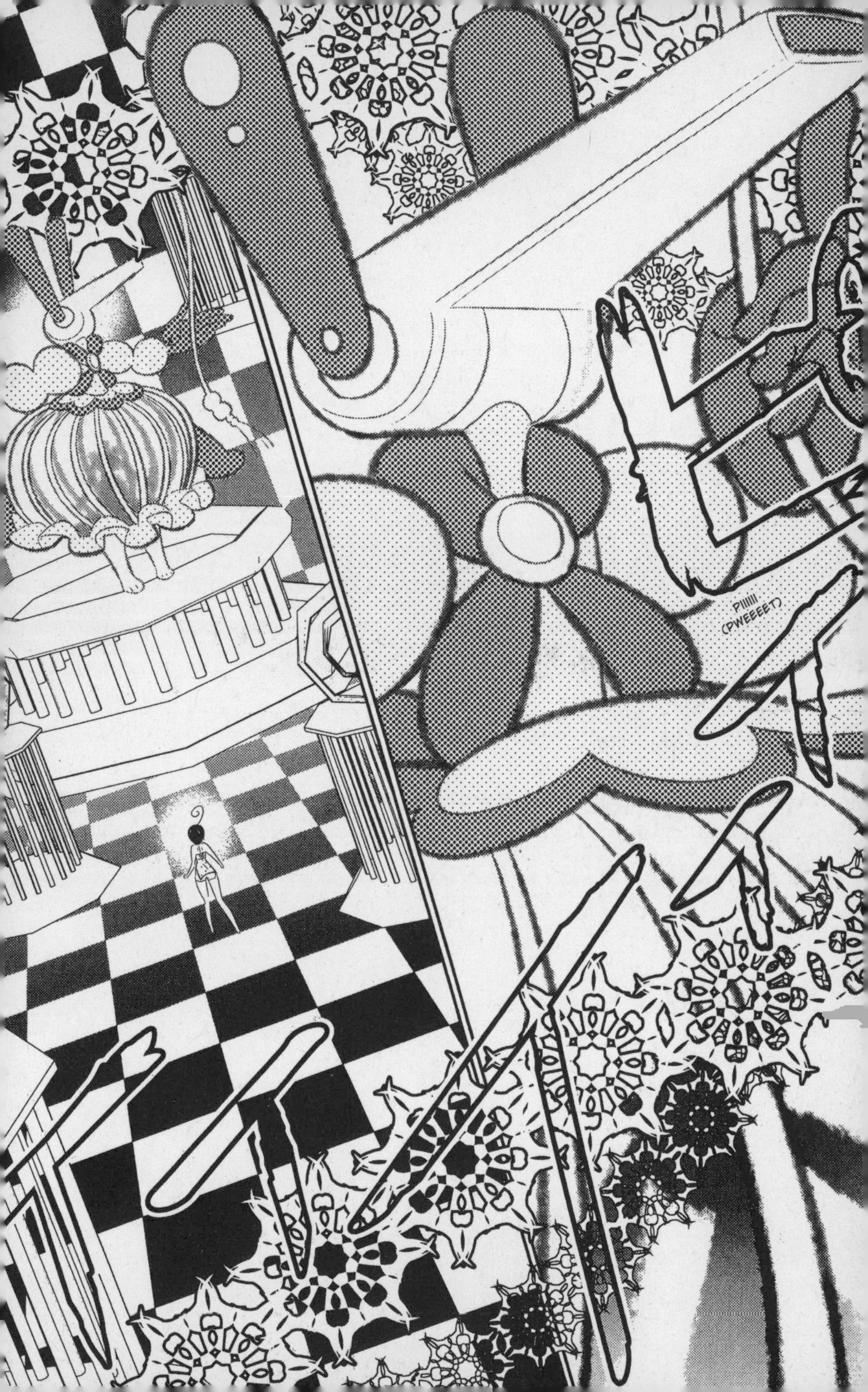
PIIIIIII
(PWEEEET)

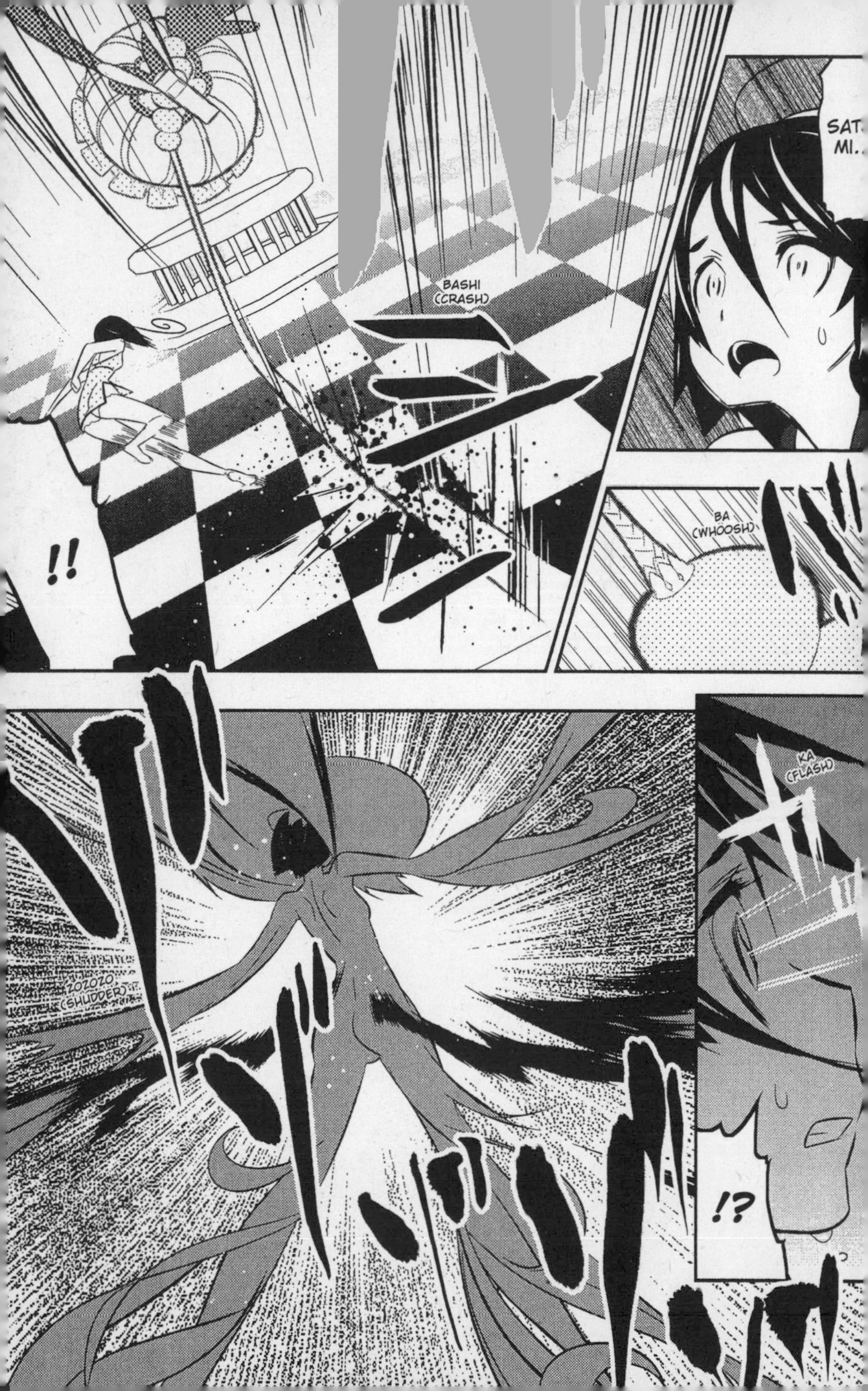
SAT
MI..
BA
(WHOOSH)
BASHI
(CRASH)
!!
KA
(FLASH)
!?
ZOZOZO
(SHUDDER)

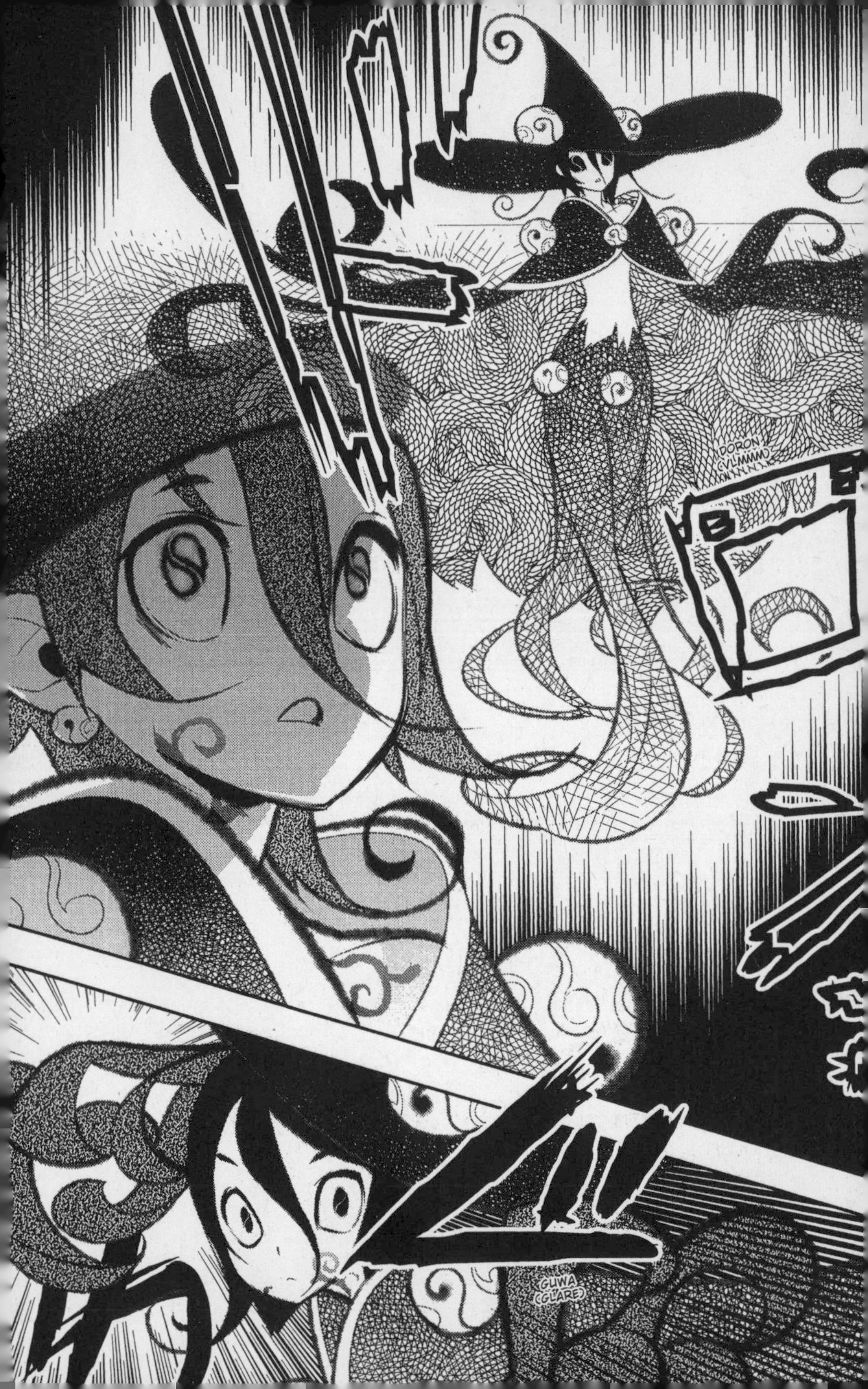
DORON (VLMMM)
GUWA (GLARE)

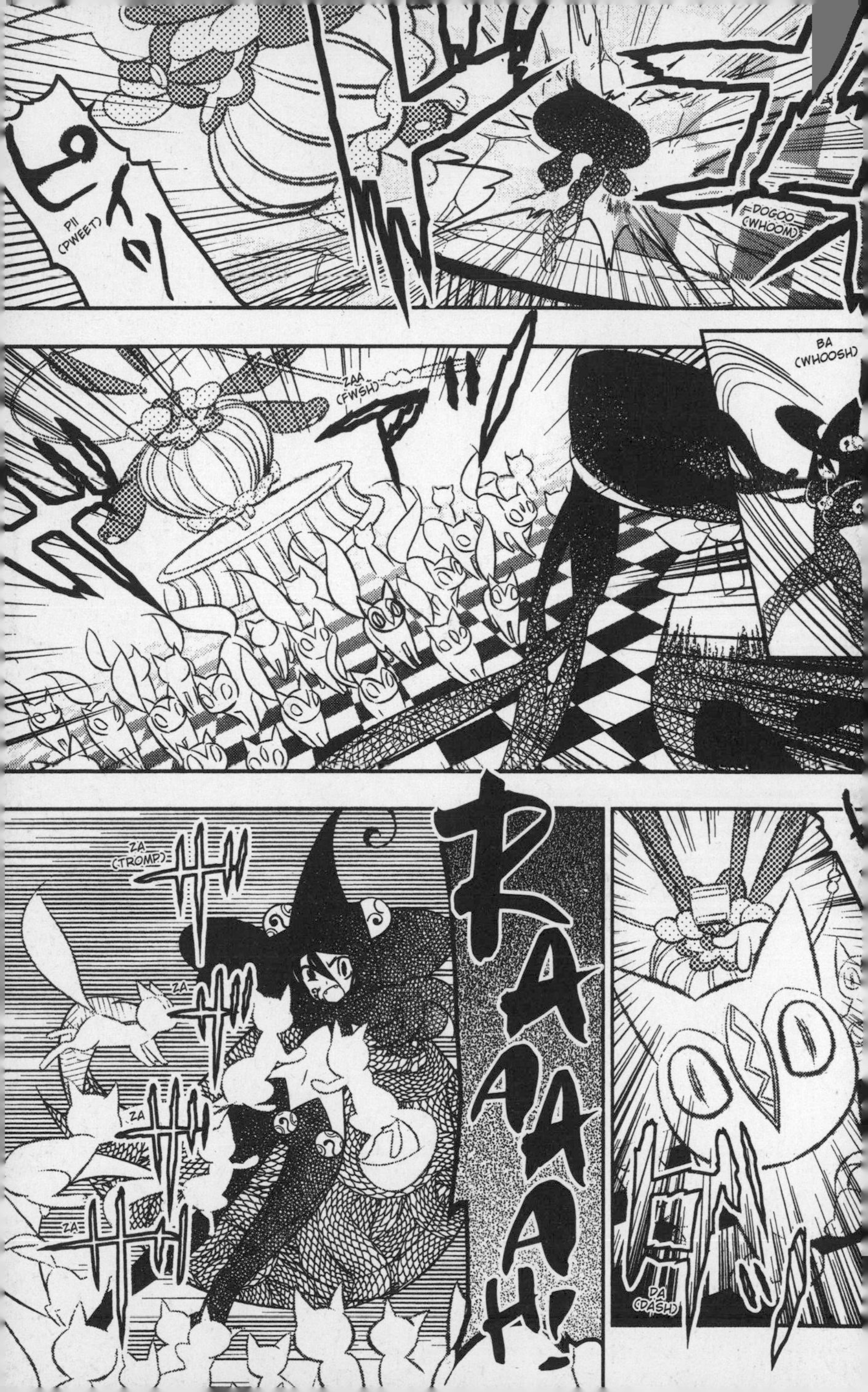
DOGOO (WHOOM)
PII (PWEET)
BA (WHOOSH)
ZAA (FWSH)
DA (DASH)
KAAAAH!
ZA (TROMP)
ZA
ZA
ZA

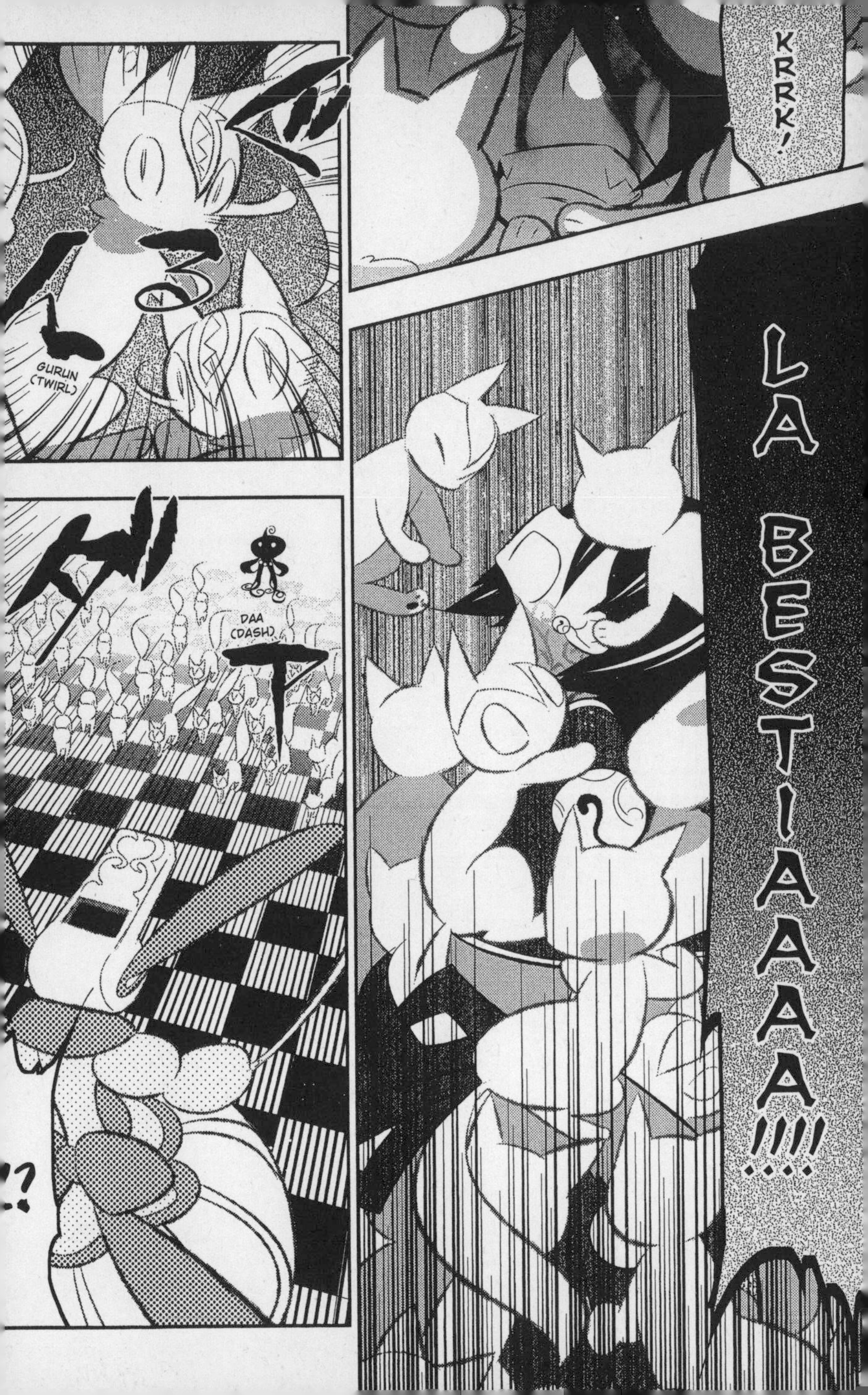
KRRK!
LA BESTIAAAA!!!!
GURUN (TWIRL)
DAA (DASH)
?!

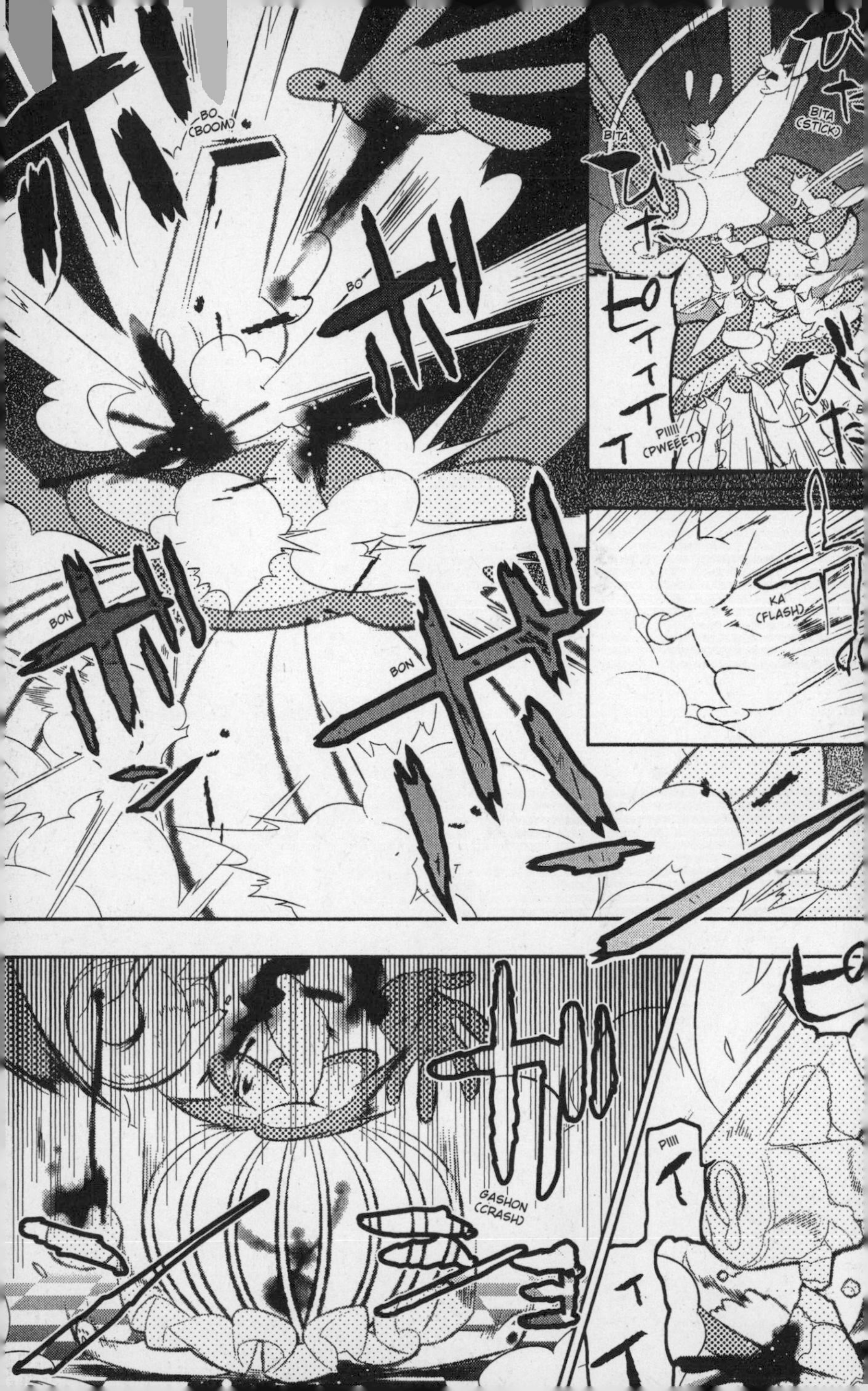
BITA (STICK)
BITA
PIIIII (PWEEET)
KA (FLASH)
BO (BOOM)
BO
BON
BON
PIIII
GASHON (CRASH)

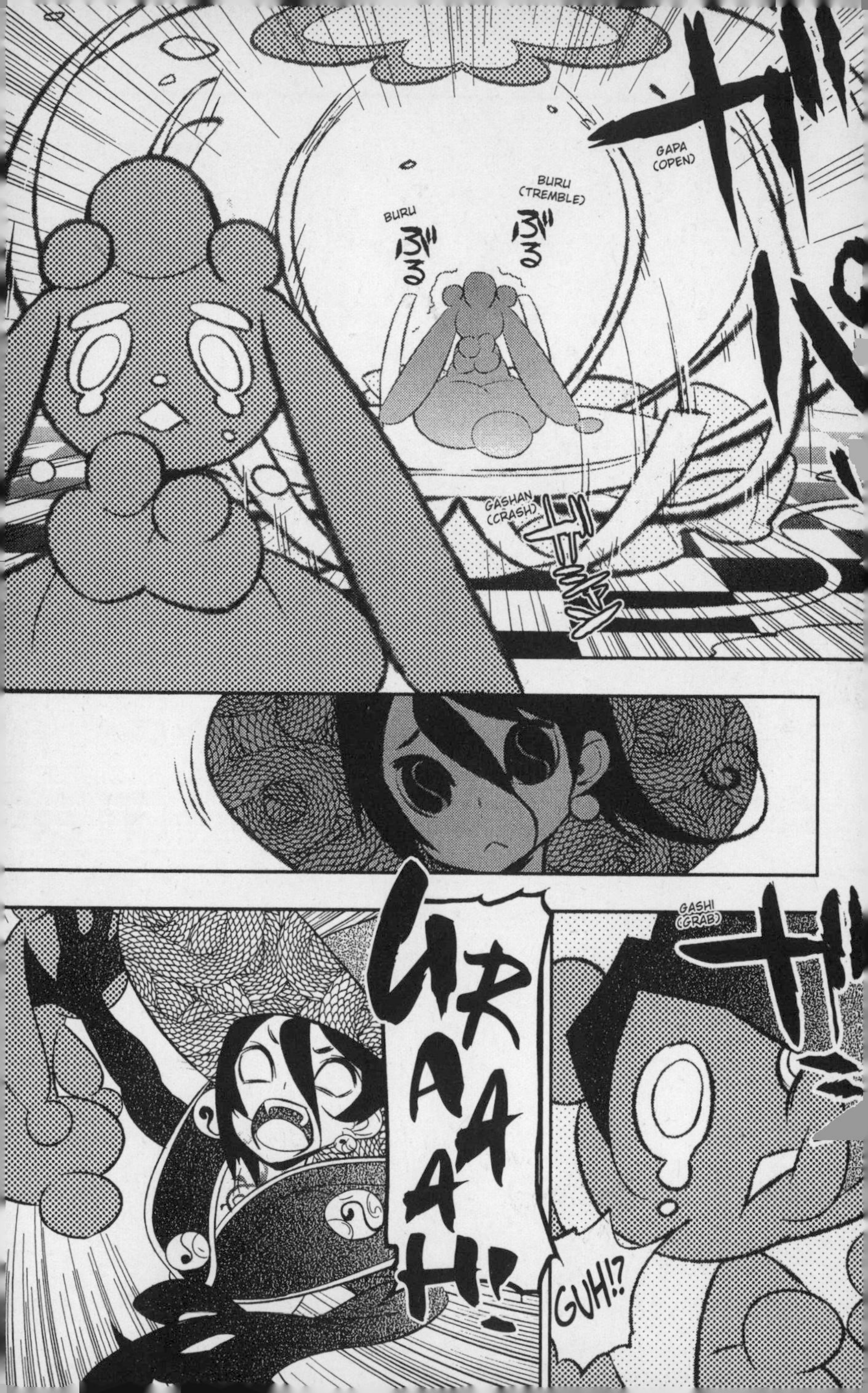
GAPA (OPEN)
BURU (TREMBLE)
BURU
GASHAN (CRASH)
GASHI (GRAB)
GUH!?
URAAAH!

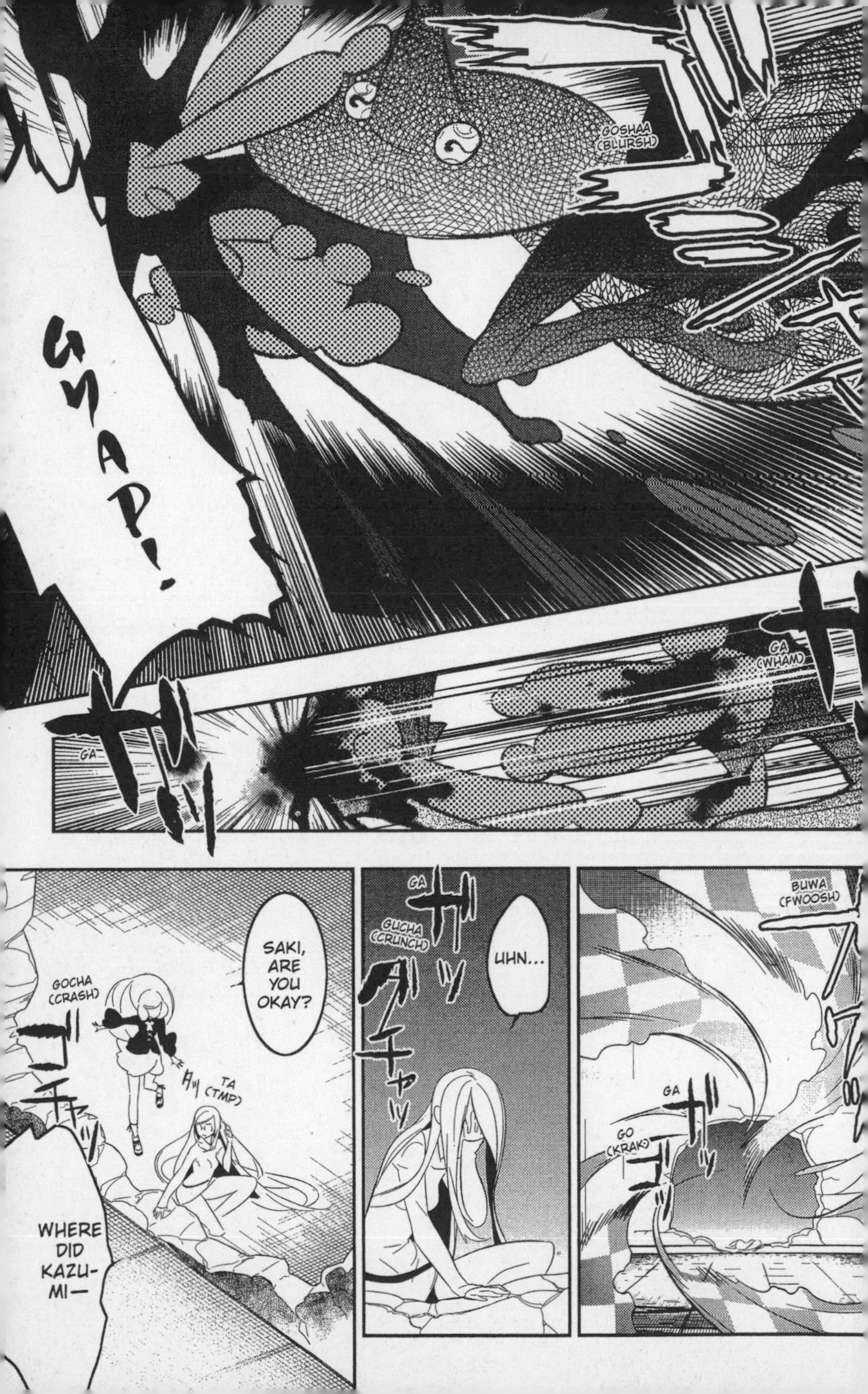
GOSHAA (BLURSH)
SNAP!
GA (WHAM)
GA
BUWA (FWOOSH)
GA
GO (KRAK)
GA
GUCHA (CRUNCH)
UHN...
SAKI, ARE YOU OKAY?
GOCHA (CRASH)
TA (TMP)
WHERE DID KAZUMI—

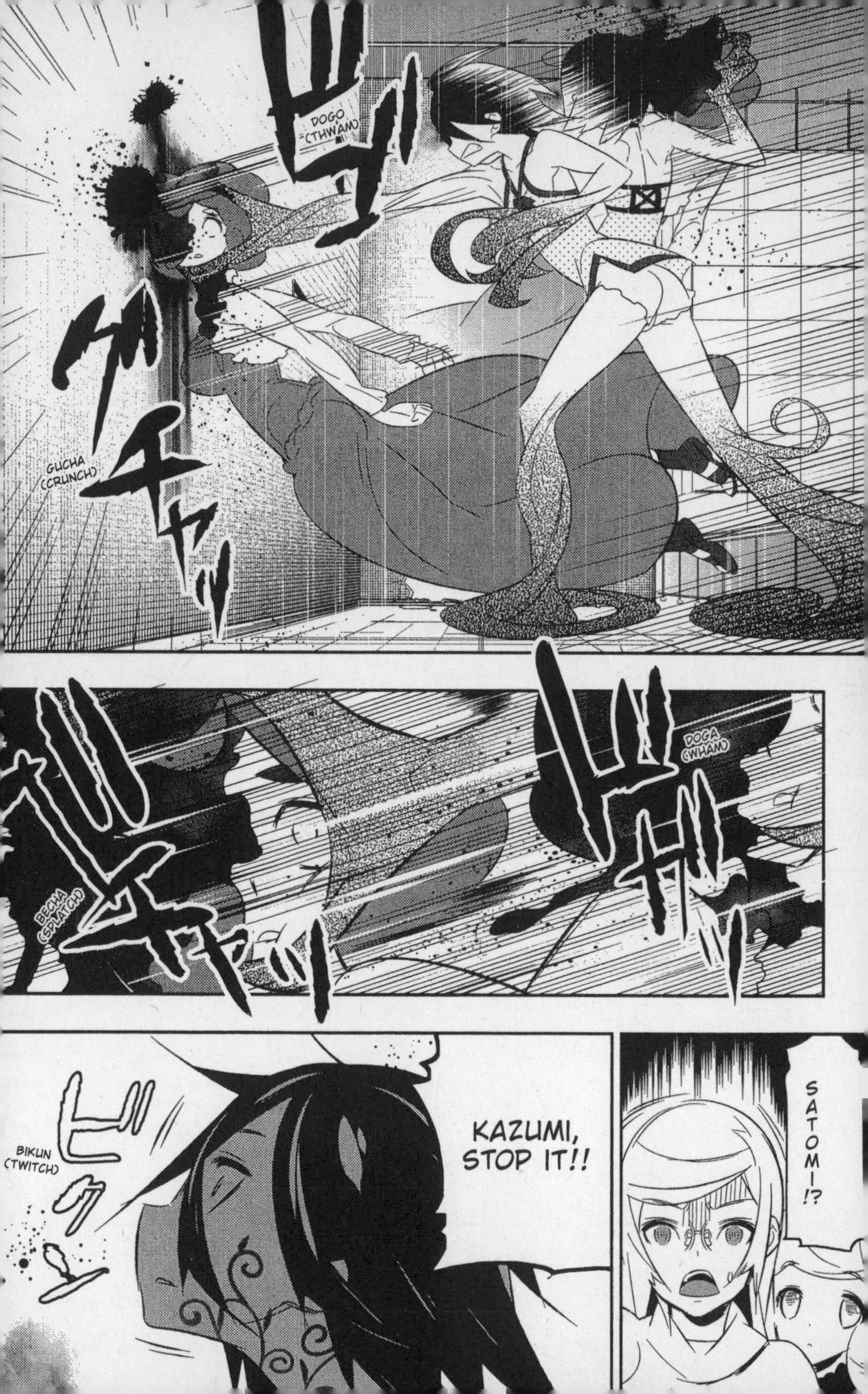
DOGO (THWAM)
GUCHA (CRUNCH)
DOGA (WHAM)
BECHA (SPLATCH)
SATOMI!?
KAZUMI, STOP IT!!
BIKUN (TWITCH)

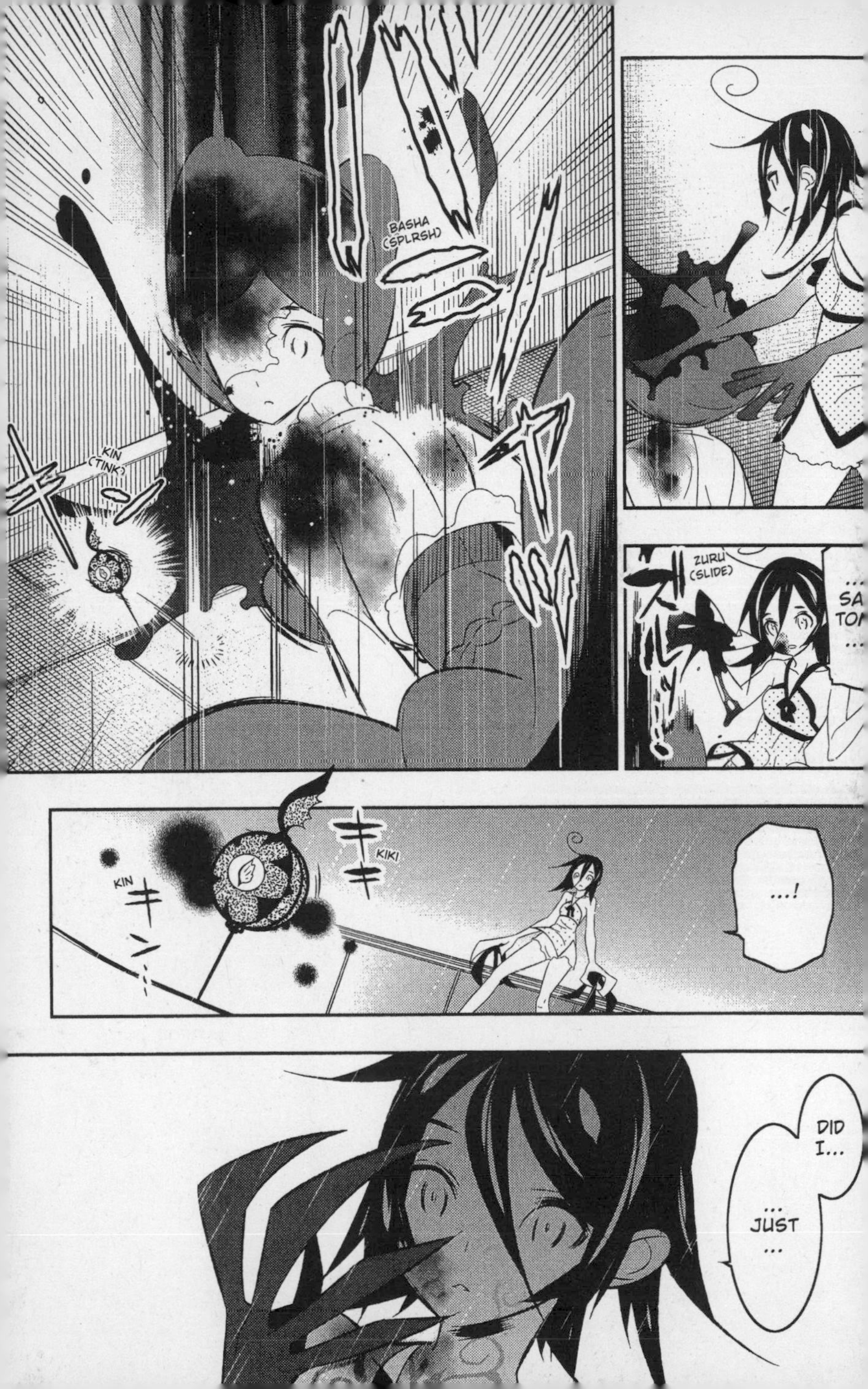
ZURU (SLIDE)
... SA TO ...
BASHA (SPLASH)
KIN (TINK)
...!
KIKI
KIN
DID I...
...JUST...

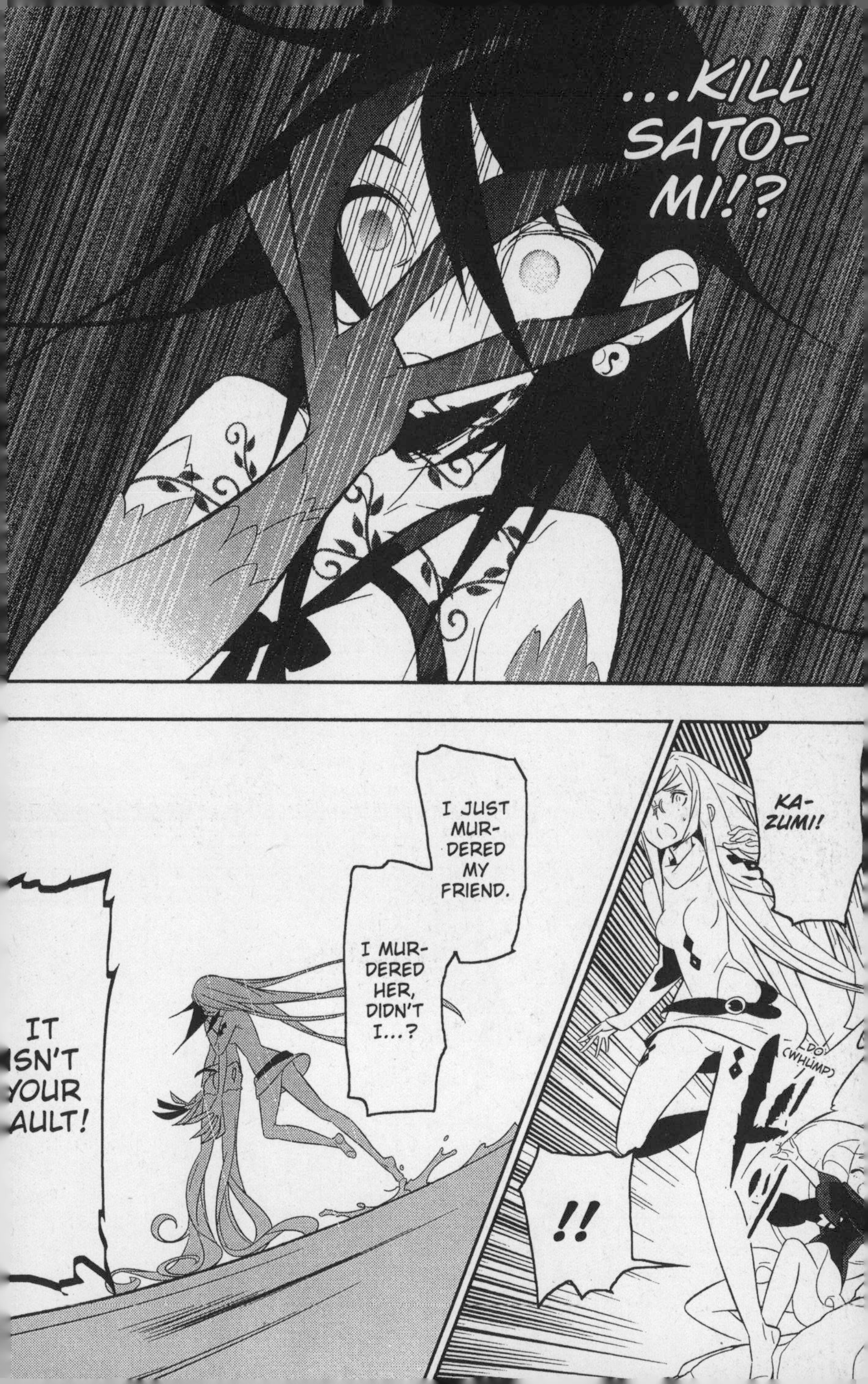
...KILL SATO-MI!?
KA-ZUMI!
DO (WHUMP)
!!
I JUST MUR-DERED MY FRIEND.
I MUR-DERED HER, DIDN'T I...?
IT ISN'T YOUR AULT!

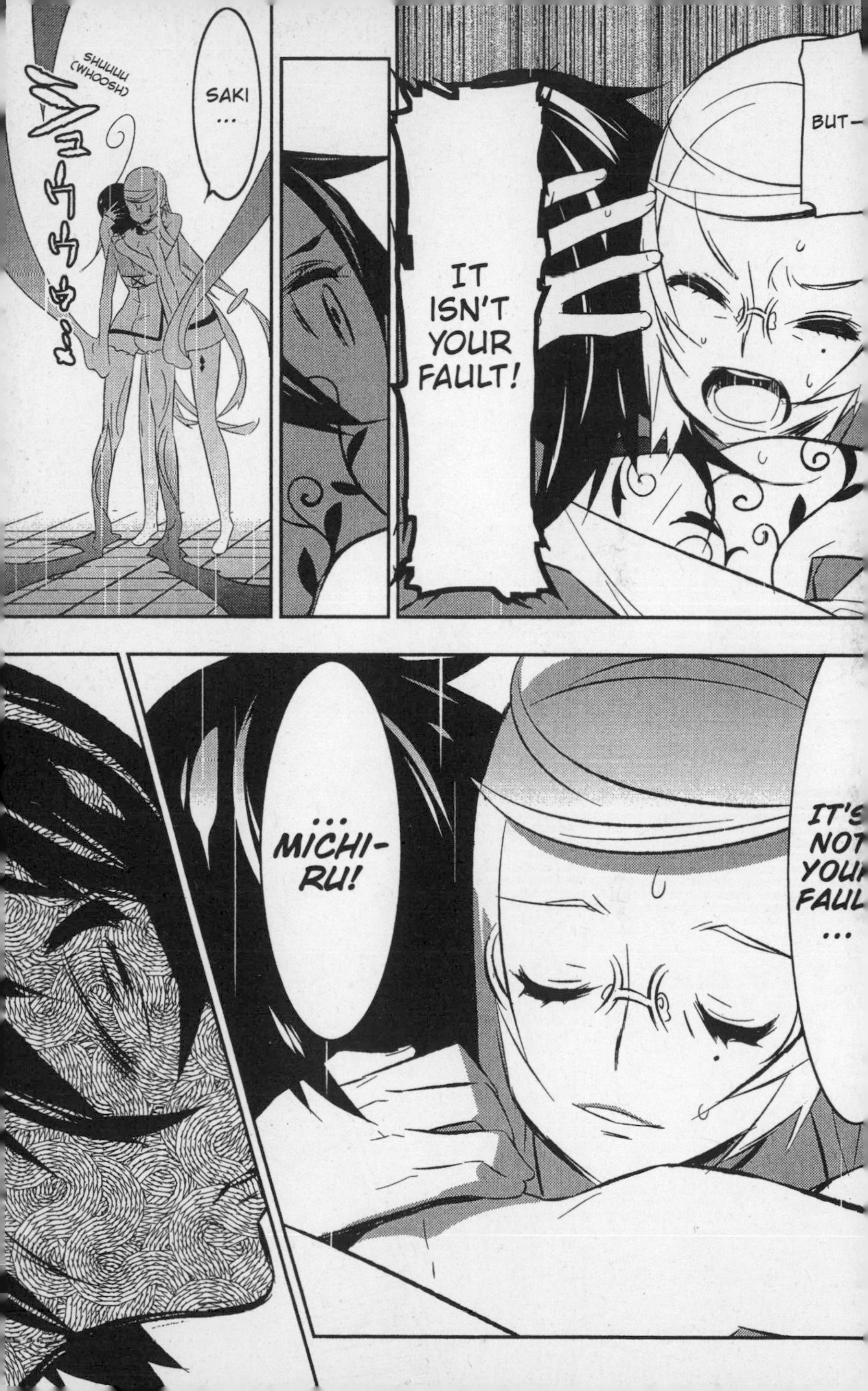
BUT–
IT ISN'T YOUR FAULT!
SAKI ...
SHUUUU (WHOOSH)
IT'S NOT YOUR FAUL...
... MICHI-RU!

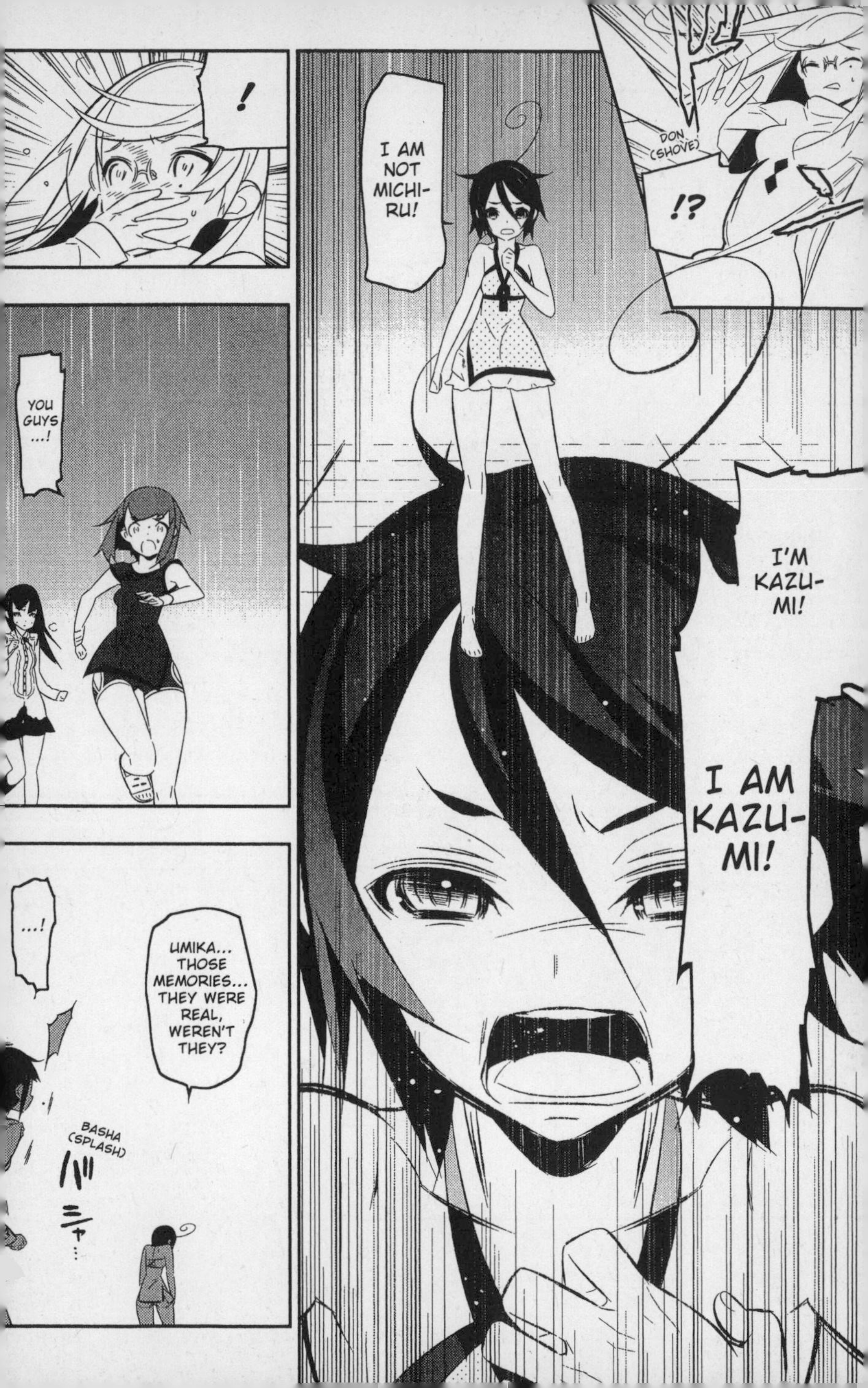
DON (SHOVE)
!?
I AM NOT MICHIRU!
I'M KAZUMI!
I AM KAZUMI!
!
YOU GUYS ...!
...!
UMIKA... THOSE MEMORIES... THEY WERE REAL, WEREN'T THEY?
BASHA (SPLASH)
バシャ…

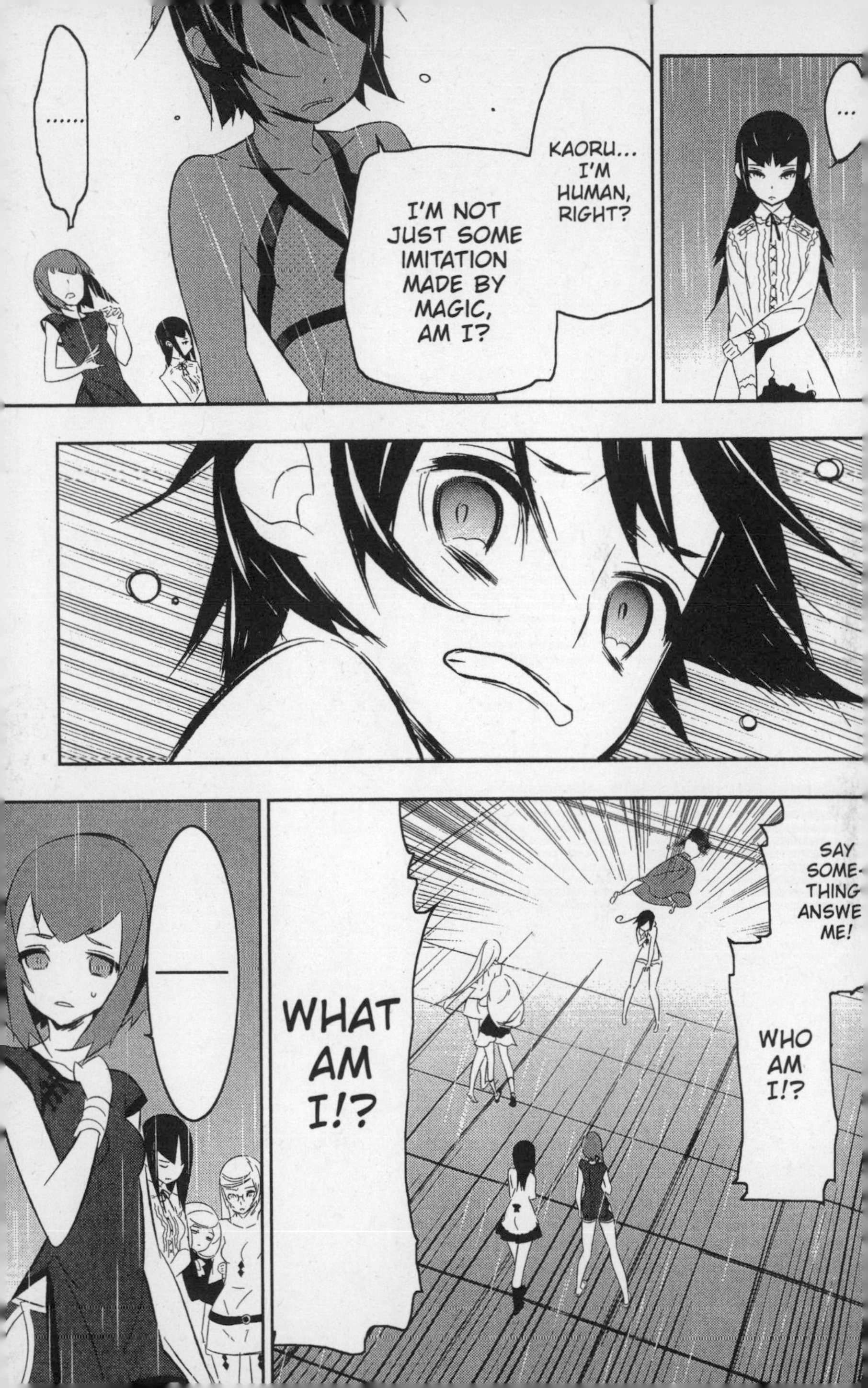
...
KAORU... I'M HUMAN, RIGHT?
I'M NOT JUST SOME IMITATION MADE BY MAGIC, AM I?
......
SAY SOMETHING ANSWE ME!
WHO AM I!?
WHAT AM I!?
——

...!!

FU
(FFT)

KAZUMI!

FUSHUN
(VWWWSH)

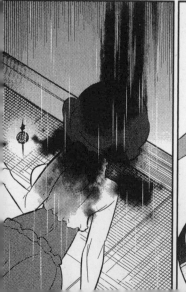

...

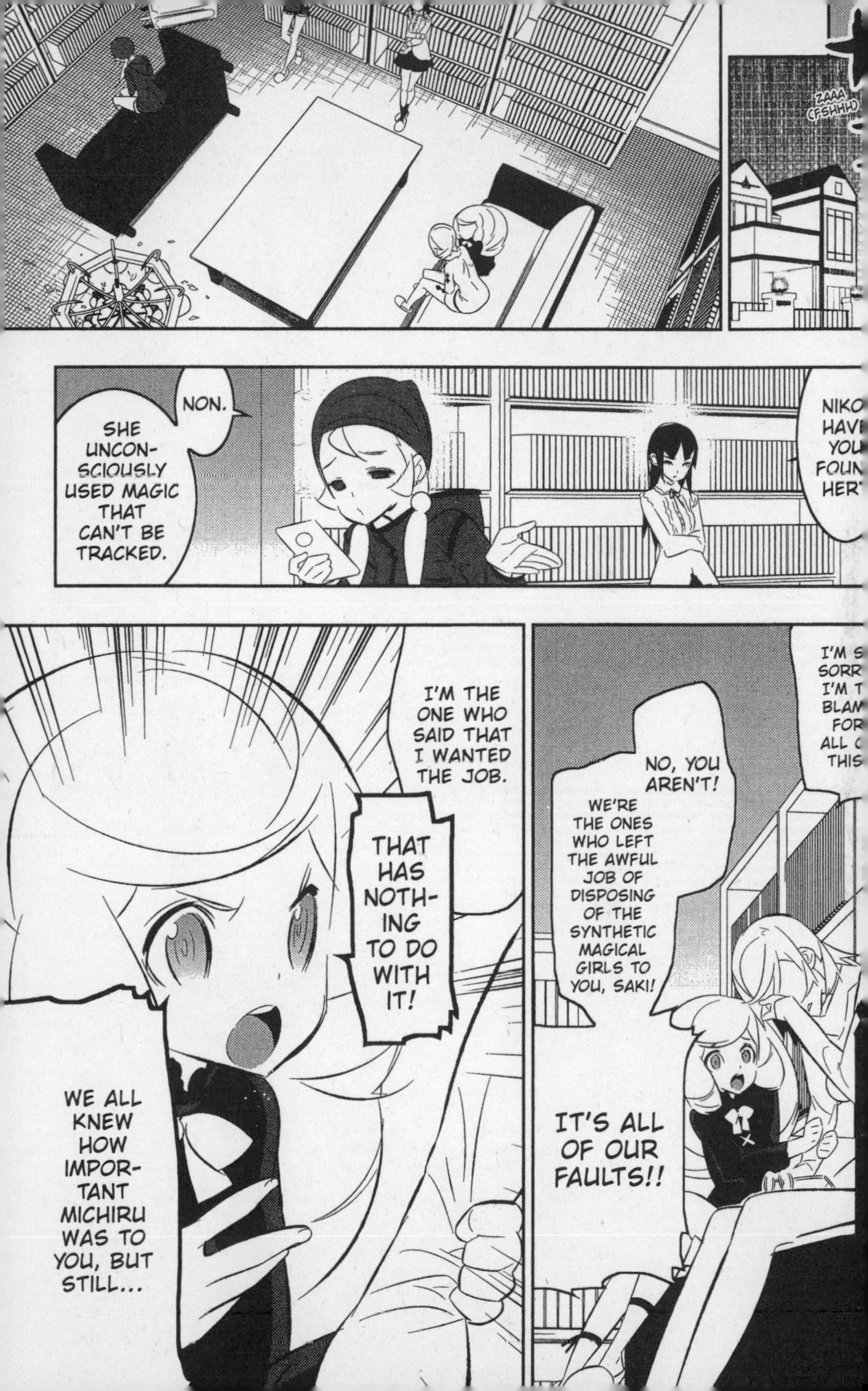
ZAAA (FSHHH)
NIKO HAVE YOU FOUN HER
NON.
SHE UNCON-SCIOUSLY USED MAGIC THAT CAN'T BE TRACKED.
I'M S SORR I'M T BLAM FOR ALL O THIS
NO, YOU AREN'T!
WE'RE THE ONES WHO LEFT THE AWFUL JOB OF DISPOSING OF THE SYNTHETIC MAGICAL GIRLS TO YOU, SAKI!
IT'S ALL OF OUR FAULTS!!
I'M THE ONE WHO SAID THAT I WANTED THE JOB.
THAT HAS NOTH-ING TO DO WITH IT!
WE ALL KNEW HOW IMPOR-TANT MICHIRU WAS TO YOU, BUT STILL...

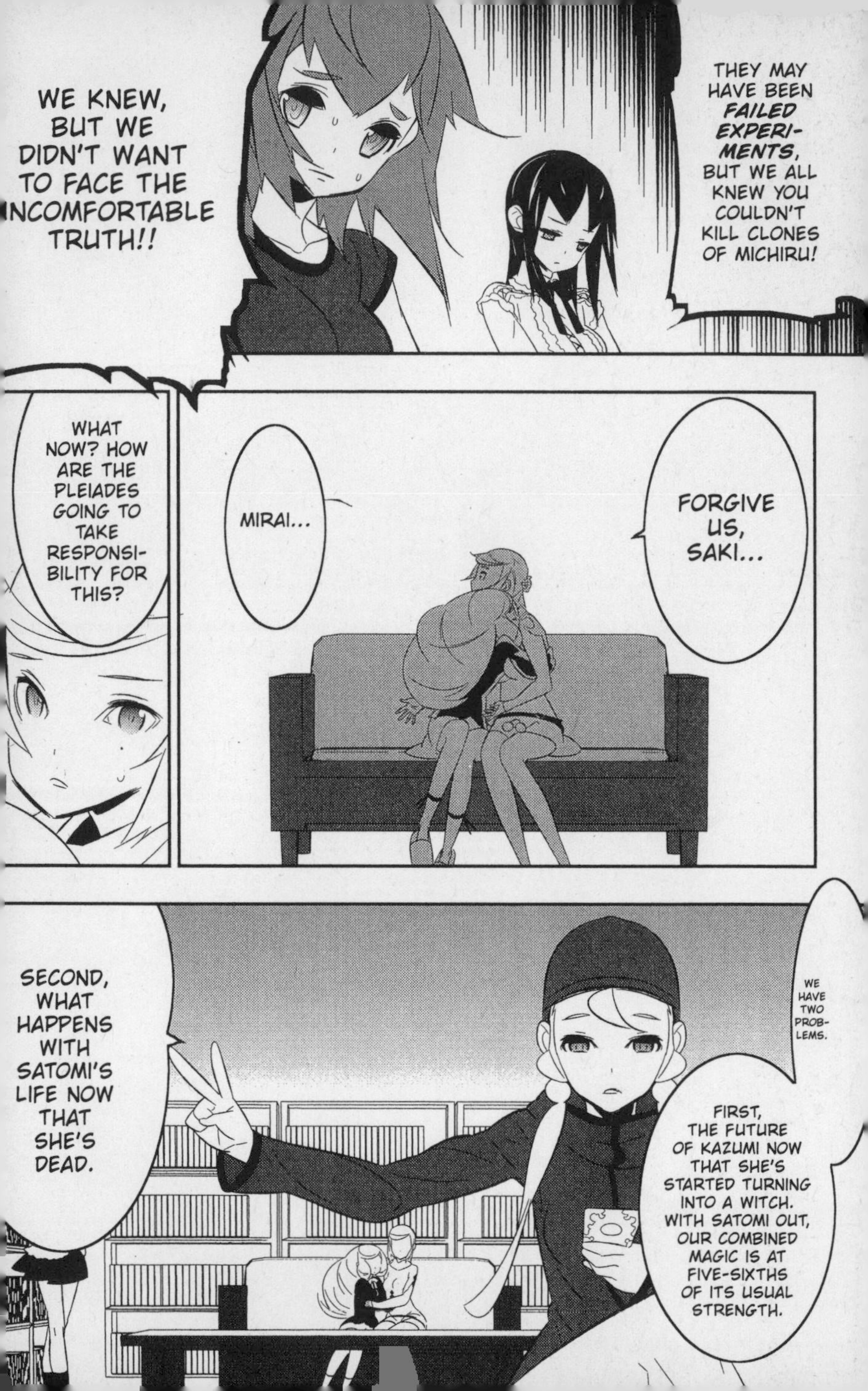
THEY MAY HAVE BEEN *FAILED EXPERIMENTS*, BUT WE ALL KNEW YOU COULDN'T KILL CLONES OF MICHIRU!
WE KNEW, BUT WE DIDN'T WANT TO FACE THE INCOMFORTABLE TRUTH!!
FORGIVE US, SAKI...
MIRAI...
WHAT NOW? HOW ARE THE PLEIADES GOING TO TAKE RESPONSIBILITY FOR THIS?
WE HAVE TWO PROBLEMS.
FIRST, THE FUTURE OF KAZUMI NOW THAT SHE'S STARTED TURNING INTO A WITCH. WITH SATOMI OUT, OUR COMBINED MAGIC IS AT FIVE-SIXTHS OF ITS USUAL STRENGTH.
SECOND, WHAT HAPPENS WITH SATOMI'S LIFE NOW THAT SHE'S DEAD.

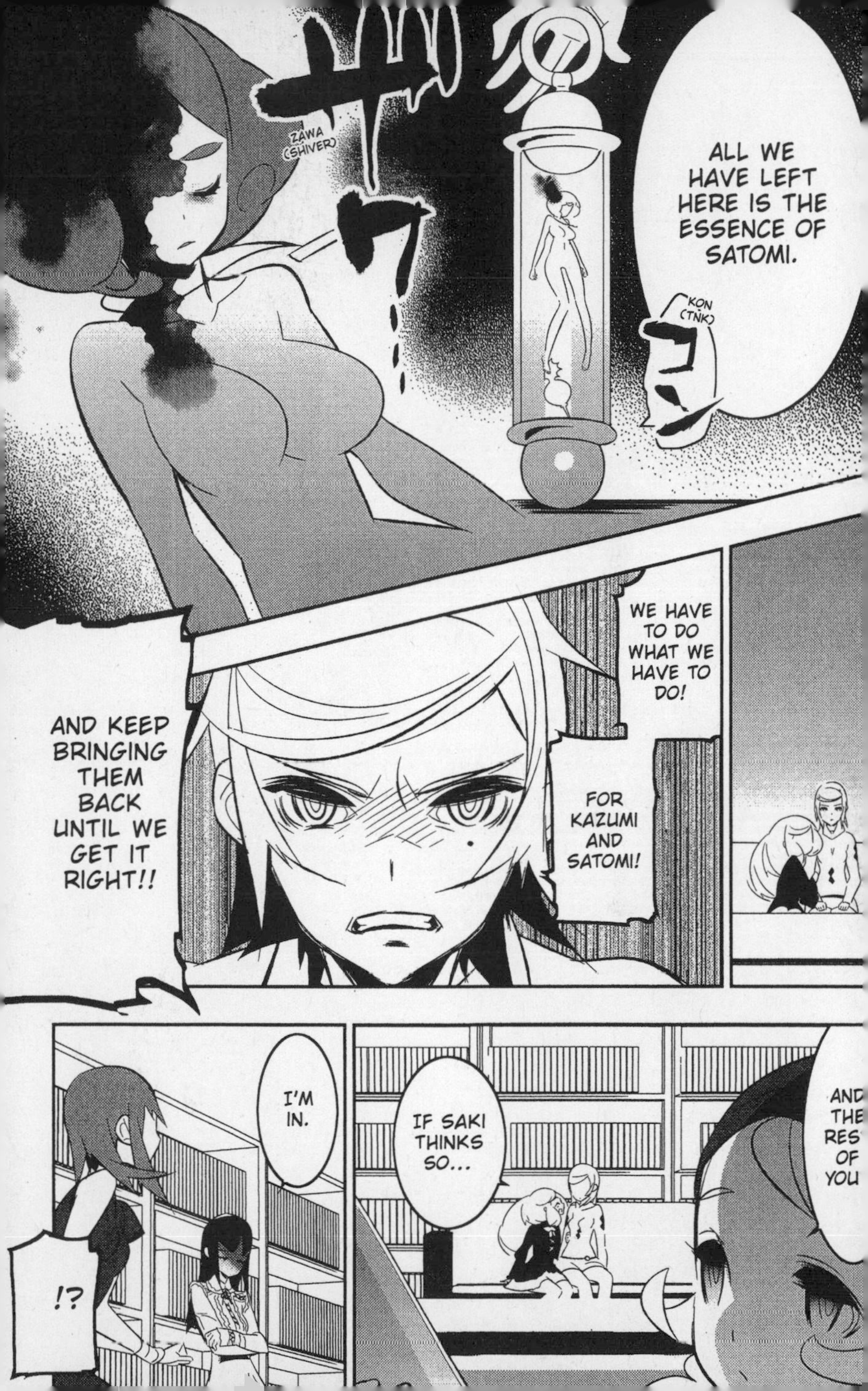
ALL WE HAVE LEFT HERE IS THE ESSENCE OF SATOMI.
KON (TNK)
ZAWA (SHIVER)
WE HAVE TO DO WHAT WE HAVE TO DO!
FOR KAZUMI AND SATOMI!
AND KEEP BRINGING THEM BACK UNTIL WE GET IT RIGHT!!
AND THE RES OF YOU
IF SAKI THINKS SO...
I'M IN.
!?

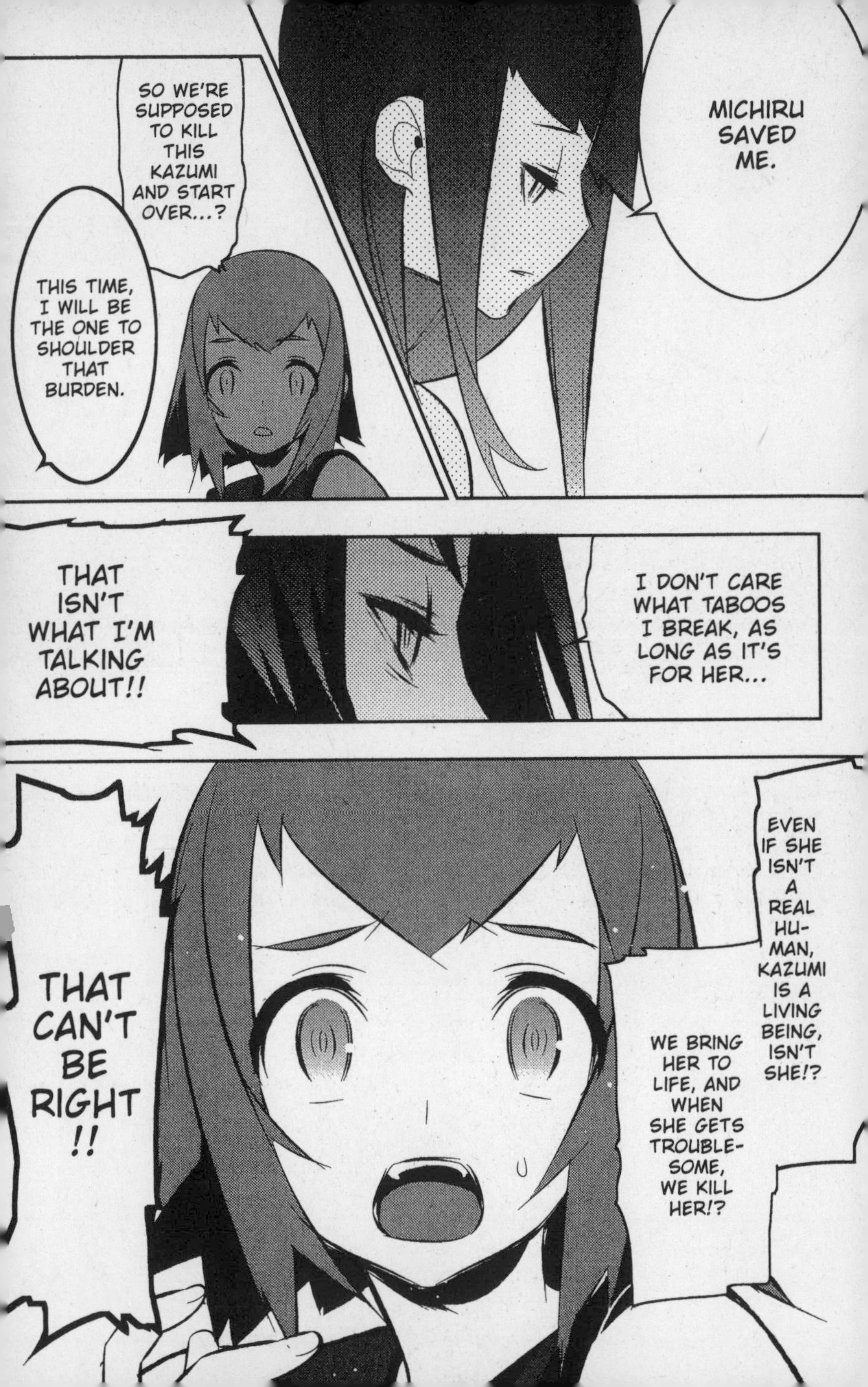
MICHIRU SAVED ME.
SO WE'RE SUPPOSED TO KILL THIS KAZUMI AND START OVER...?
THIS TIME, I WILL BE THE ONE TO SHOULDER THAT BURDEN.
I DON'T CARE WHAT TABOOS I BREAK, AS LONG AS IT'S FOR HER...
THAT ISN'T WHAT I'M TALKING ABOUT!!
EVEN IF SHE ISN'T A REAL HU-MAN, KAZUMI IS A LIVING BEING, ISN'T SHE!?
WE BRING HER TO LIFE, AND WHEN SHE GETS TROUBLE-SOME, WE KILL HER!?
THAT CAN'T BE RIGHT!!

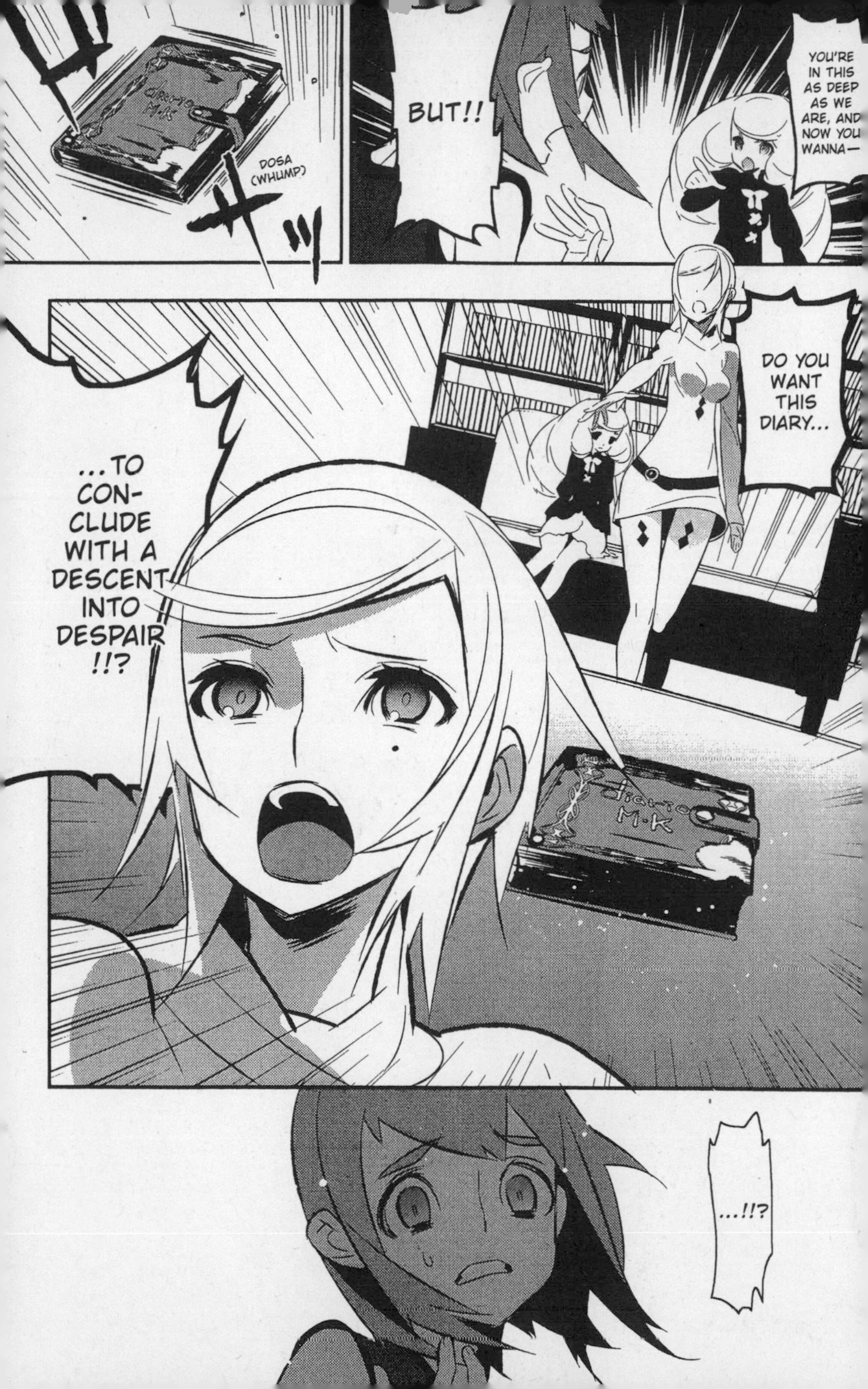
YOU'RE IN THIS AS DEEP AS WE ARE, AND NOW YOU WANNA—
BUT!!
DOSA (WHUMP)
DO YOU WANT THIS DIARY...
...TO CON-CLUDE WITH A DESCENT INTO DESPAIR !!?
...!!?

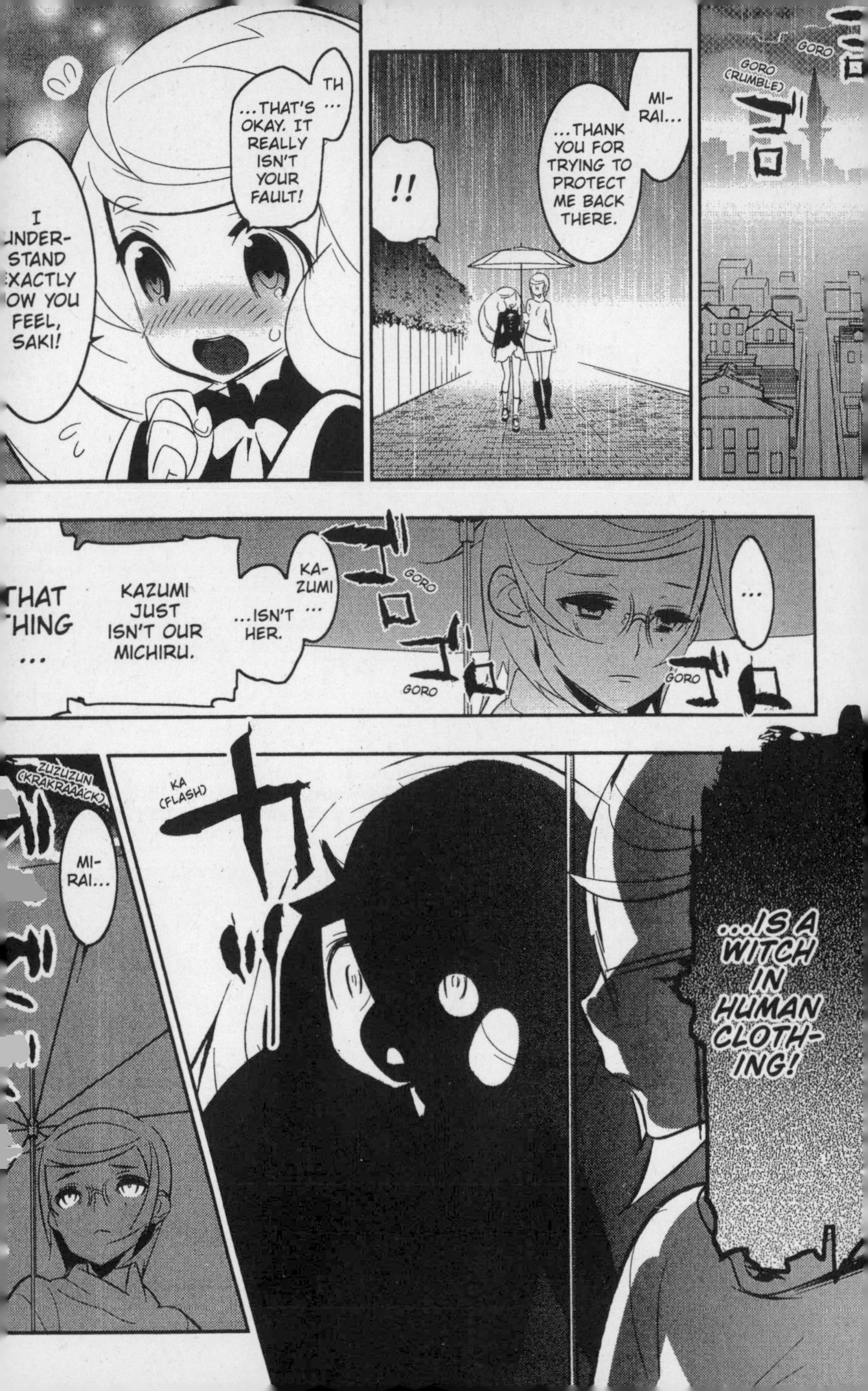
GORO
GORO (RUMBLE)
MI-RAI...
...THANK YOU FOR TRYING TO PROTECT ME BACK THERE.
!!
TH...
...THAT'S OKAY. IT REALLY ISN'T YOUR FAULT!
I NDER-STAND XACTLY OW YOU FEEL, SAKI!
...
GORO
GORO
KA-ZUMI...
GORO
...ISN'T HER.
KAZUMI JUST ISN'T OUR MICHIRU.
THAT HING...
...IS A WITCH IN HUMAN CLOTH-ING!
KA (FLASH)
ZUZUZUN (KRAKRAAACK)
MI-RAI...

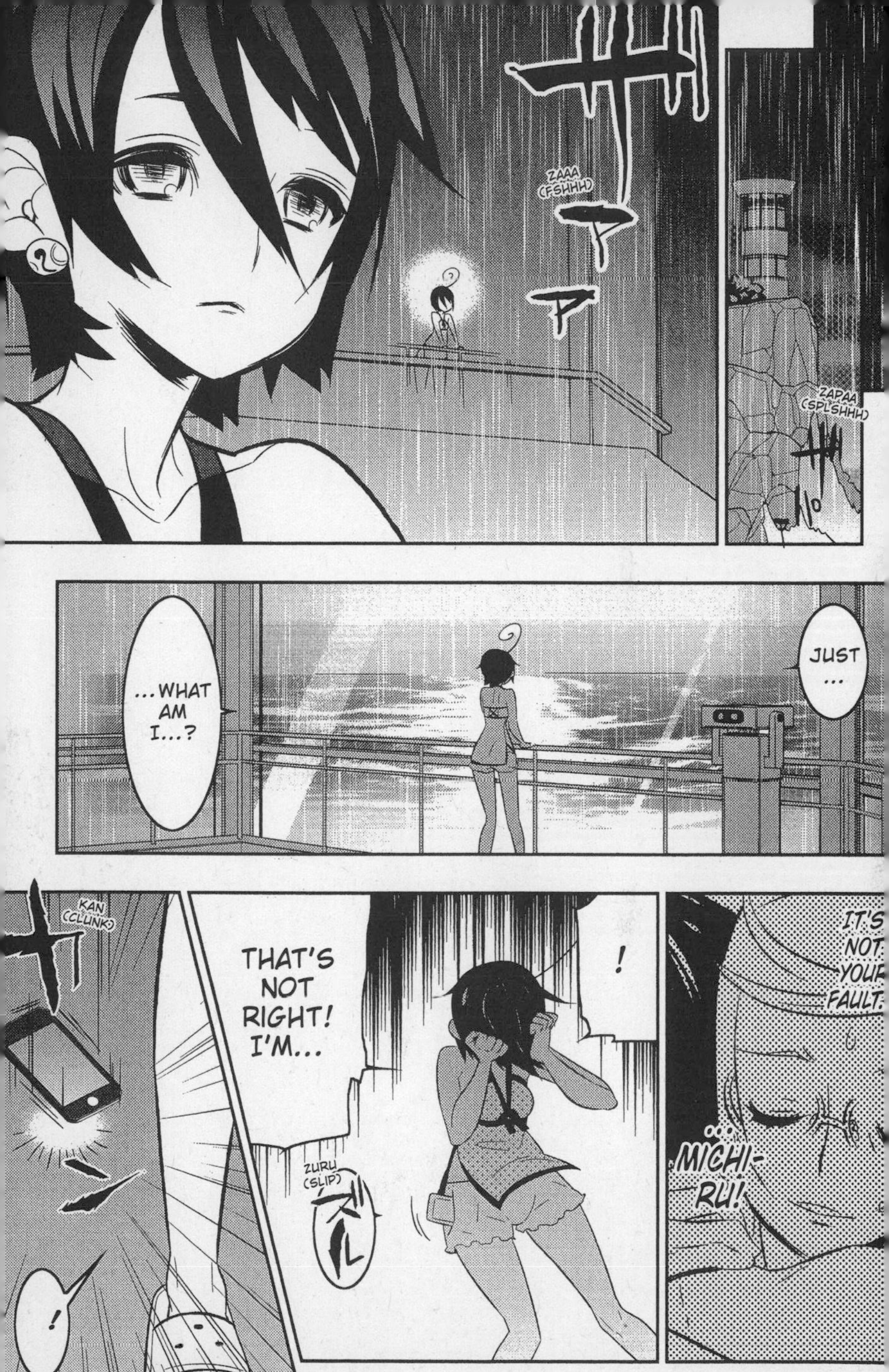
ZAPAA (SPLSHHH)
ZAAA (FSHHH)
JUST...
...WHAT AM I...?
IT'S NOT YOUR FAULT.
...MICHI-RU!
!
THAT'S NOT RIGHT! I'M...
ZURU (SLIP)
KAN (CLUNK)
!

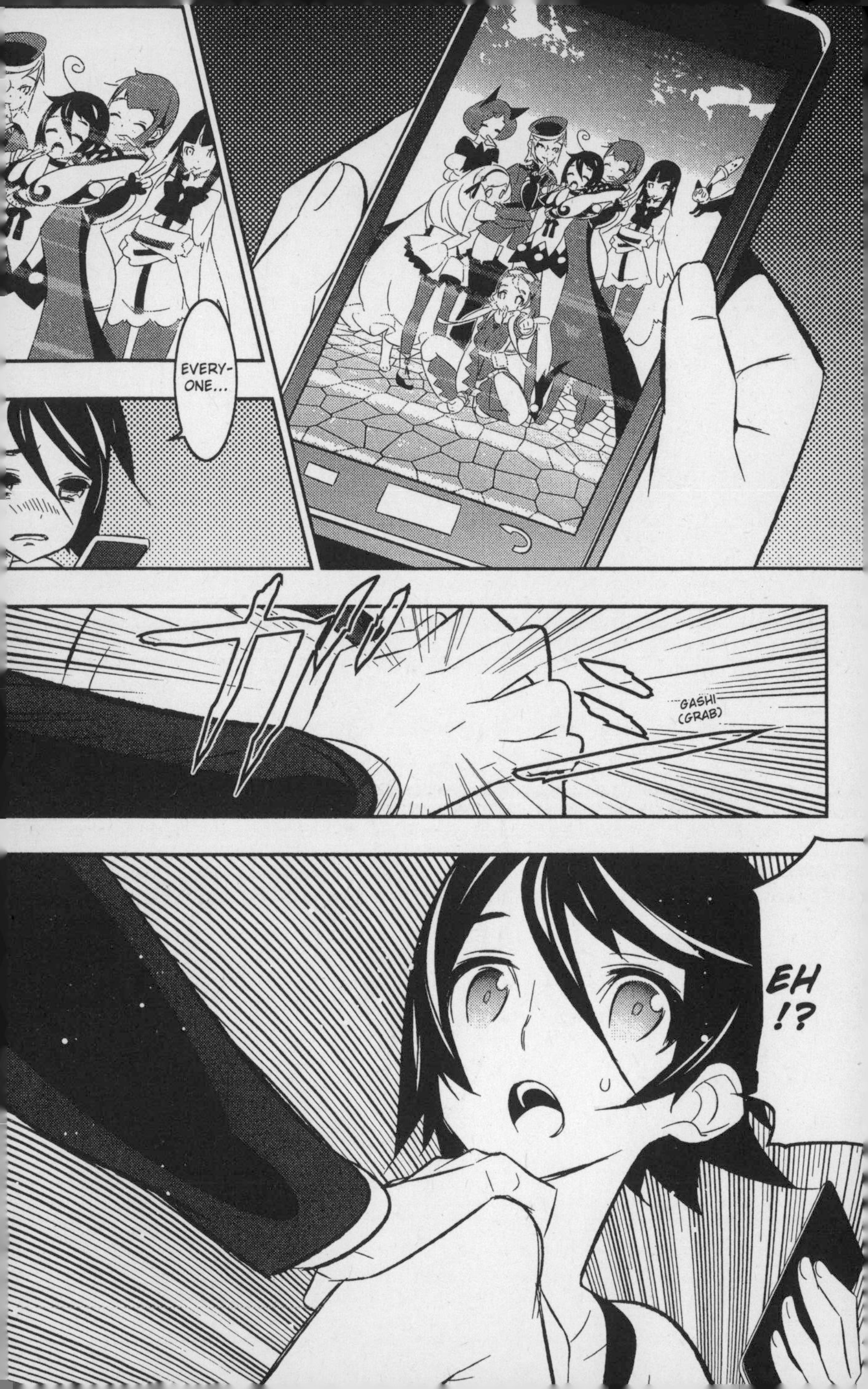
EVERY-ONE...
GASHI (GRAB)
EH!?

Witch Field Guide

Satomi Witch

The design direction from Hiramatsu-san was, "On the outside she's a beast summoner, but on the inside she's a frightened bunny."

So very Satomi-like.

PUELLA MAGI
KAZUMI ★ MAGICA
The innocent malice

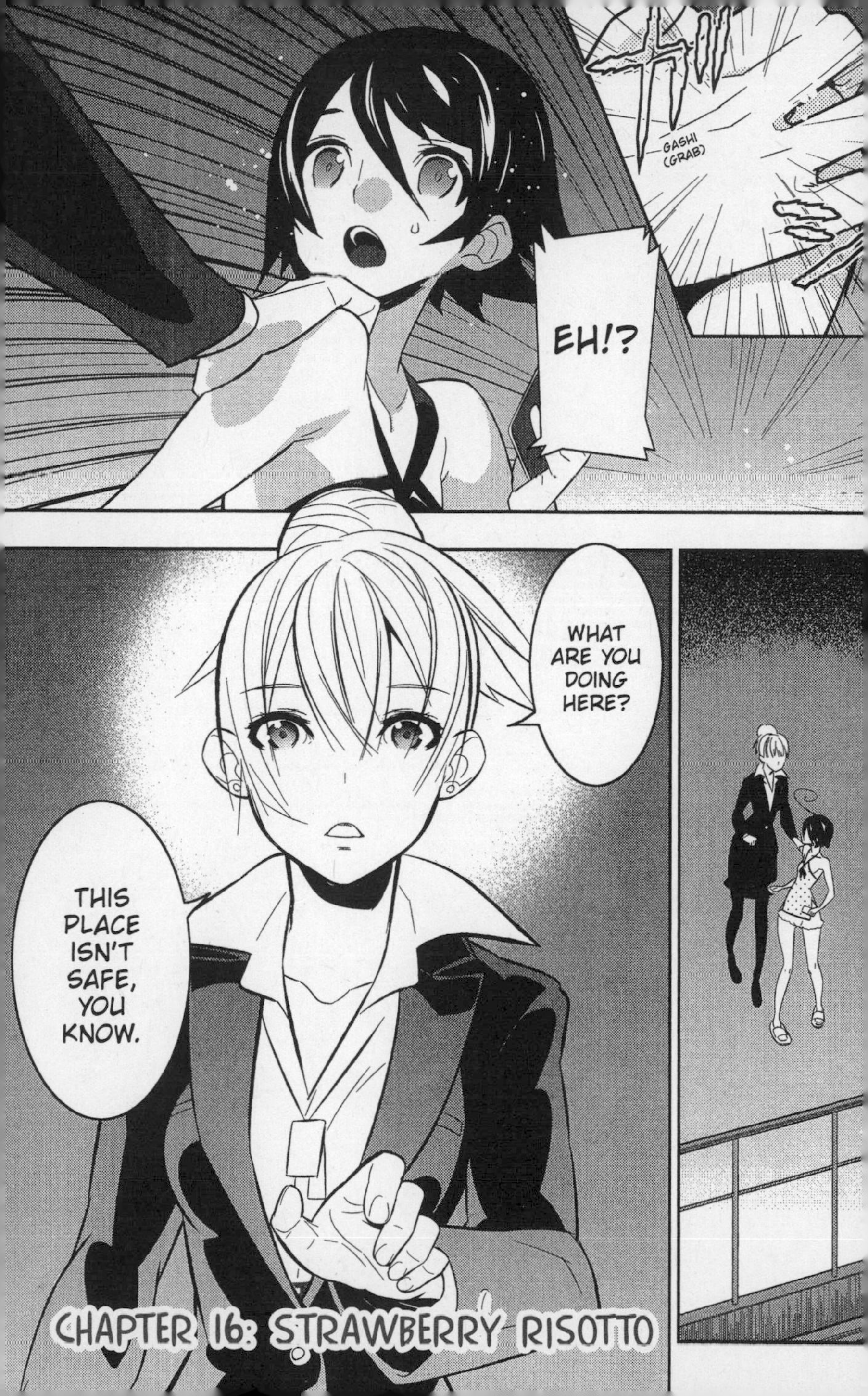
GASHI (GRAB)
EH!?
WHAT ARE YOU DOING HERE?
THIS PLACE ISN'T SAFE, YOU KNOW.
CHAPTER 16: STRAWBERRY RISOTTO

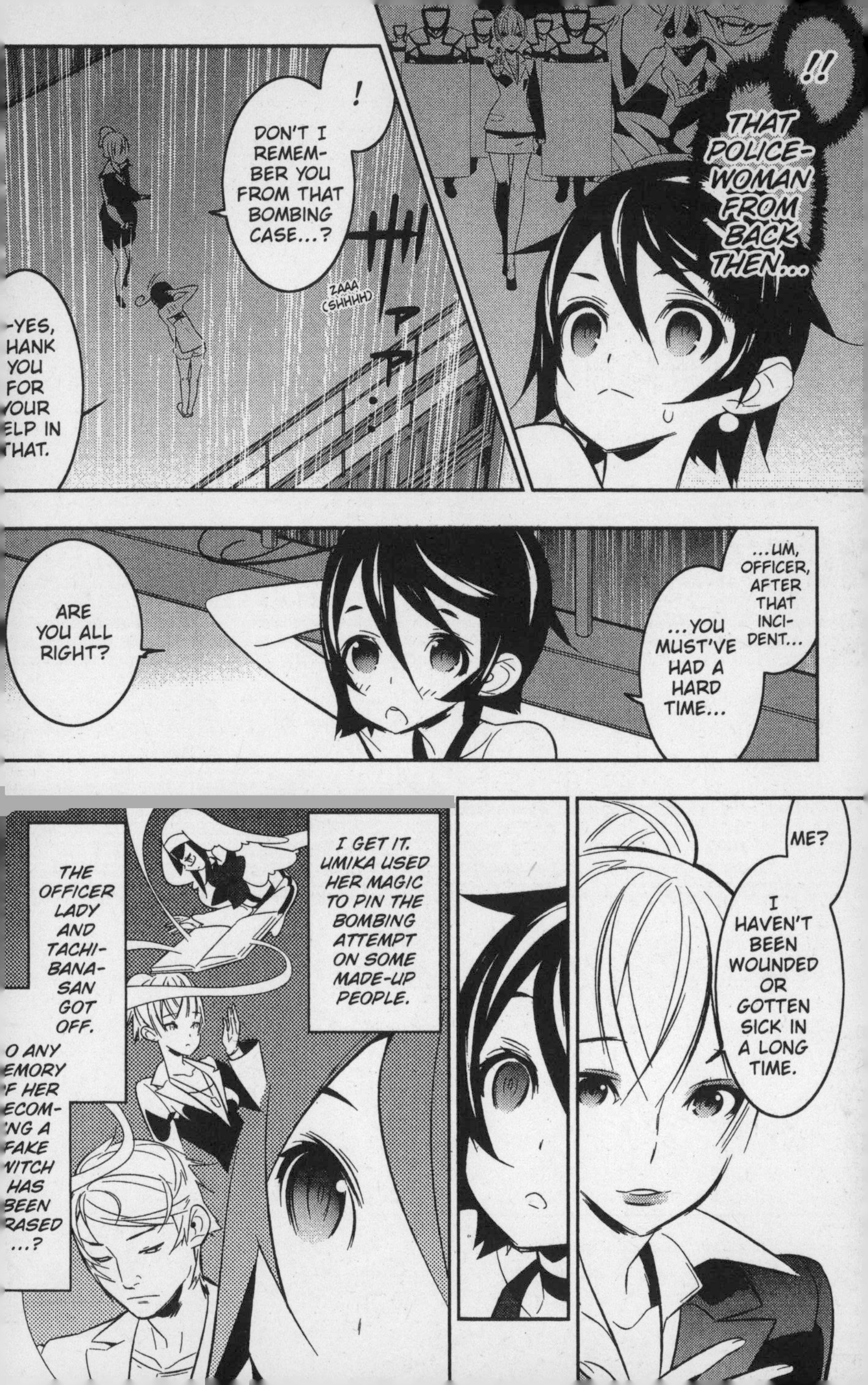
!!
THAT POLICE-WOMAN FROM BACK THEN...
!
DON'T I REMEM-BER YOU FROM THAT BOMBING CASE...?
ZAAA (SHHHH)
-YES, HANK YOU FOR YOUR ELP IN THAT.
...UM, OFFICER, AFTER THAT INCI-DENT...
...YOU MUST'VE HAD A HARD TIME...
ARE YOU ALL RIGHT?
ME?
I HAVEN'T BEEN WOUNDED OR GOTTEN SICK IN A LONG TIME.
I GET IT. UMIKA USED HER MAGIC TO PIN THE BOMBING ATTEMPT ON SOME MADE-UP PEOPLE.
THE OFFICER LADY AND TACHI-BANA-SAN GOT OFF.
O ANY EMORY F HER ECOM-NG A FAKE WITCH HAS BEEN RASED ...?

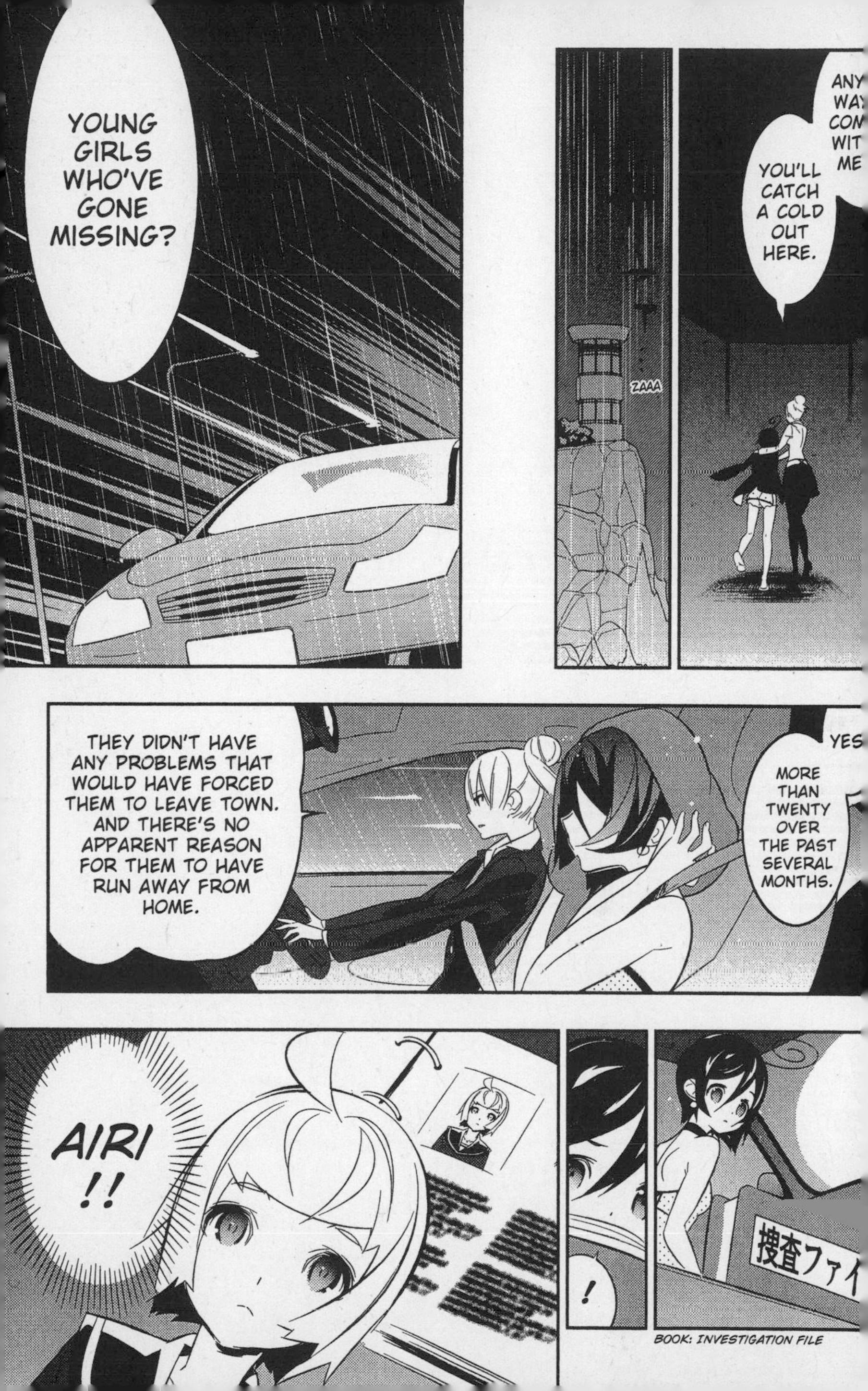
ANY WAY COM WIT ME
YOU'LL CATCH A COLD OUT HERE.
ZAAA
YOUNG GIRLS WHO'VE GONE MISSING?
YES
MORE THAN TWENTY OVER THE PAST SEVERAL MONTHS.
THEY DIDN'T HAVE ANY PROBLEMS THAT WOULD HAVE FORCED THEM TO LEAVE TOWN. AND THERE'S NO APPARENT REASON FOR THEM TO HAVE RUN AWAY FROM HOME.
捜査ファイ
BOOK: INVESTIGATION FILE
!
AIRI !!

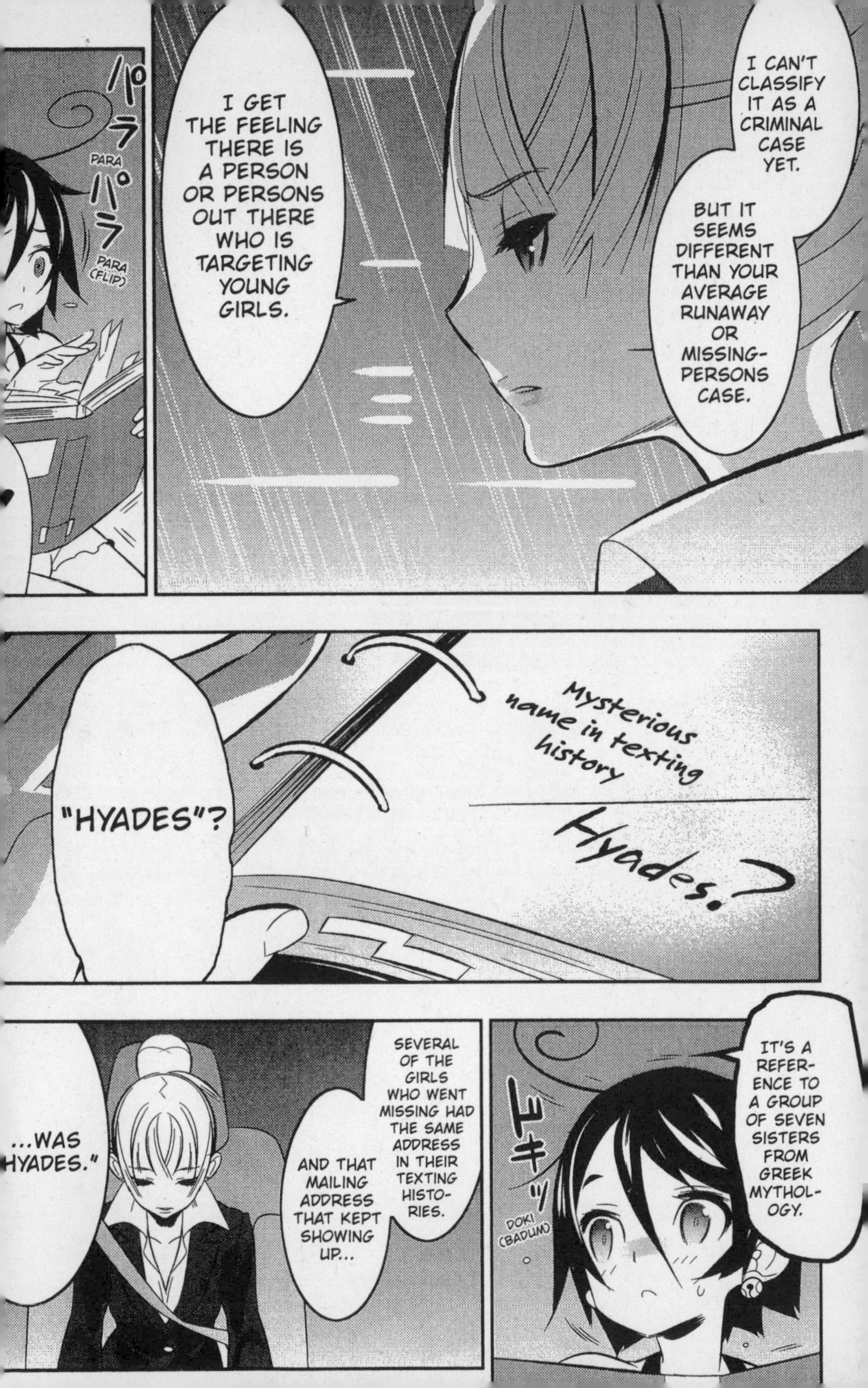
I CAN'T CLASSIFY IT AS A CRIMINAL CASE YET.
BUT IT SEEMS DIFFERENT THAN YOUR AVERAGE RUNAWAY OR MISSING-PERSONS CASE.
I GET THE FEELING THERE IS A PERSON OR PERSONS OUT THERE WHO IS TARGETING YOUNG GIRLS.
パラ
PARA
パラ
PARA (FLIP)
Mysterious name in texting history
Hyades?
"HYADES"?
IT'S A REFERENCE TO A GROUP OF SEVEN SISTERS FROM GREEK MYTHOLOGY.
ドキッ
DOKI (BADUM)
SEVERAL OF THE GIRLS WHO WENT MISSING HAD THE SAME ADDRESS IN THEIR TEXTING HISTORIES.
AND THAT MAILING ADDRESS THAT KEPT SHOWING UP...
...WAS HYADES."

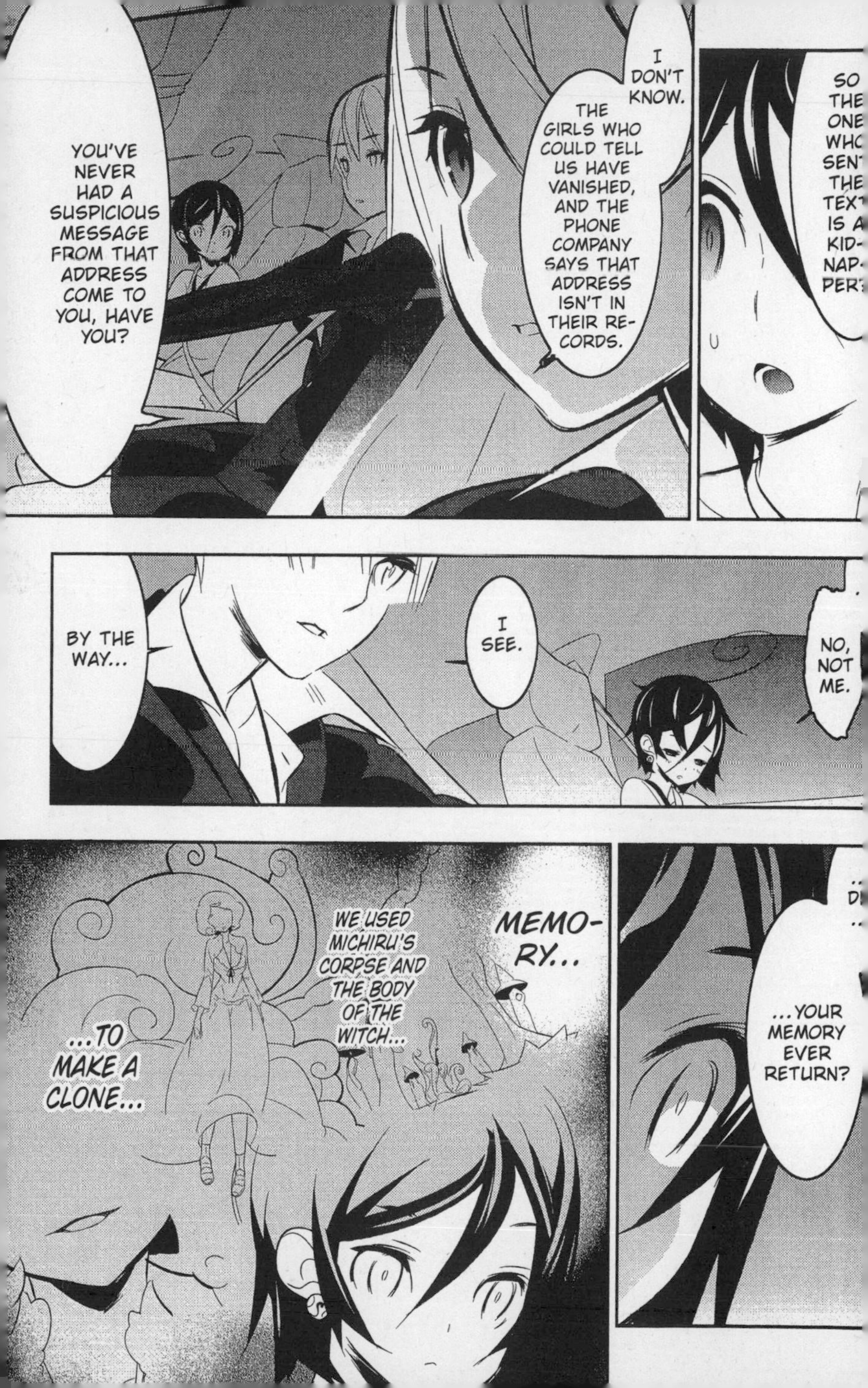
SO THE ONE WHO SENT THE TEXT IS A KIDNAPPER?
I DON'T KNOW.
THE GIRLS WHO COULD TELL US HAVE VANISHED, AND THE PHONE COMPANY SAYS THAT ADDRESS ISN'T IN THEIR RECORDS.
YOU'VE NEVER HAD A SUSPICIOUS MESSAGE FROM THAT ADDRESS COME TO YOU, HAVE YOU?
NO, NOT ME.
I SEE.
BY THE WAY...
...YOUR MEMORY EVER RETURN?
MEMORY...
WE USED MICHIRU'S CORPSE AND THE BODY OF THE WITCH...
...TO MAKE A CLONE...

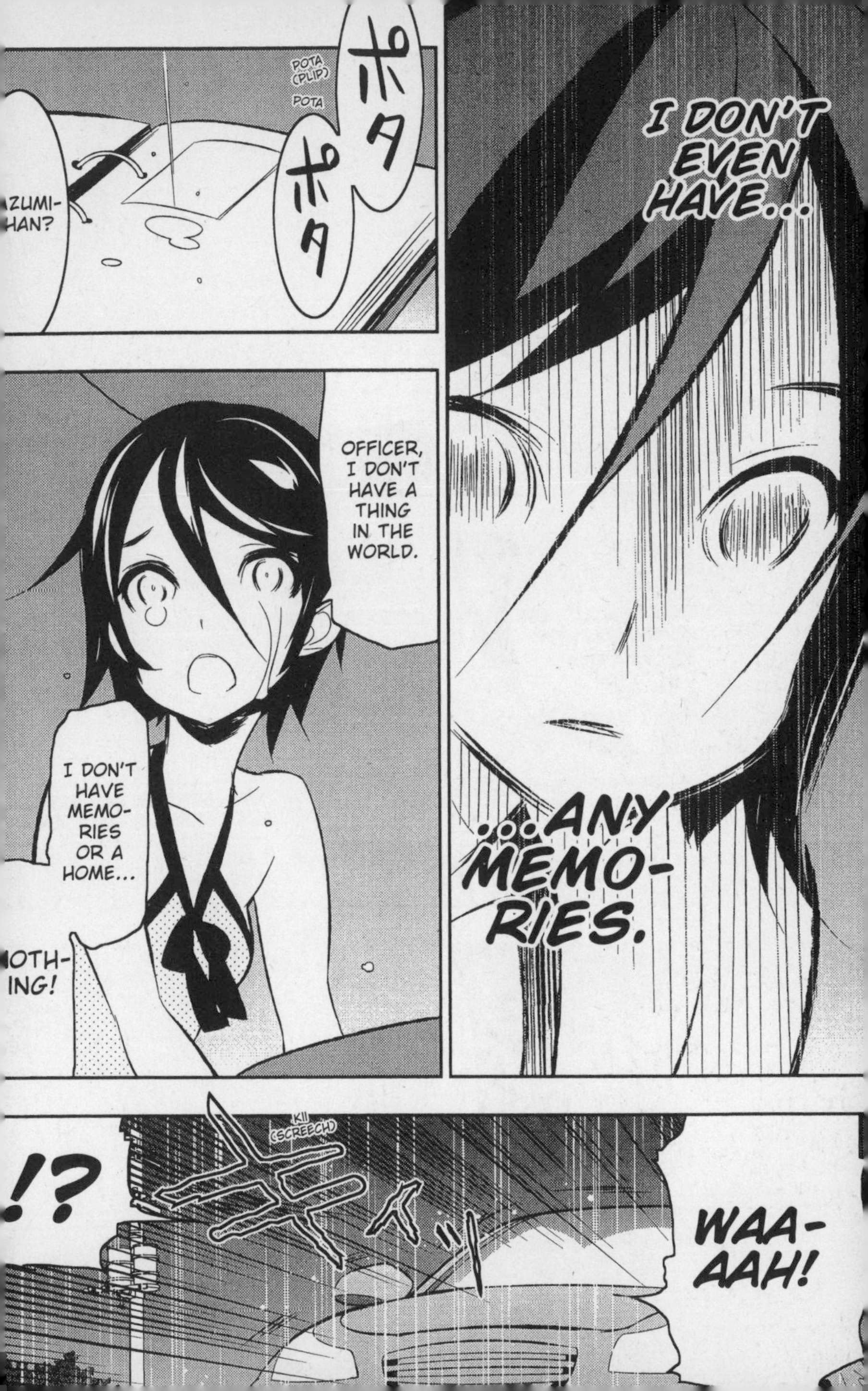
I DON'T EVEN HAVE...
...ANY MEMO-RIES.
ポタ
ポタ
POTA (PLIP)
POTA
ZUMI-HAN?
OFFICER, I DON'T HAVE A THING IN THE WORLD.
I DON'T HAVE MEMO-RIES OR A HOME...
OTH-ING!
WAA-AAH!
KII (SCREECH)
キイッ
!?

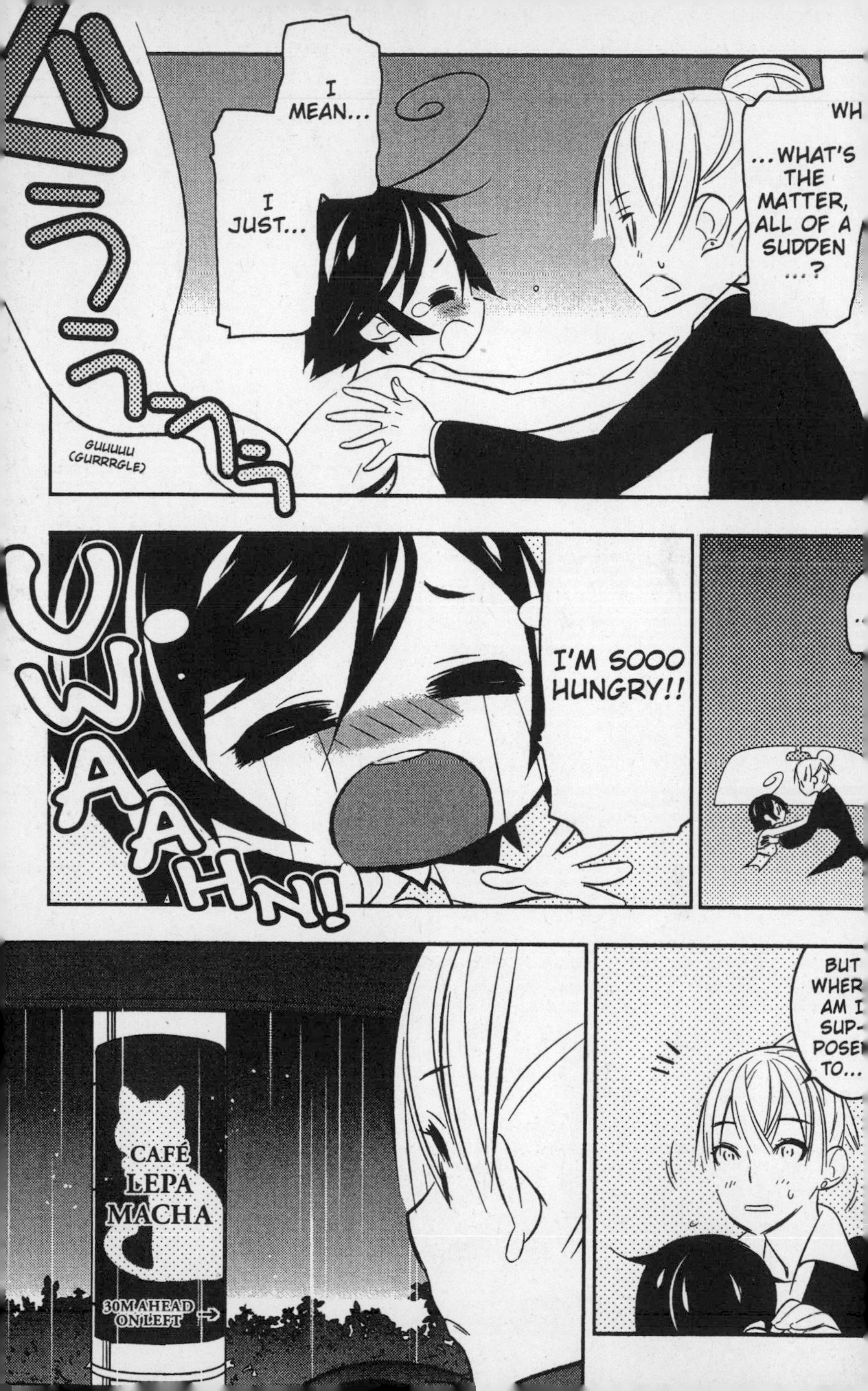
WH
...WHAT'S THE MATTER, ALL OF A SUDDEN ...?
I MEAN...
I JUST...
GUUUUU (GURRRGLE)
...
I'M SOOO HUNGRY!!
UWAAAHN!
BUT WHER AM I SUP-POSE TO...
CAFÉ LEPA MACHA
30M AHEAD ON LEFT

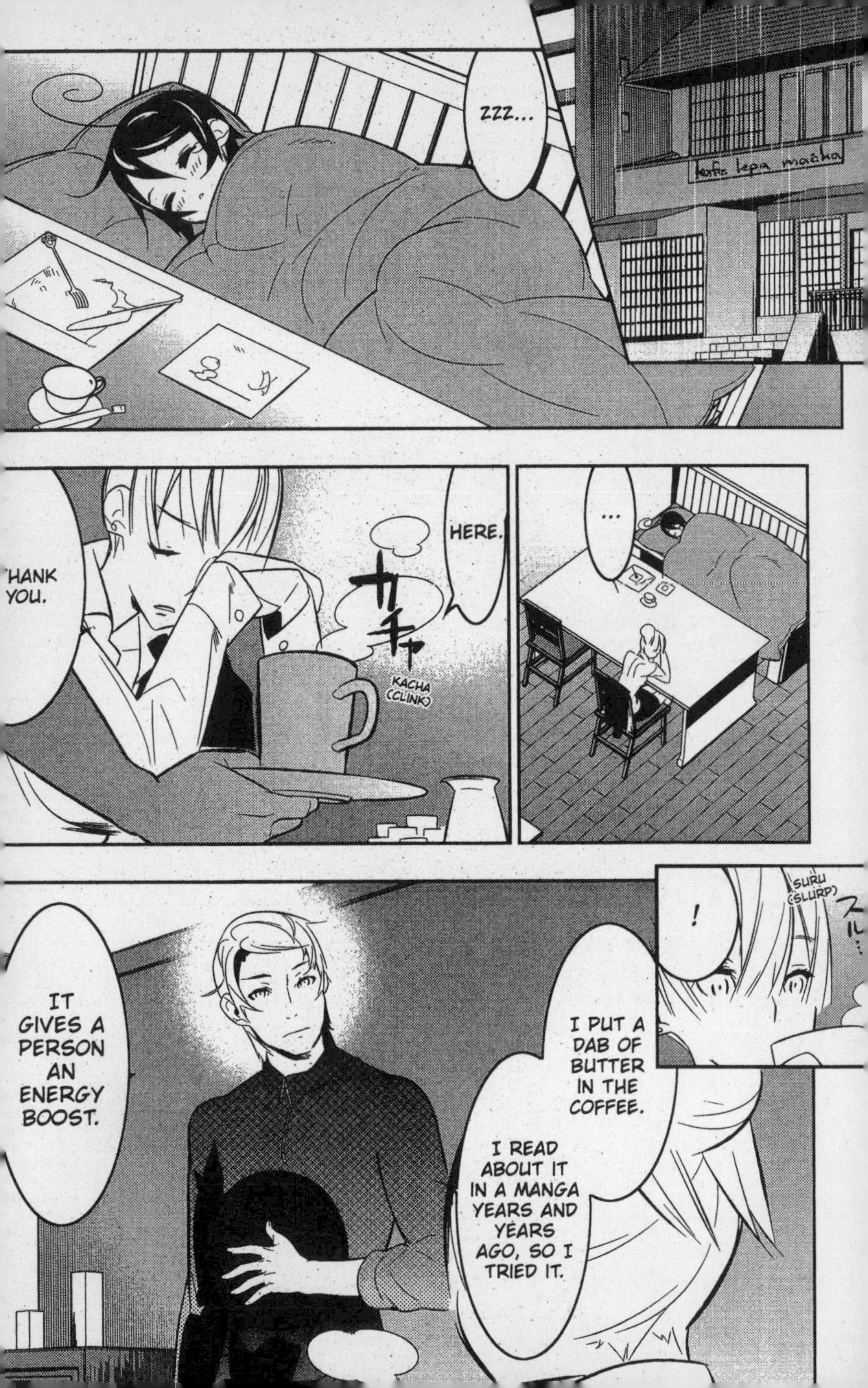
ZZZ...
...
HERE.
カチャ
KACHA (CLINK)
HANK YOU.
!
SURU (SLURP)
スル…
I PUT A DAB OF BUTTER IN THE COFFEE.
I READ ABOUT IT IN A MANGA YEARS AND YEARS AGO, SO I TRIED IT.
IT GIVES A PERSON AN ENERGY BOOST.

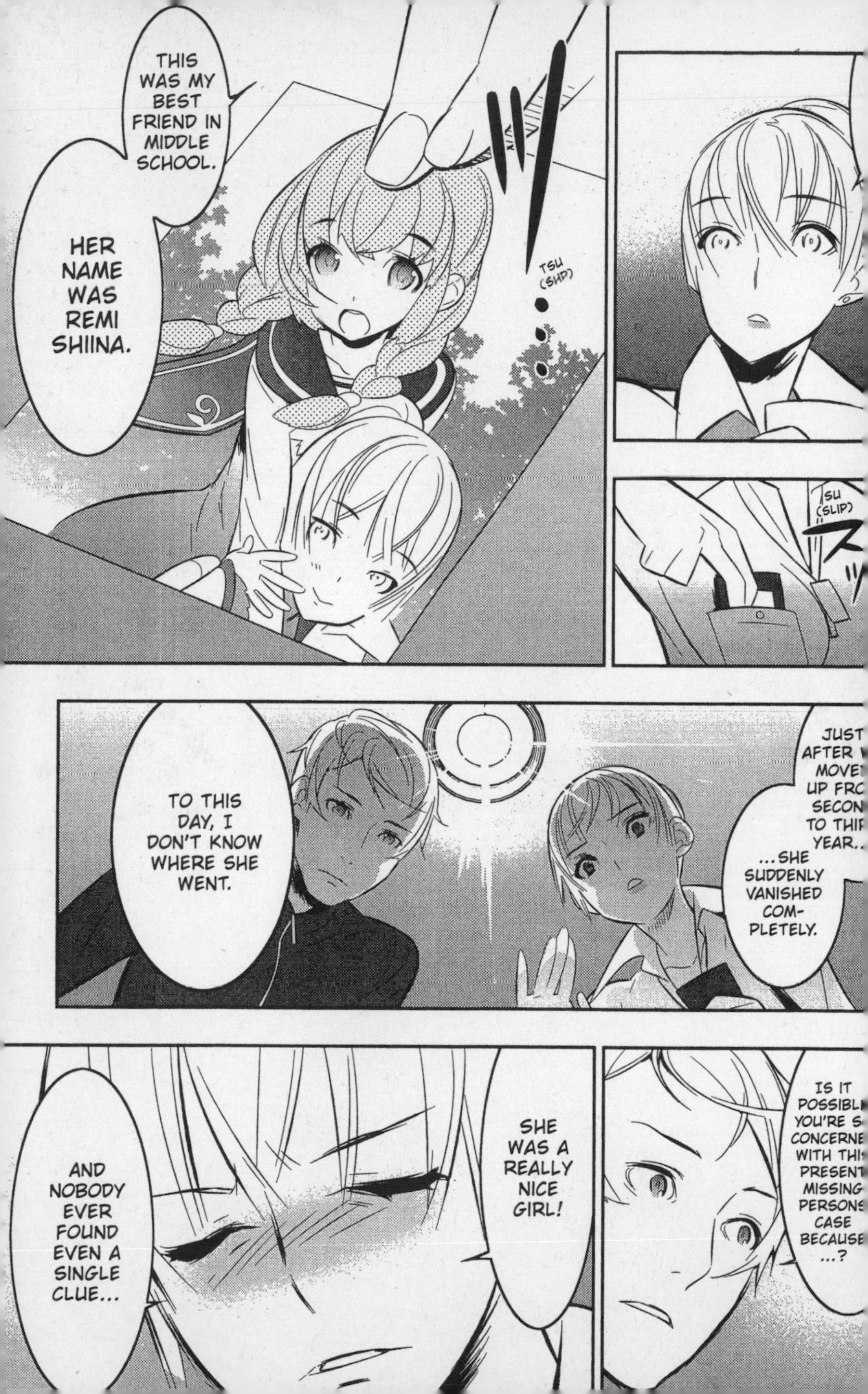
TSU (SLIP)
THIS WAS MY BEST FRIEND IN MIDDLE SCHOOL.
HER NAME WAS REMI SHIINA.
TSU (SHP)
JUST AFTER MOVE UP FRO SECON TO THIR YEAR..
...SHE SUDDENLY VANISHED COM-PLETELY.
TO THIS DAY, I DON'T KNOW WHERE SHE WENT.
IS IT POSSIBL YOU'RE S CONCERNE WITH THIS PRESENT MISSING PERSONS CASE BECAUSE ...?
SHE WAS A REALLY NICE GIRL!
AND NOBODY EVER FOUND EVEN A SINGLE CLUE...

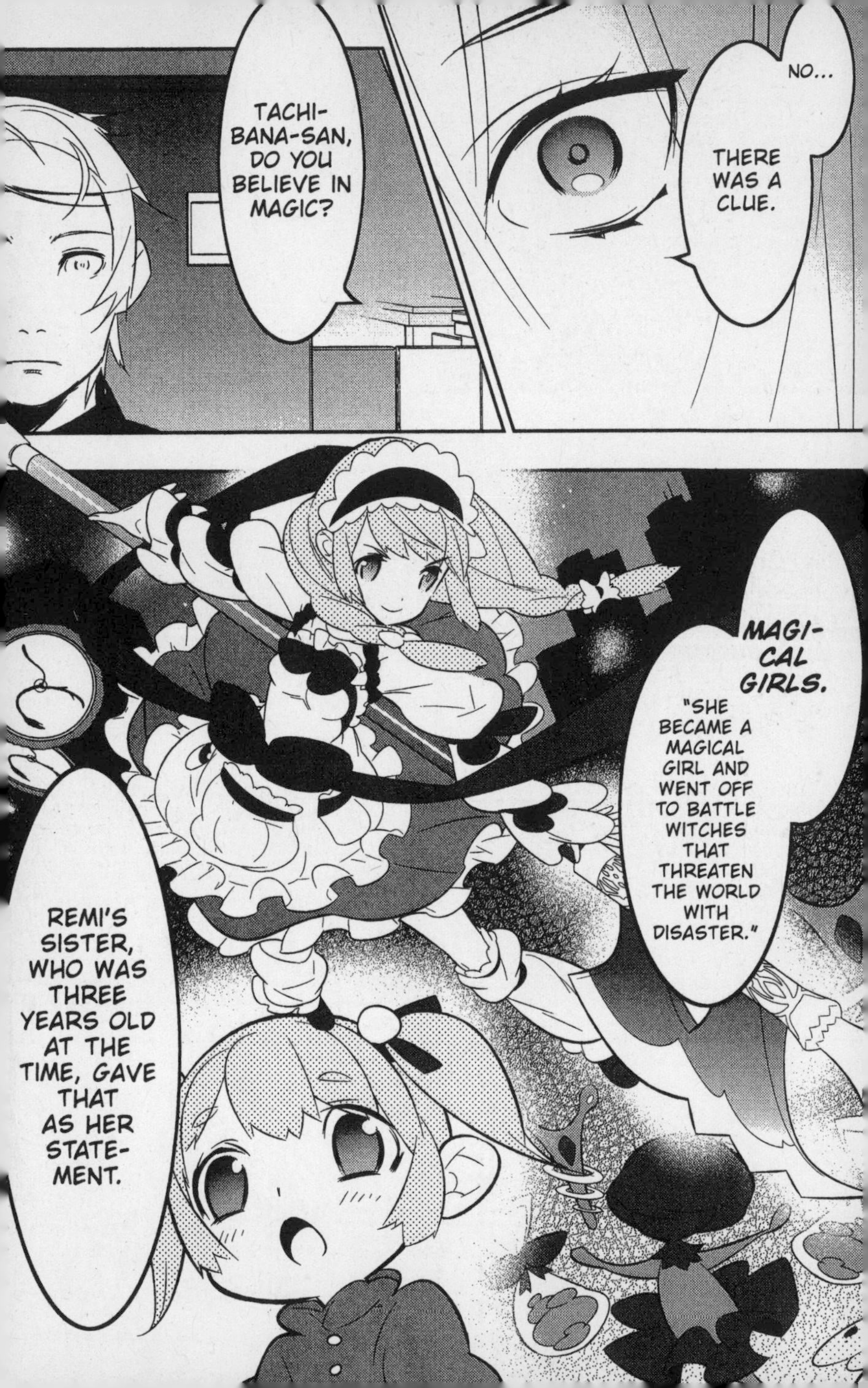
NO...
THERE WAS A CLUE.
TACHI-BANA-SAN, DO YOU BELIEVE IN MAGIC?
MAGI-CAL GIRLS.
"SHE BECAME A MAGICAL GIRL AND WENT OFF TO BATTLE WITCHES THAT THREATEN THE WORLD WITH DISASTER."
REMI'S SISTER, WHO WAS THREE YEARS OLD AT THE TIME, GAVE THAT AS HER STATE-MENT.

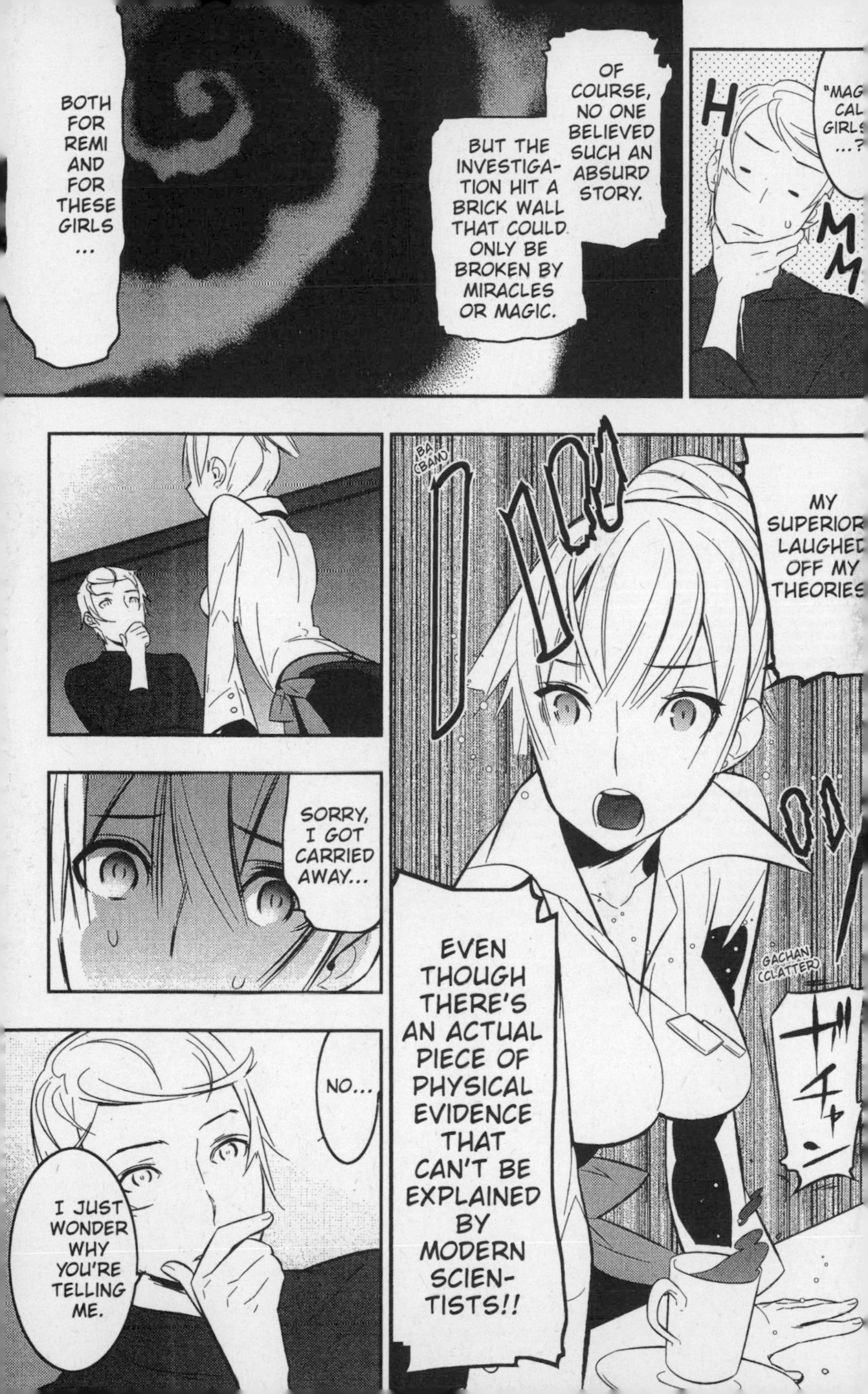

"MAG CAL GIRLS ...?
HMM
OF COURSE, NO ONE BELIEVED SUCH AN ABSURD STORY.
BUT THE INVESTIGATION HIT A BRICK WALL THAT COULD ONLY BE BROKEN BY MIRACLES OR MAGIC.
BOTH FOR REMI AND FOR THESE GIRLS...
BA (BAM)
MY SUPERIOR LAUGHED OFF MY THEORIES
EVEN THOUGH THERE'S AN ACTUAL PIECE OF PHYSICAL EVIDENCE THAT CAN'T BE EXPLAINED BY MODERN SCIENTISTS!!
GACHAN (CLATTER)
SORRY, I GOT CARRIED AWAY...
NO...
I JUST WONDER WHY YOU'RE TELLING ME.

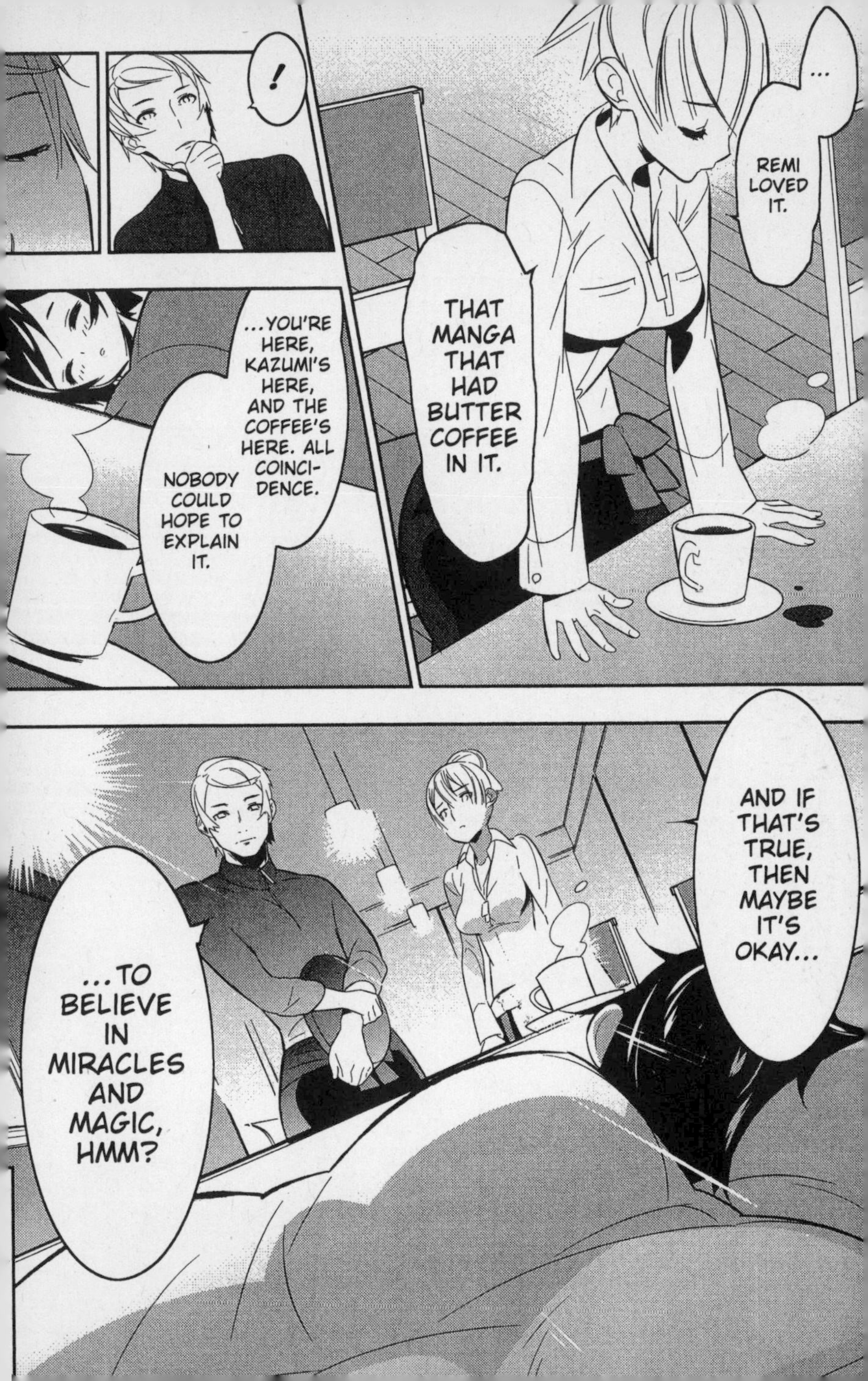
...
REMI LOVED IT.
THAT MANGA THAT HAD BUTTER COFFEE IN IT.
!
...YOU'RE HERE, KAZUMI'S HERE, AND THE COFFEE'S HERE. ALL COINCIDENCE.
NOBODY COULD HOPE TO EXPLAIN IT.
AND IF THAT'S TRUE, THEN MAYBE IT'S OKAY...
...TO BELIEVE IN MIRACLES AND MAGIC, HMM?

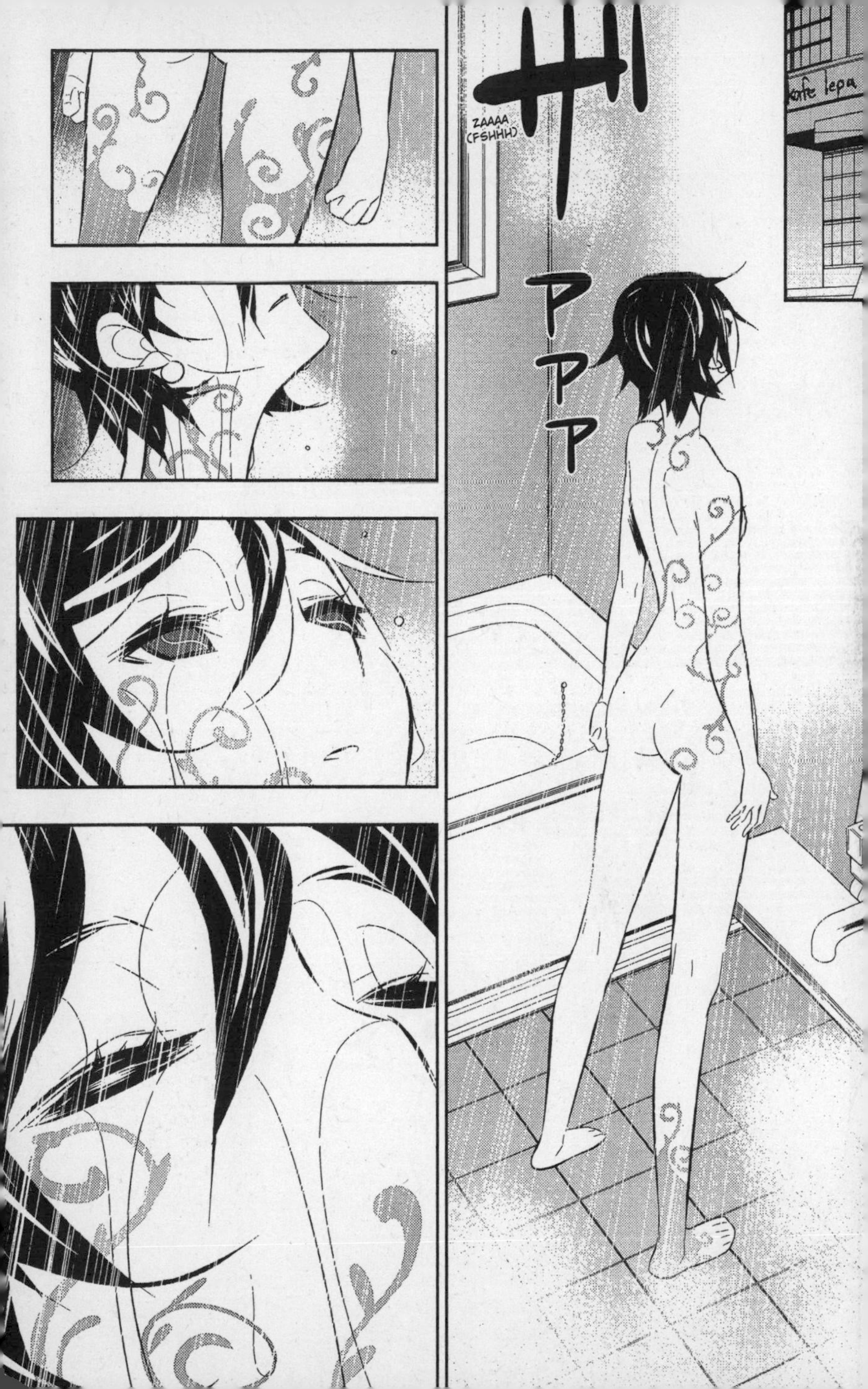
ZAAAA (FSHHH)
afe lepa

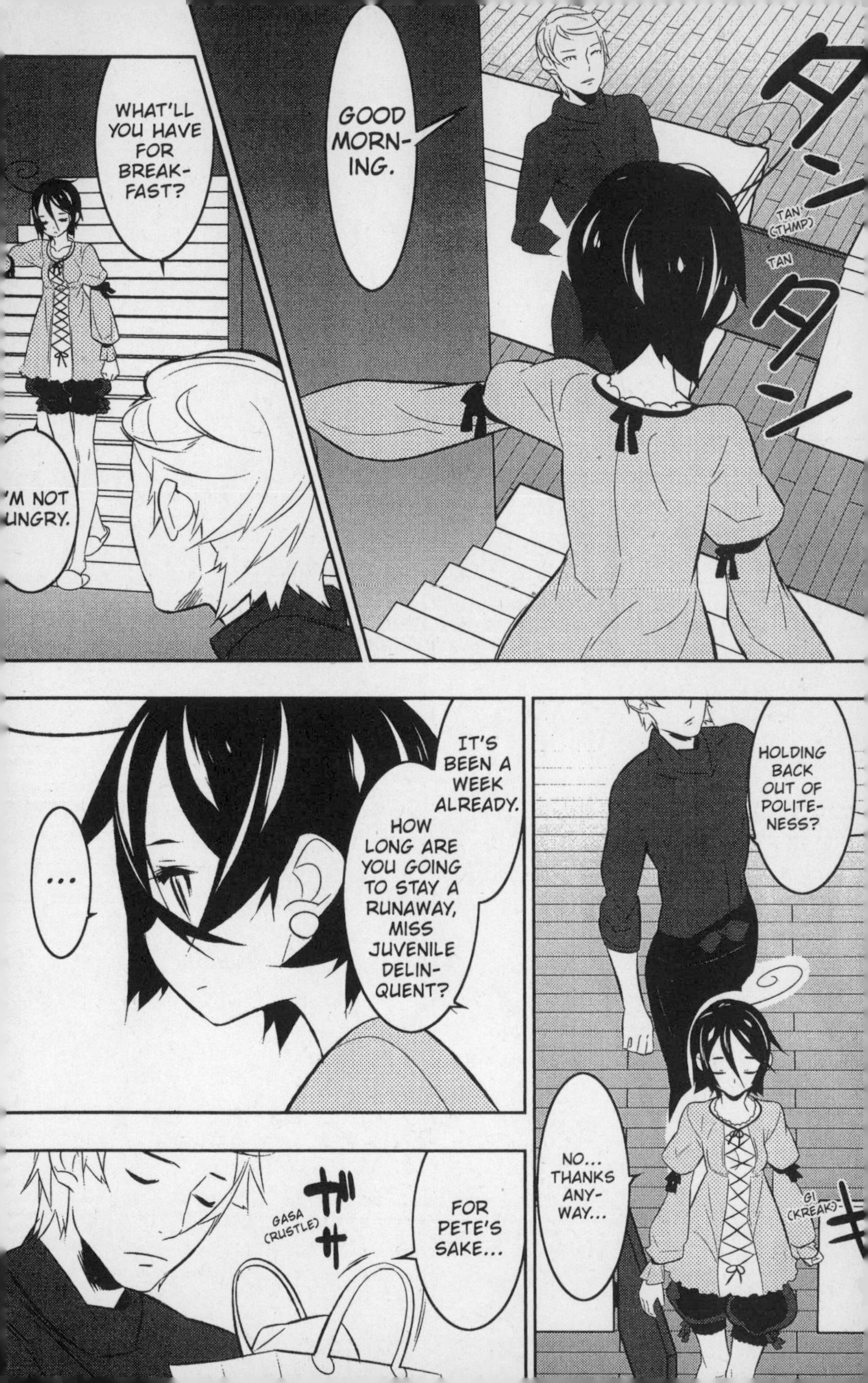

TAN (THMP)
TAN
GOOD MORNING.
WHAT'LL YOU HAVE FOR BREAKFAST?
'M NOT UNGRY.
HOLDING BACK OUT OF POLITENESS?
GI (KREAK)
NO... THANKS ANYWAY...
IT'S BEEN A WEEK ALREADY.
HOW LONG ARE YOU GOING TO STAY A RUNAWAY, MISS JUVENILE DELINQUENT?
...
FOR PETE'S SAKE...
GASA (RUSTLE)

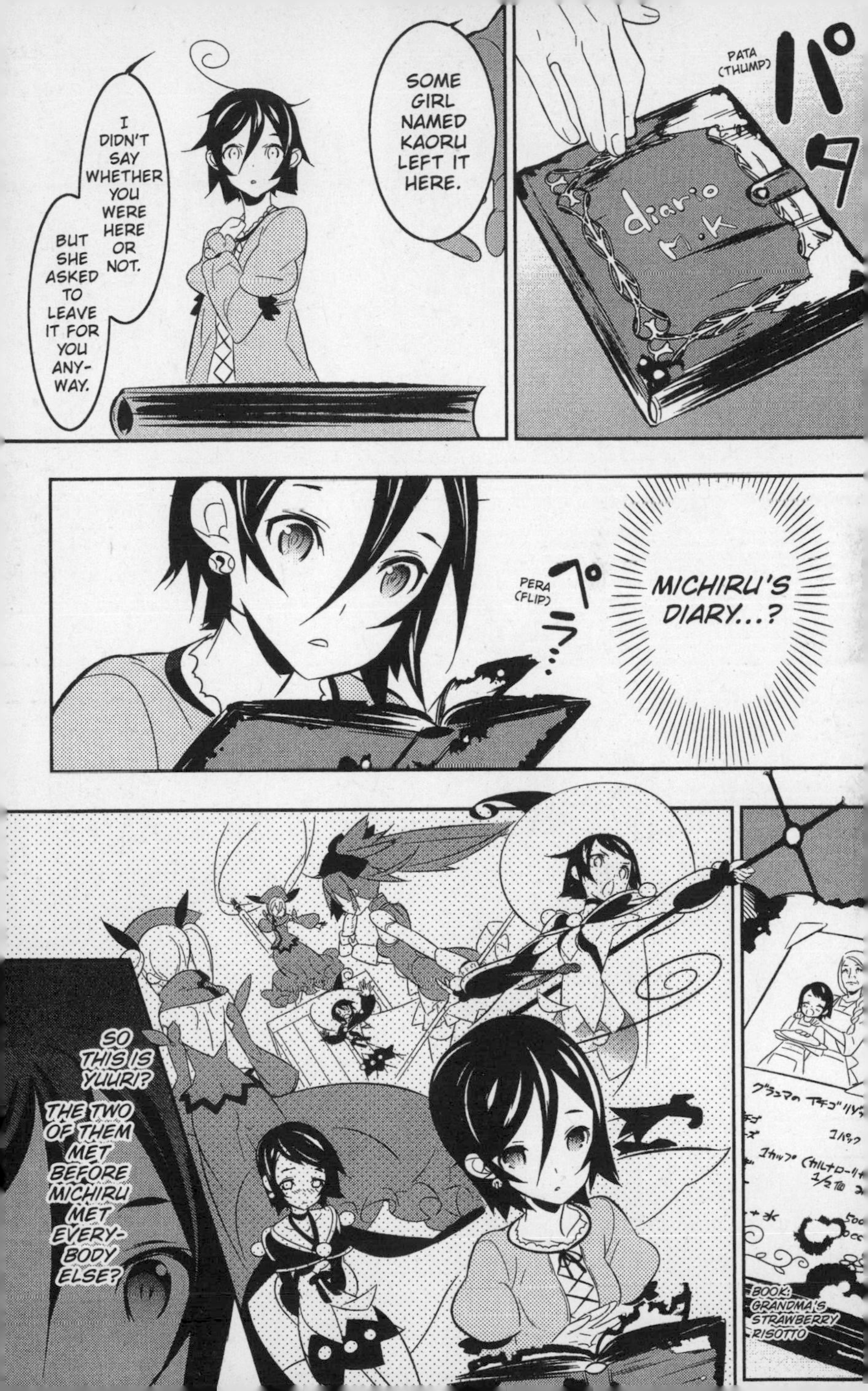
PATA (THUMP)
SOME GIRL NAMED KAORU LEFT IT HERE.
I DIDN'T SAY WHETHER YOU WERE HERE OR NOT.
BUT SHE ASKED TO LEAVE IT FOR YOU ANYWAY.
MICHIRU'S DIARY...?
PERA (FLIP)
BOOK: GRANDMA'S STRAWBERRY RISOTTO
SO THIS IS YUURI?
THE TWO OF THEM MET BEFORE MICHIRU MET EVERYBODY ELSE?

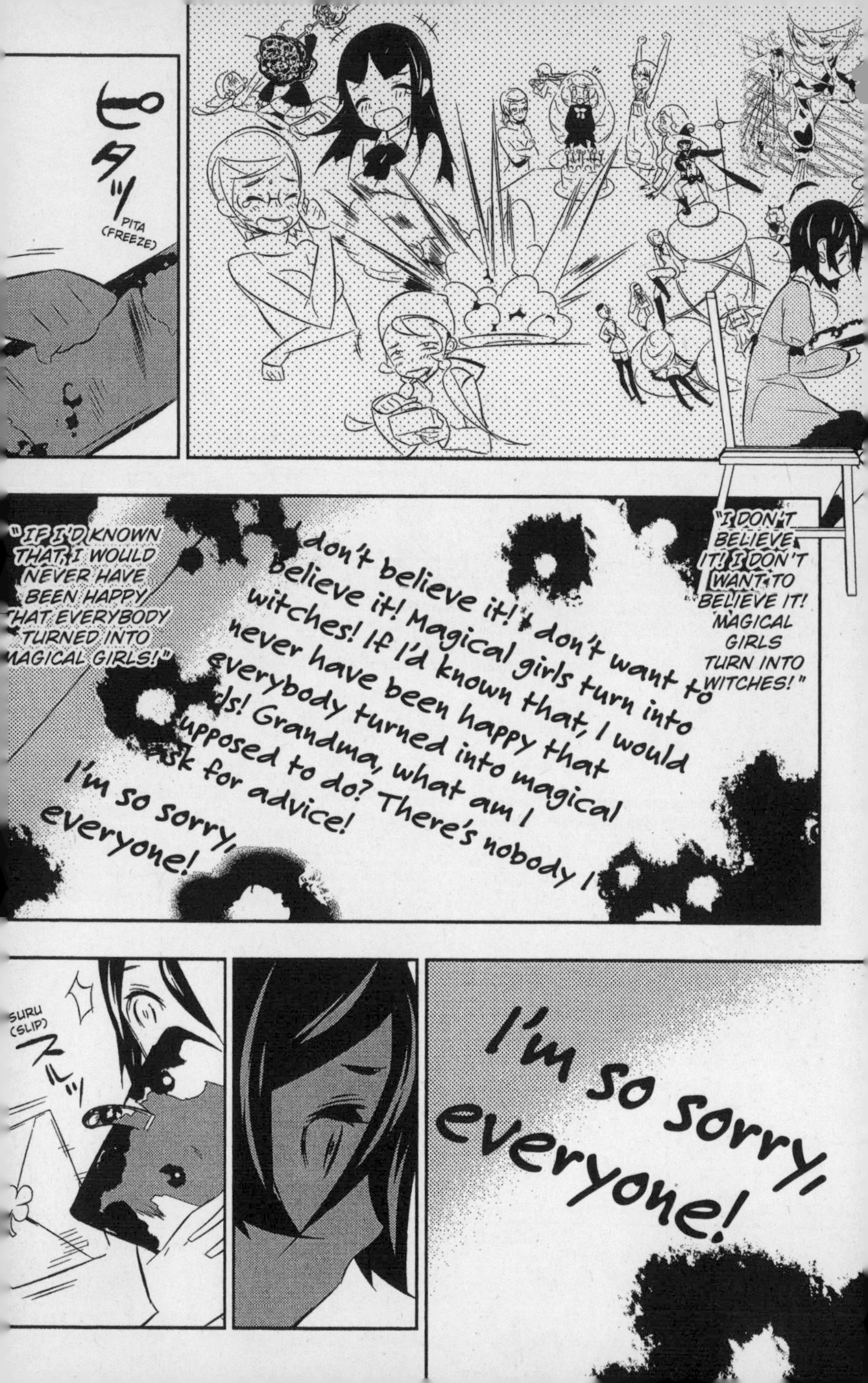
ピタッ
PITA (FREEZE)
"I DON'T BELIEVE IT! I DON'T WANT TO BELIEVE IT! MAGICAL GIRLS TURN INTO WITCHES!"
don't believe it! I don't want to believe it! Magical girls turn into witches! If I'd known that, I would never have been happy that everybody turned into magical rls! Grandma, what am I upposed to do? There's nobody I sk for advice!
I'm so sorry, everyone!
"IF I'D KNOWN THAT, I WOULD NEVER HAVE BEEN HAPPY THAT EVERYBODY TURNED INTO MAGICAL GIRLS!"
I'm so sorry, everyone!
SURU (SLIP)
スルッ

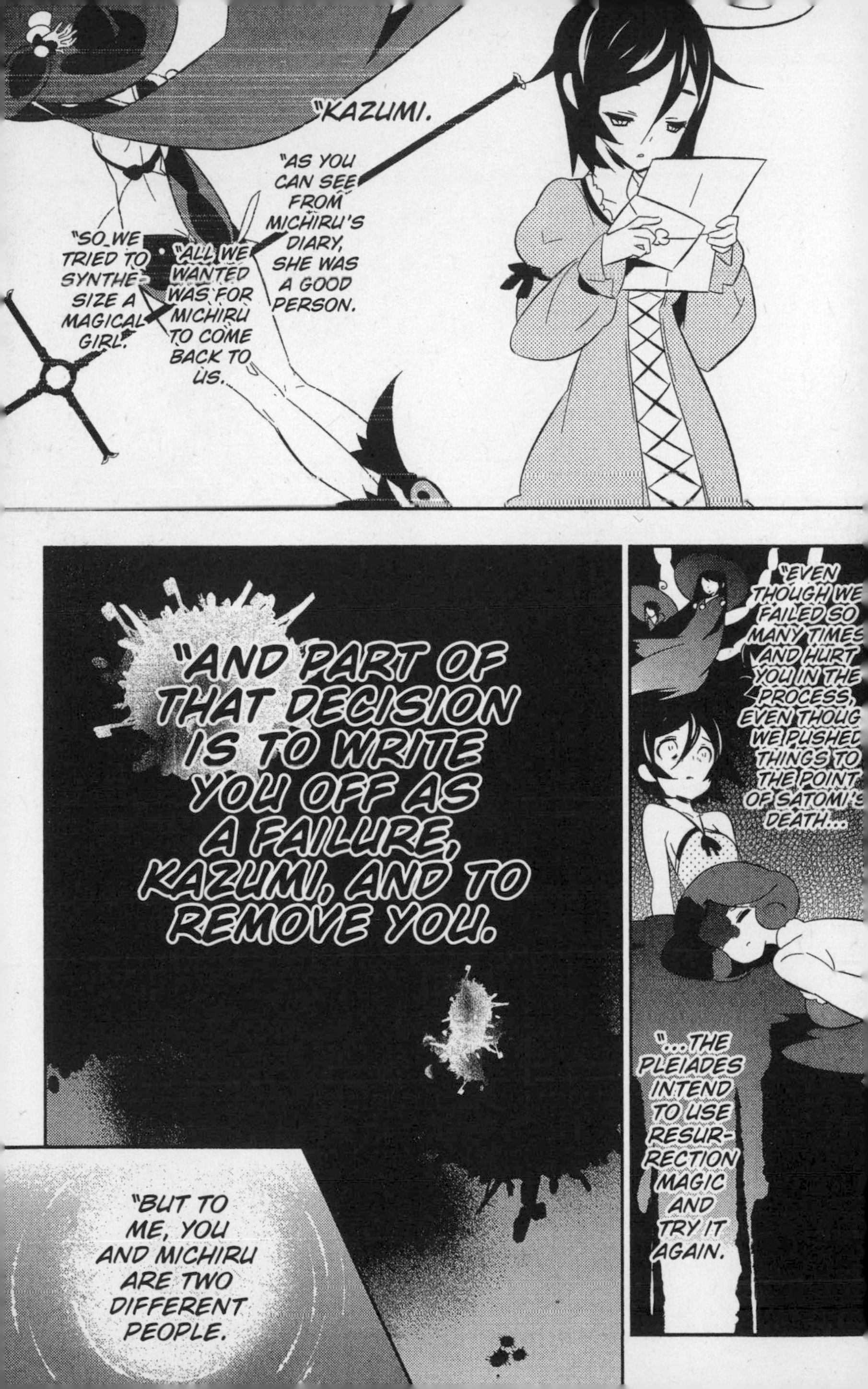
"KAZUMI.
"AS YOU CAN SEE FROM MICHIRU'S DIARY, SHE WAS A GOOD PERSON.
"ALL WE WANTED WAS FOR MICHIRU TO COME BACK TO US.
"SO WE TRIED TO SYNTHESIZE A MAGICAL GIRL.
"EVEN THOUGH WE FAILED SO MANY TIMES AND HURT YOU IN THE PROCESS, EVEN THOUG WE PUSHED THINGS TO THE POINT OF SATOMI'S DEATH...
"...THE PLEIADES INTEND TO USE RESURRECTION MAGIC AND TRY IT AGAIN.
"AND PART OF THAT DECISION IS TO WRITE YOU OFF AS A FAILURE, KAZUMI, AND TO REMOVE YOU.
"BUT TO ME, YOU AND MICHIRU ARE TWO DIFFERENT PEOPLE.

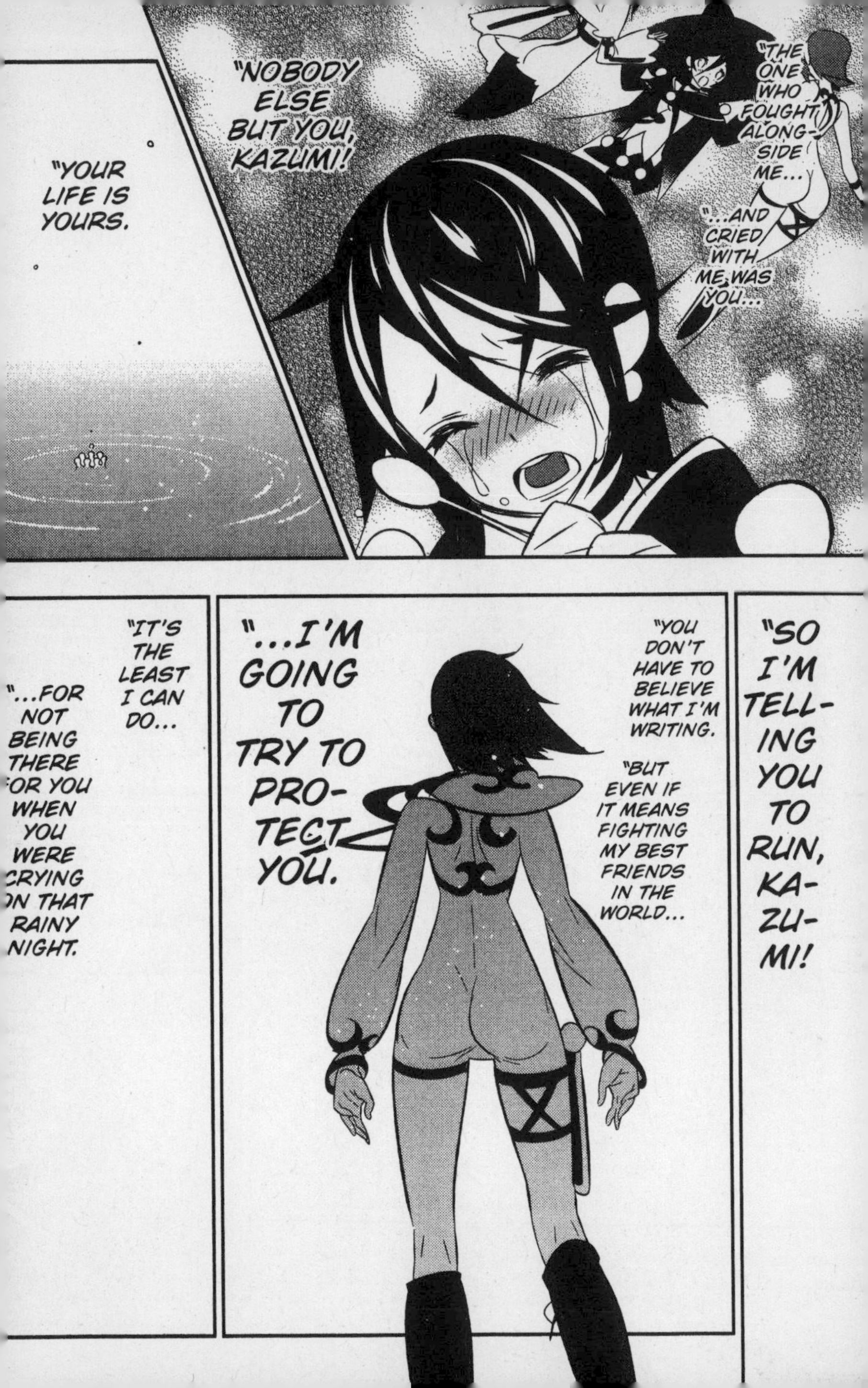
"THE ONE WHO FOUGHT ALONGSIDE ME...
"...AND CRIED WITH ME WAS YOU...
"NOBODY ELSE BUT YOU, KAZUMI!
"YOUR LIFE IS YOURS.
"SO I'M TELLING YOU TO RUN, KAZUMI!
"YOU DON'T HAVE TO BELIEVE WHAT I'M WRITING.
"BUT EVEN IF IT MEANS FIGHTING MY BEST FRIENDS IN THE WORLD...
"...I'M GOING TO TRY TO PROTECT YOU.
"IT'S THE LEAST I CAN DO...
"...FOR NOT BEING THERE FOR YOU WHEN YOU WERE CRYING ON THAT RAINY NIGHT.

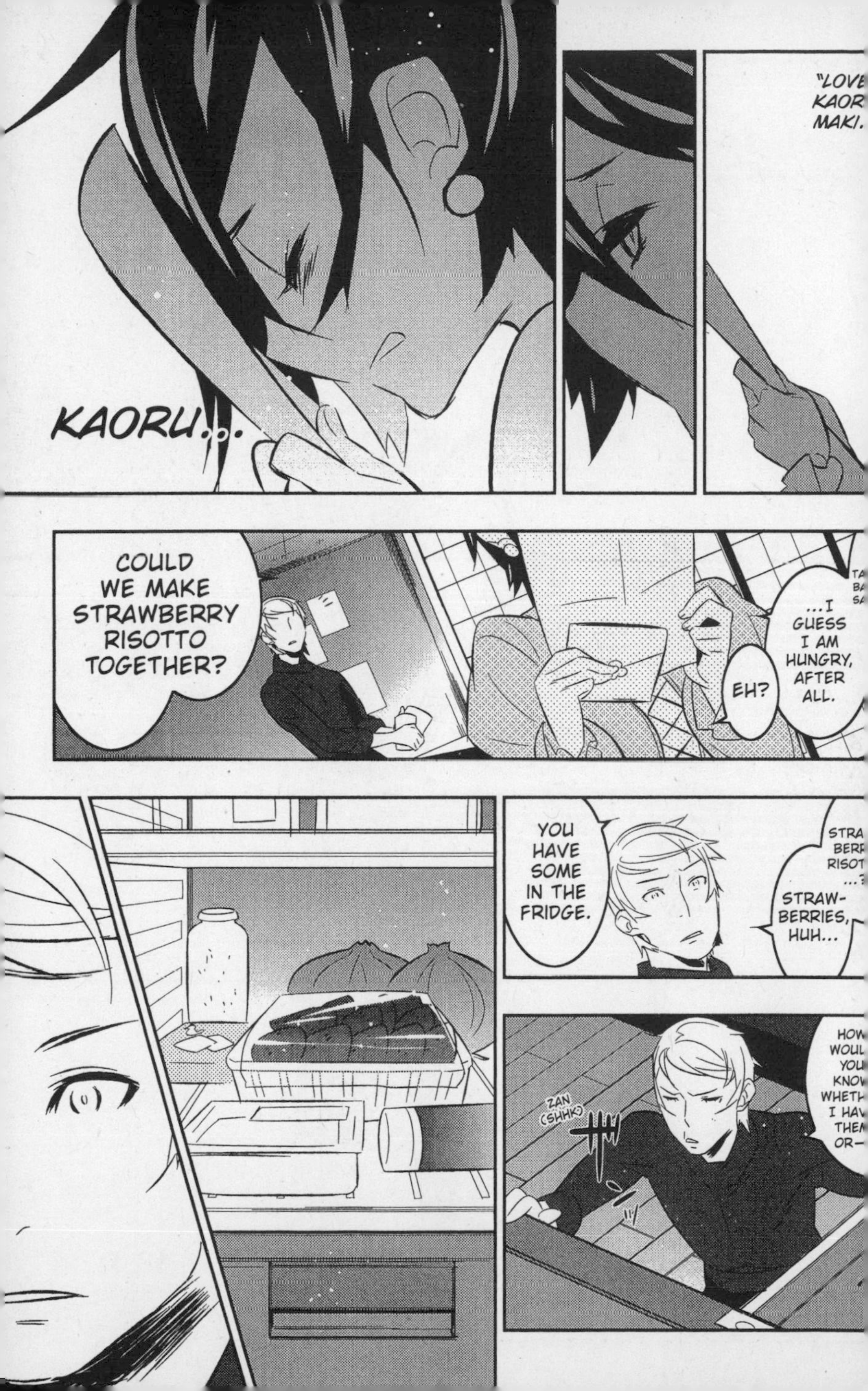
"LOVE KAOR MAKI.
KAORU...
...I GUESS I AM HUNGRY, AFTER ALL.
EH?
COULD WE MAKE STRAWBERRY RISOTTO TOGETHER?
STRA BERR RISOT ...?
STRAW-BERRIES, HUH...
YOU HAVE SOME IN THE FRIDGE.
HOW WOUL YOU KNOW WHETH I HAV THEM OR—
ZAN (SHHK)

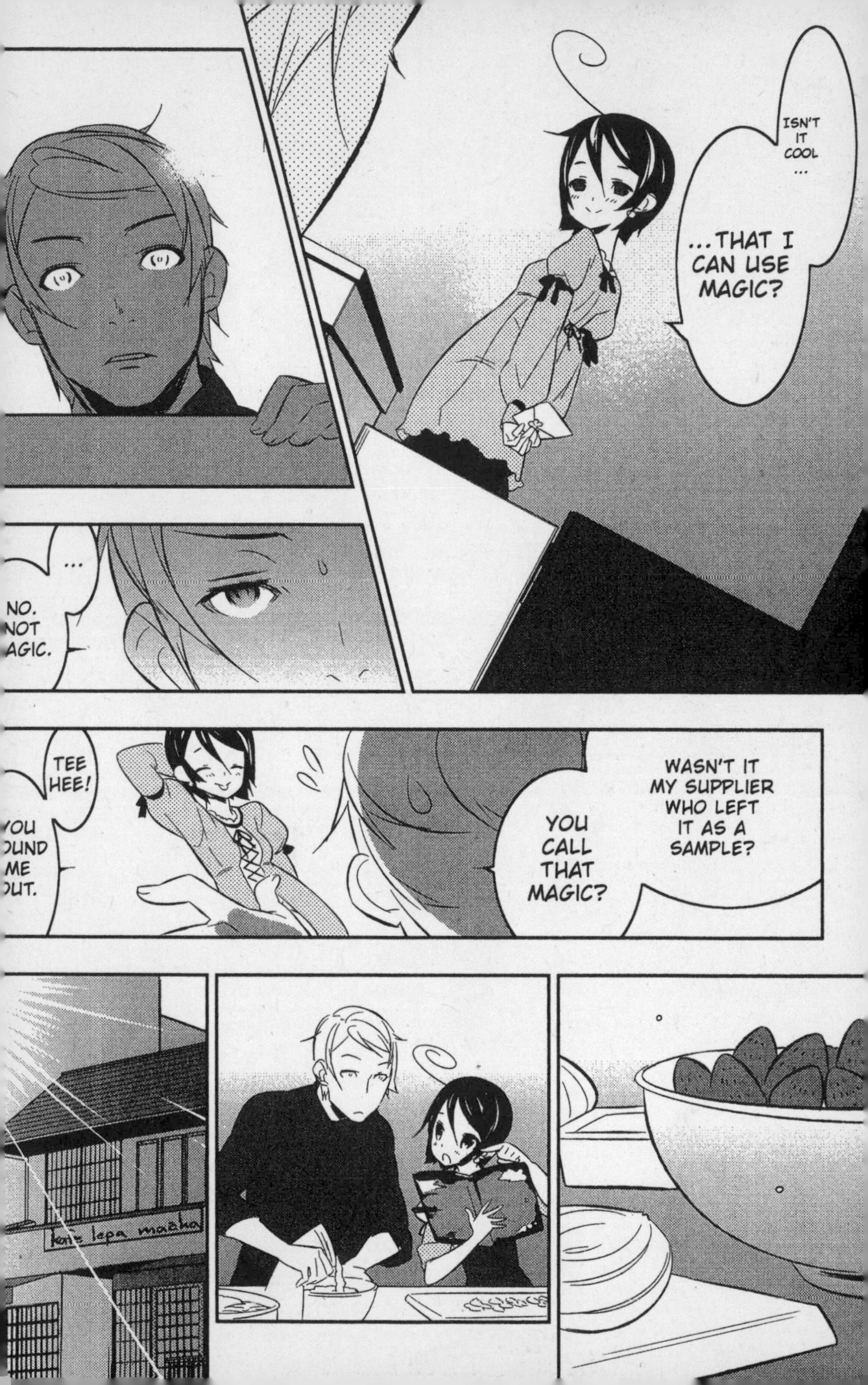
ISN'T IT COOL ...
...THAT I CAN USE MAGIC?
...
NO. NOT AGIC.
WASN'T IT MY SUPPLIER WHO LEFT IT AS A SAMPLE?
YOU CALL THAT MAGIC?
TEE HEE!
OU OUND ME UT.

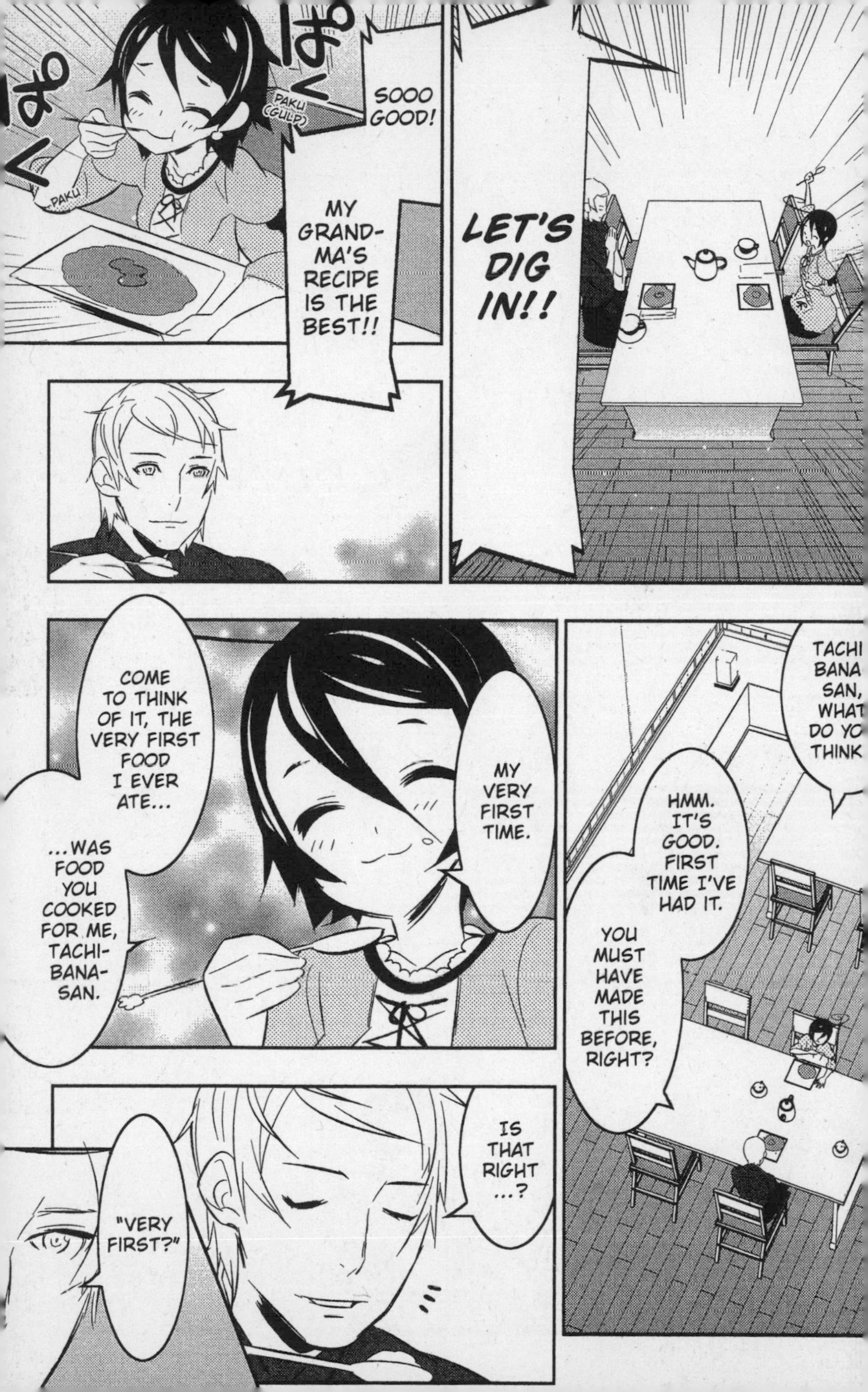
LET'S DIG IN!!
ぱく
PAKU (GULP)
SOOO GOOD!
ぱく
PAKU
MY GRAND-MA'S RECIPE IS THE BEST!!
TACHI BANA SAN, WHAT DO YO THINK
HMM. IT'S GOOD. FIRST TIME I'VE HAD IT.
YOU MUST HAVE MADE THIS BEFORE, RIGHT?
MY VERY FIRST TIME.
COME TO THINK OF IT, THE VERY FIRST FOOD I EVER ATE...
...WAS FOOD YOU COOKED FOR ME, TACHI-BANA-SAN.
IS THAT RIGHT...?
"VERY FIRST?"

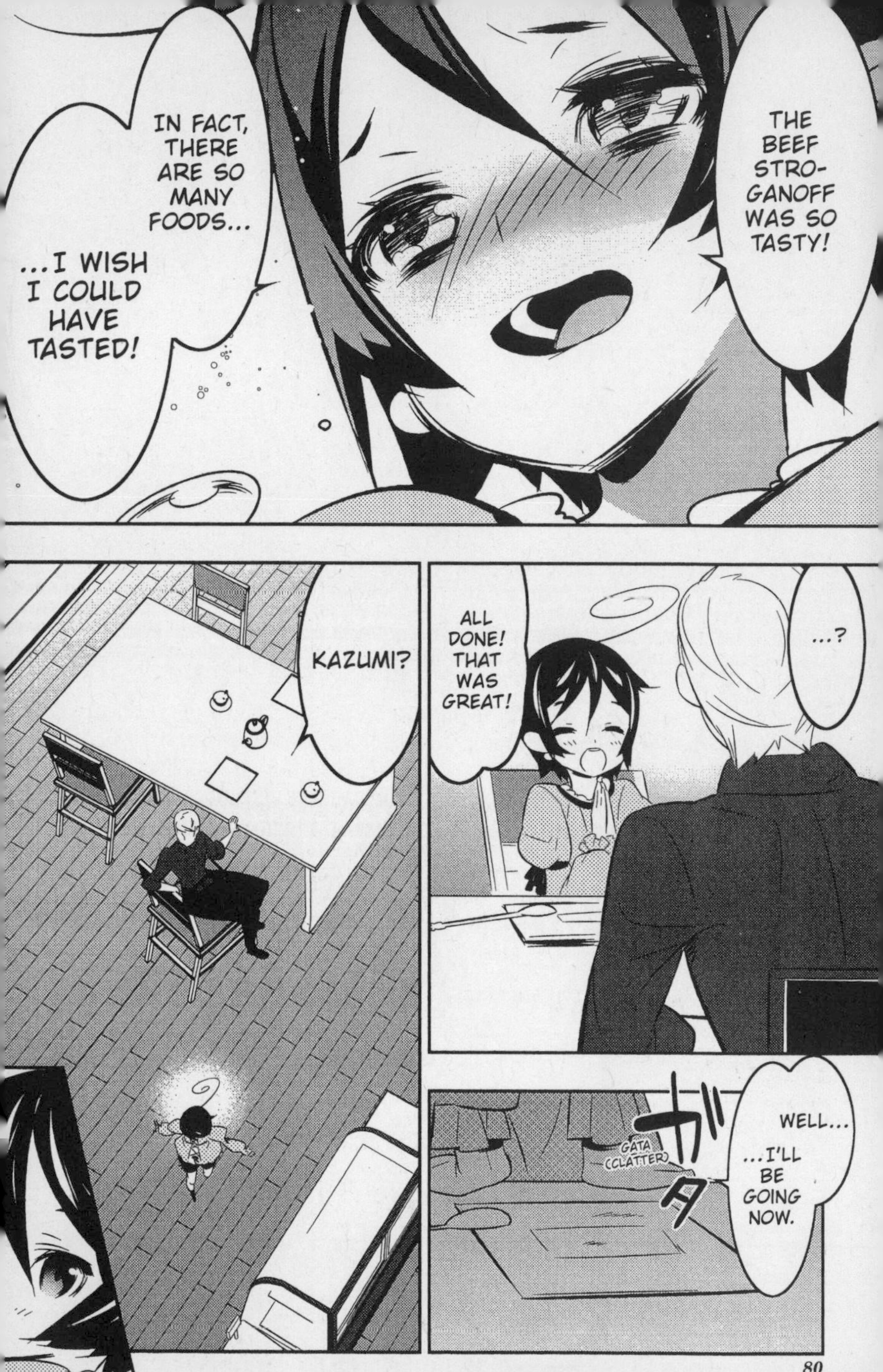
THE BEEF STROGANOFF WAS SO TASTY!
IN FACT, THERE ARE SO MANY FOODS...
...I WISH I COULD HAVE TASTED!
...?
ALL DONE! THAT WAS GREAT!
WELL...
...I'LL BE GOING NOW.
GATA (CLATTER)
KAZUMI?

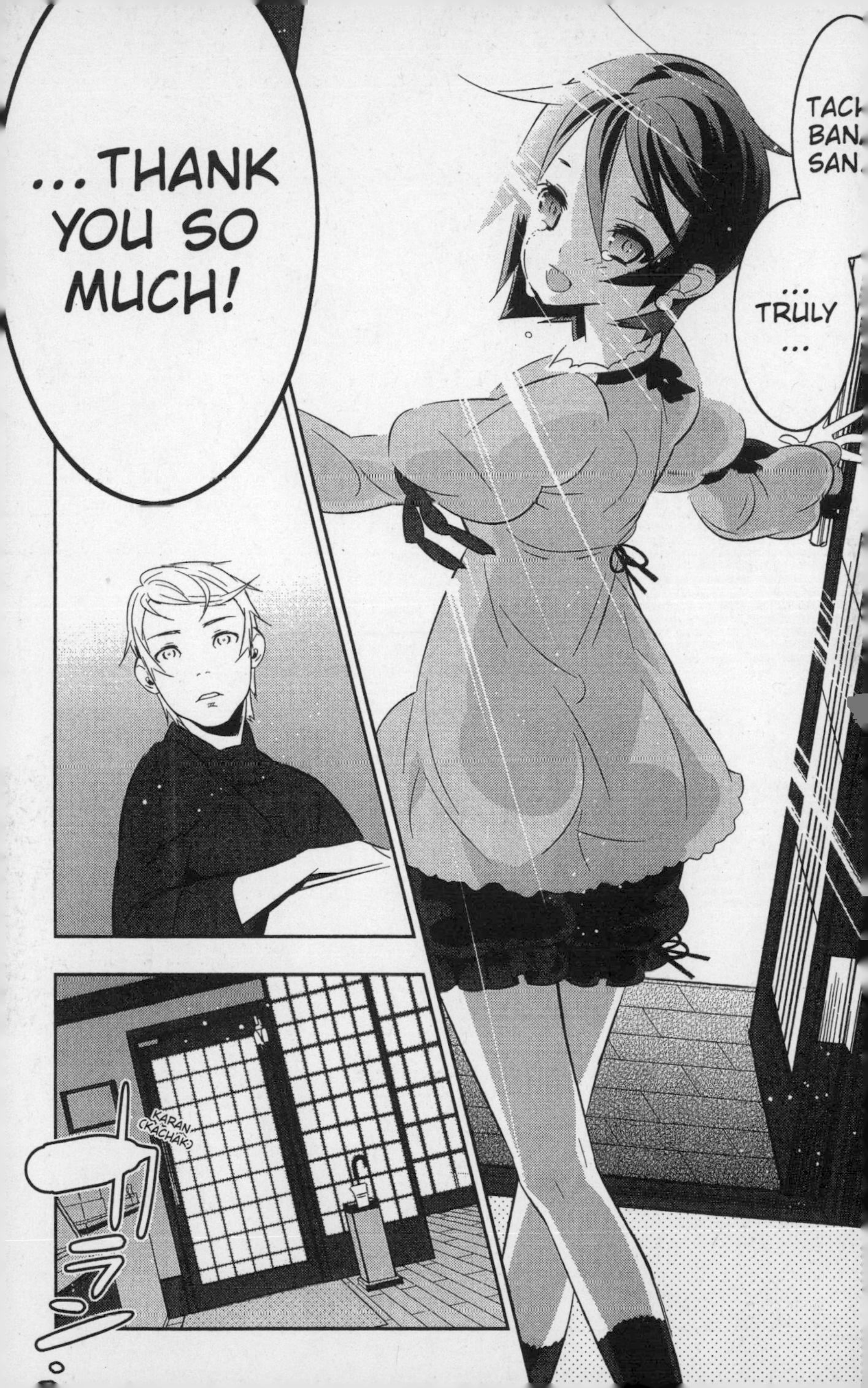
TACH
BAN
SAN
...TRULY...
...THANK YOU SO MUCH!
KARAN (KACHAK)

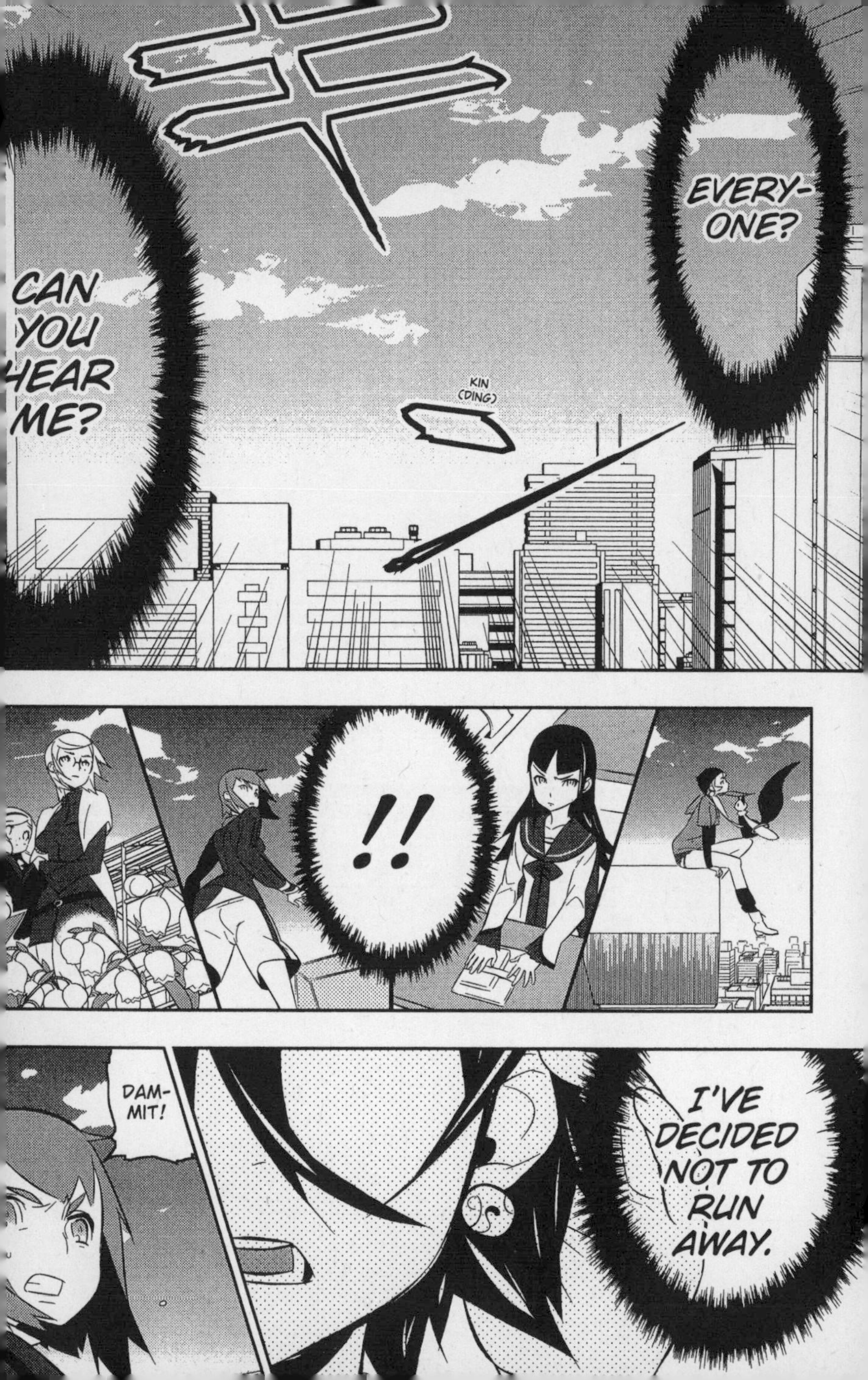
EVERY-ONE?
CAN YOU HEAR ME?
KIN (DING)
!!
I'VE DECIDED NOT TO RUN AWAY.
DAM-MIT!

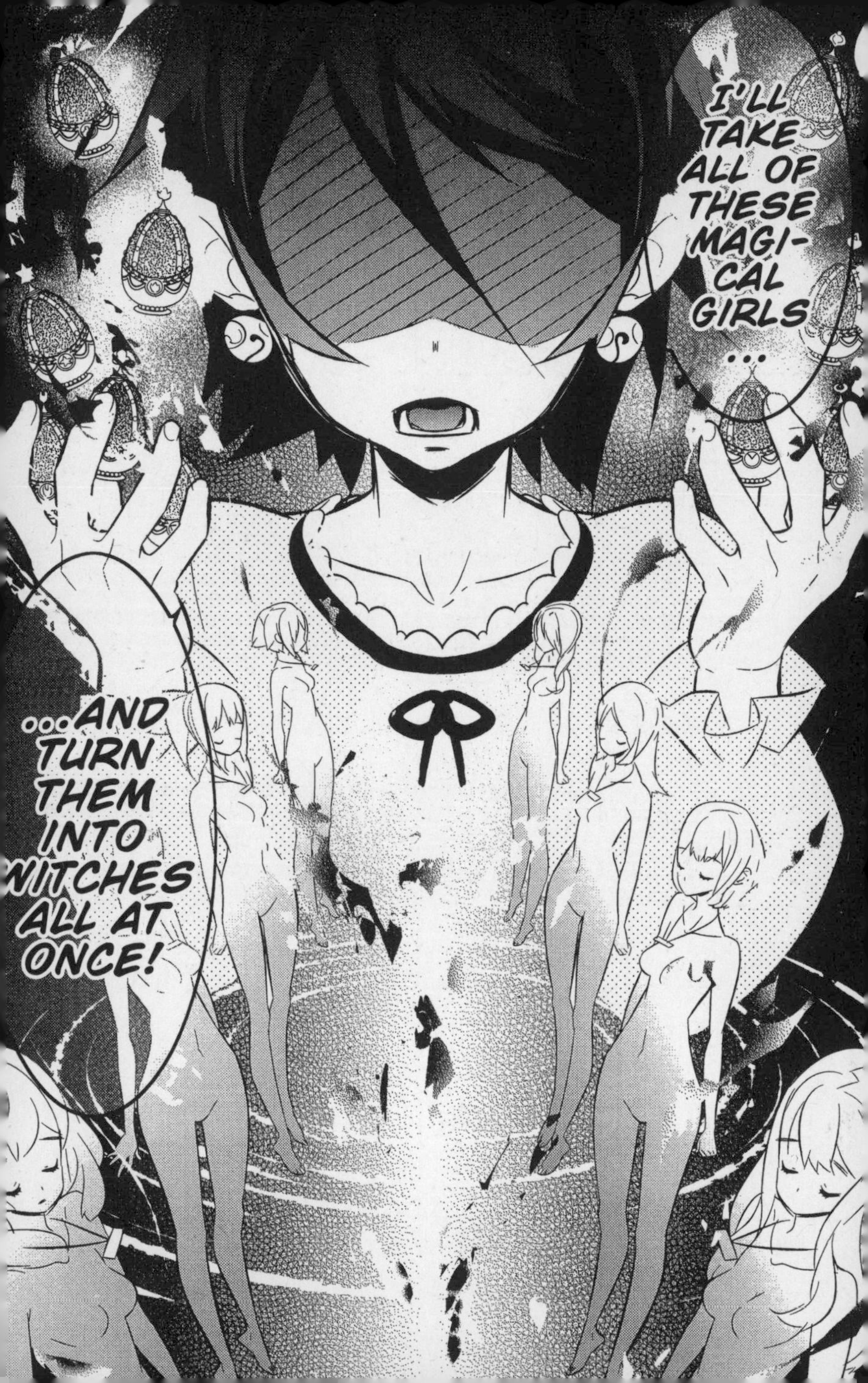
I'LL TAKE ALL OF THESE MAGI-CAL GIRLS...
...AND TURN THEM INTO WITCHES ALL AT ONCE!

MY BEST FRIEND... HER NAME WAS REMI SHIINA.
SHE WAS A REALLY NICE GIRL!
AND NOBODY EVER FOUND EVEN A SINGLE CLUE...
BUN (SHAKE)
YOU JUST DID A DOUBLE TAKE, DIDN'T YOU?
BUN
YES. I-I MEAN NO!
THIS LADY DETECTIVE IS PRETTY YOUNG! (TACHIBANA)

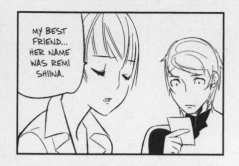

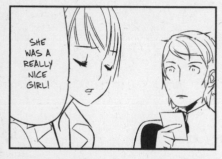

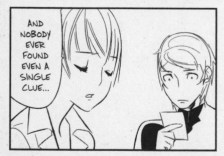

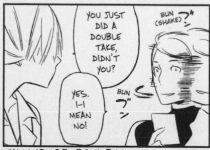

PUELLA MAGI
KAZUMI ★ MAGICA
The innocent malice

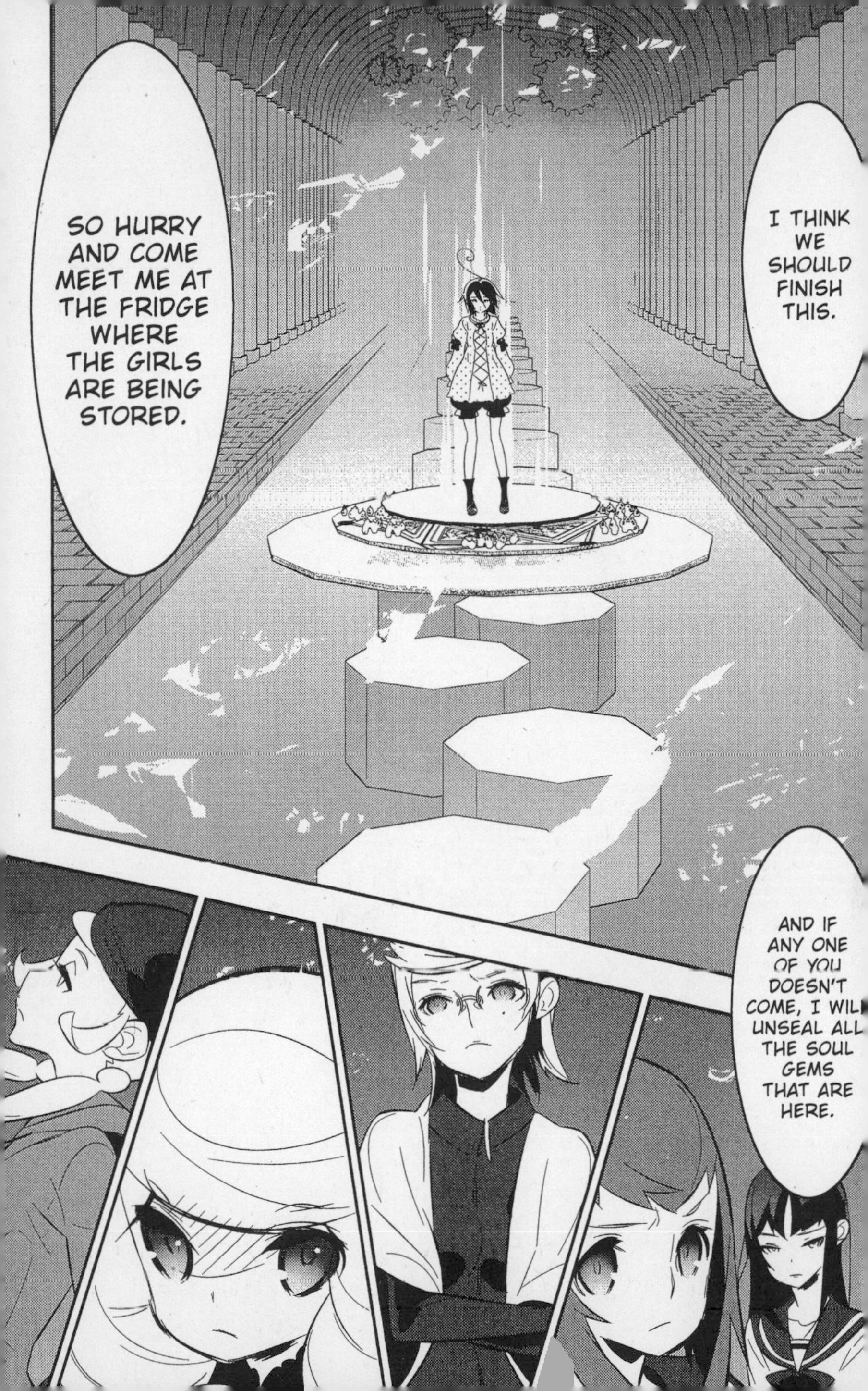
I THINK WE SHOULD FINISH THIS.
SO HURRY AND COME MEET ME AT THE FRIDGE WHERE THE GIRLS ARE BEING STORED.
AND IF ANY ONE OF YOU DOESN'T COME, I WIL UNSEAL ALL THE SOUL GEMS THAT ARE HERE.

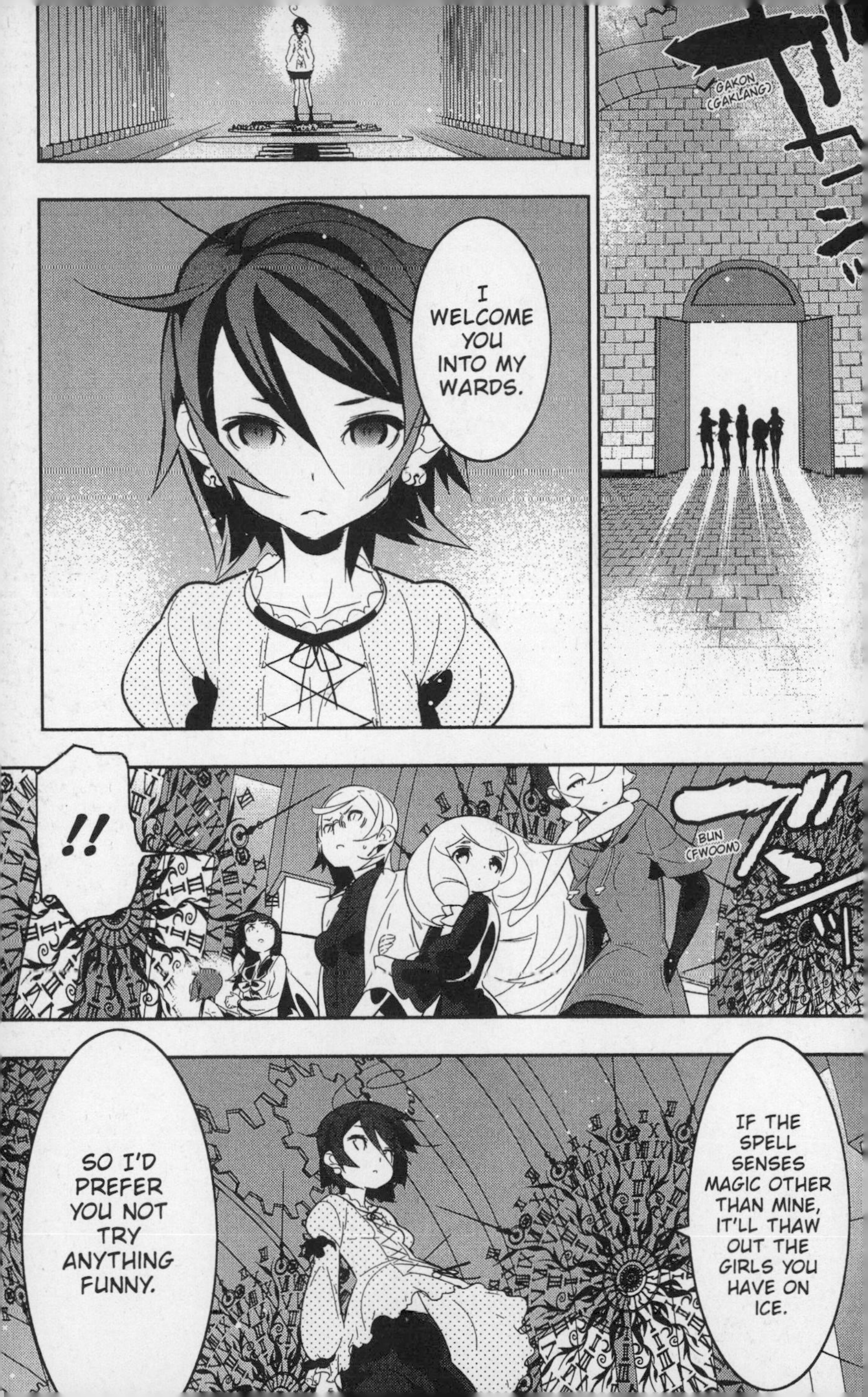
GAKON (GAKLANG)
I WELCOME YOU INTO MY WARDS.
BUN (FWOOM)
!!
IF THE SPELL SENSES MAGIC OTHER THAN MINE, IT'LL THAW OUT THE GIRLS YOU HAVE ON ICE.
SO I'D PREFER YOU NOT TRY ANYTHING FUNNY.

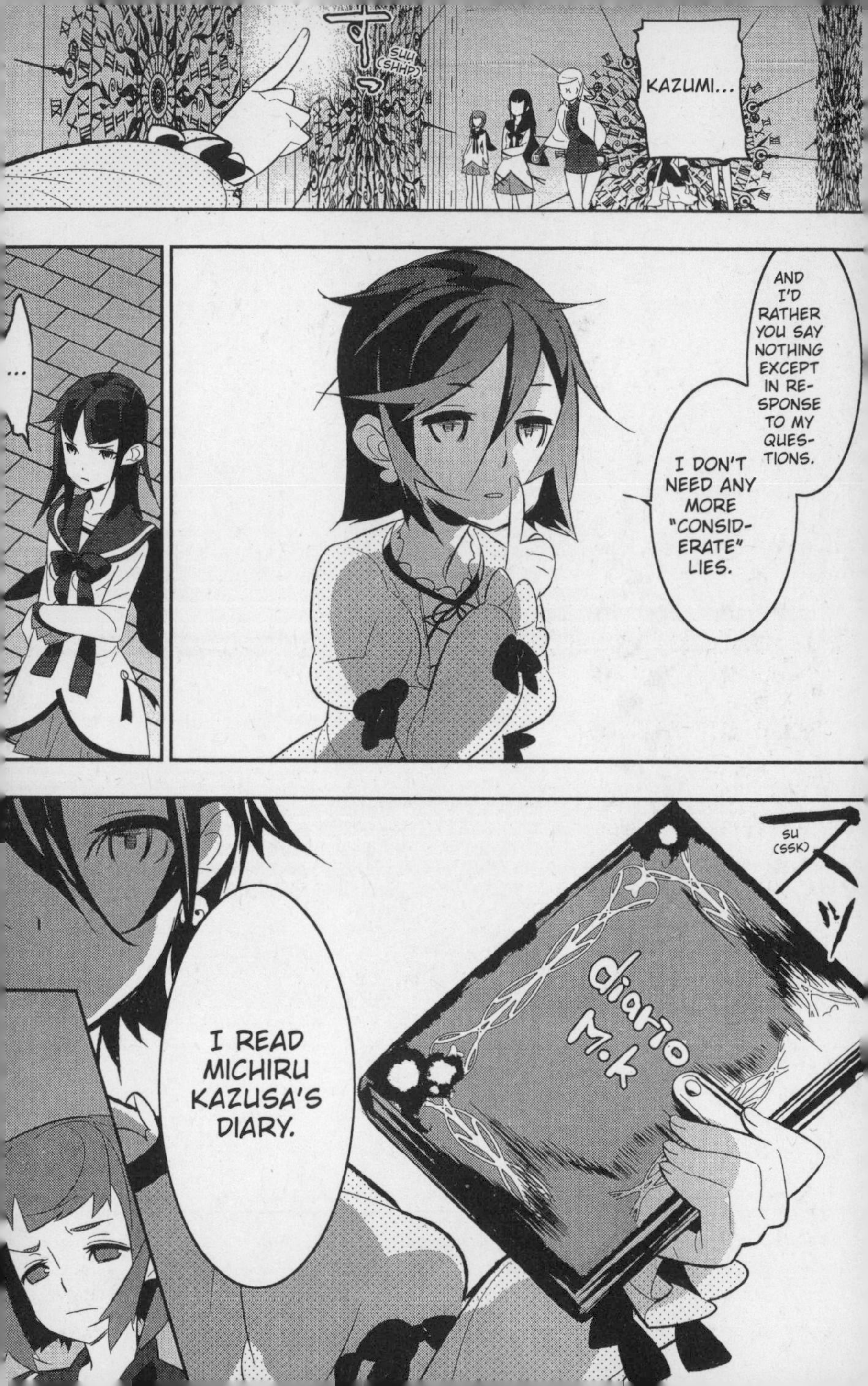
KAZUMI...
SUU (SHHP)
AND I'D RATHER YOU SAY NOTHING EXCEPT IN RESPONSE TO MY QUESTIONS.
I DON'T NEED ANY MORE "CONSIDERATE" LIES.
...
SU (SSK)
diario M.k
I READ MICHIRU KAZUSA'S DIARY.

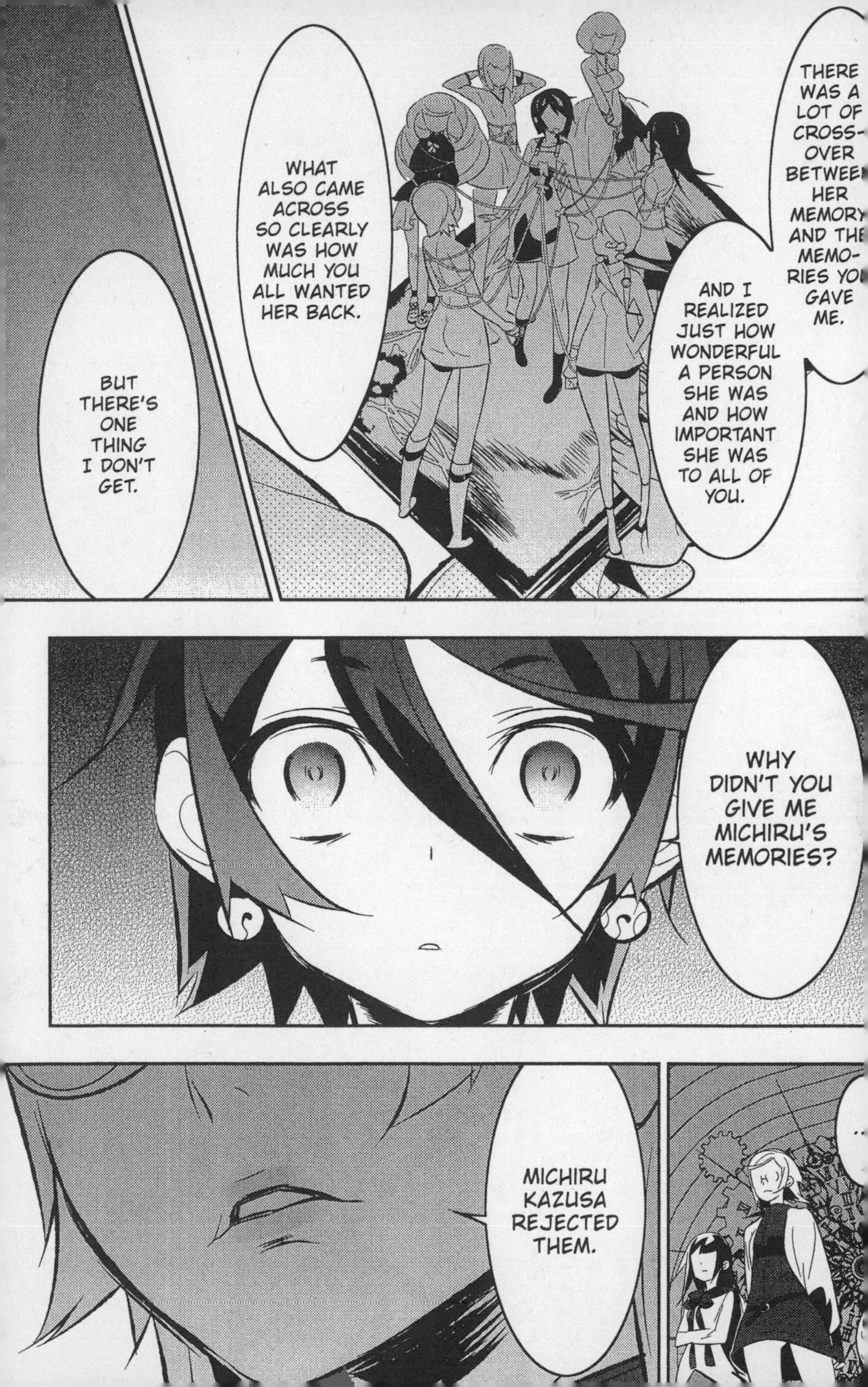
THERE WAS A LOT OF CROSS-OVER BETWEEN HER MEMORY AND THE MEMORIES YOU GAVE ME.
AND I REALIZED JUST HOW WONDERFUL A PERSON SHE WAS AND HOW IMPORTANT SHE WAS TO ALL OF YOU.
WHAT ALSO CAME ACROSS SO CLEARLY WAS HOW MUCH YOU ALL WANTED HER BACK.
BUT THERE'S ONE THING I DON'T GET.
WHY DIDN'T YOU GIVE ME MICHIRU'S MEMORIES?
...
MICHIRU KAZUSA REJECTED THEM.

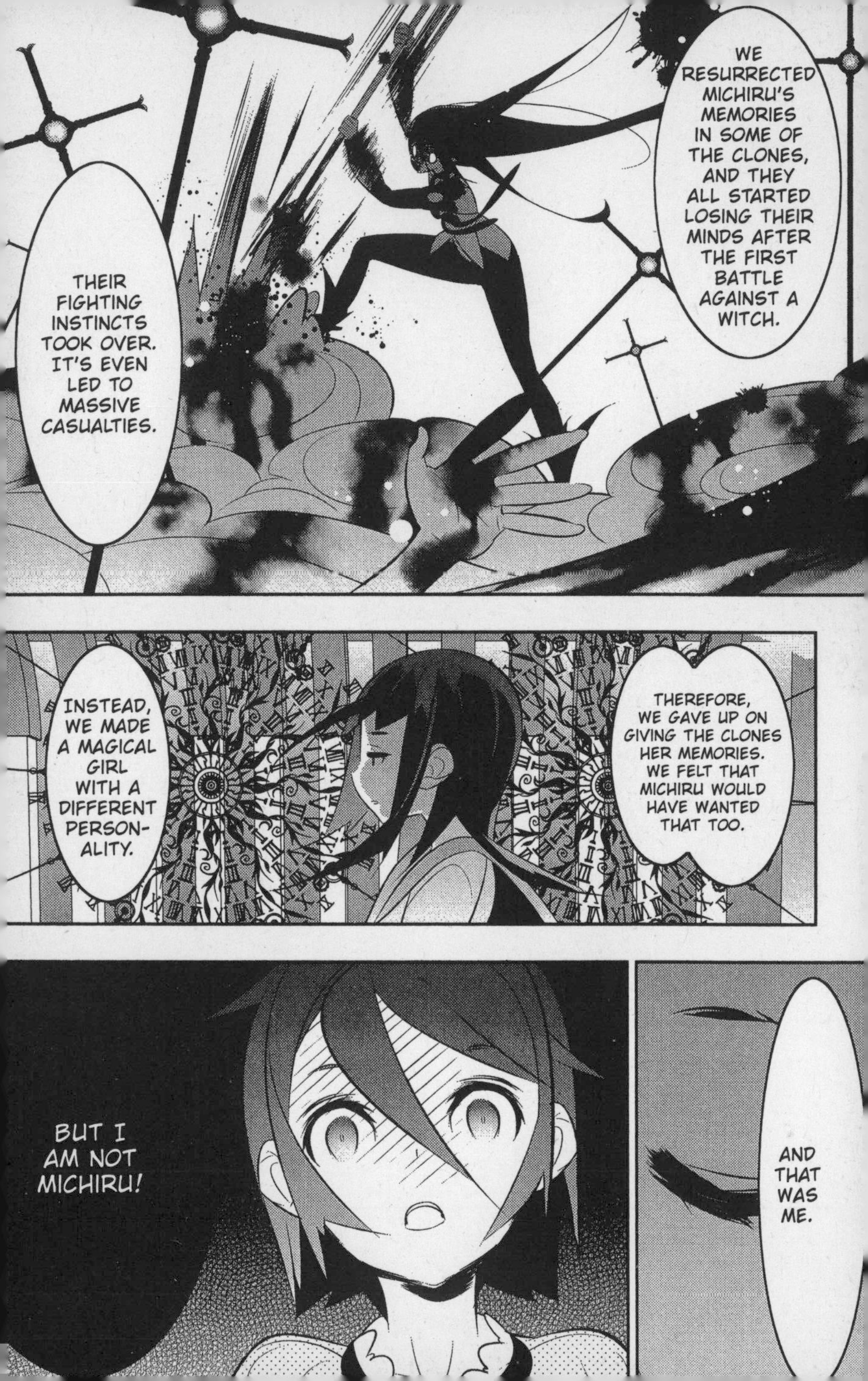
WE RESURRECTED MICHIRU'S MEMORIES IN SOME OF THE CLONES, AND THEY ALL STARTED LOSING THEIR MINDS AFTER THE FIRST BATTLE AGAINST A WITCH.
THEIR FIGHTING INSTINCTS TOOK OVER. IT'S EVEN LED TO MASSIVE CASUALTIES.
THEREFORE, WE GAVE UP ON GIVING THE CLONES HER MEMORIES. WE FELT THAT MICHIRU WOULD HAVE WANTED THAT TOO.
INSTEAD, WE MADE A MAGICAL GIRL WITH A DIFFERENT PERSON-ALITY.
AND THAT WAS ME.
BUT I AM NOT MICHIRU!

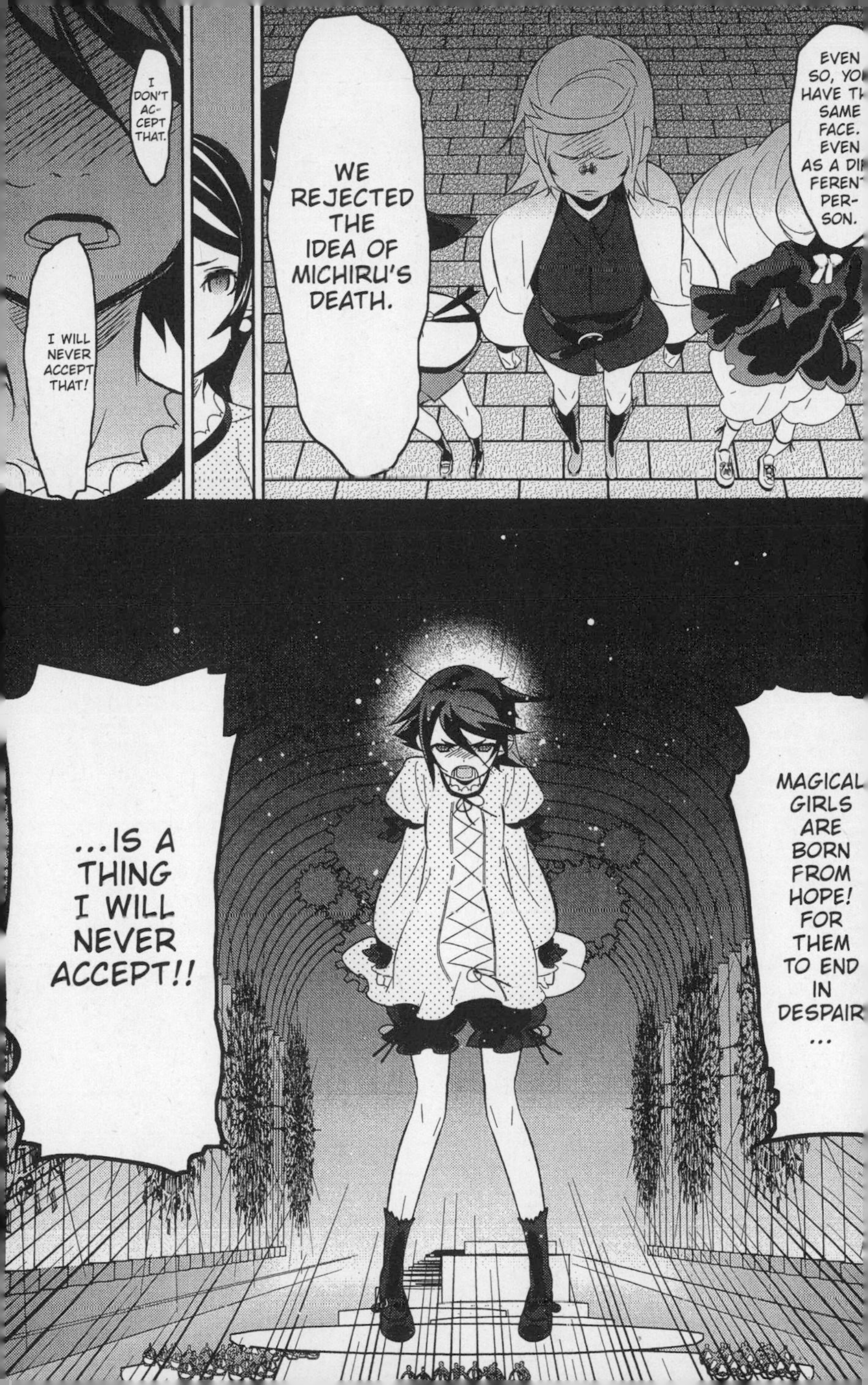
EVEN SO, YO HAVE TH SAME FACE. EVEN AS A DI FERENT PER-SON.
WE REJECTED THE IDEA OF MICHIRU'S DEATH.
I DON'T AC-CEPT THAT.
I WILL NEVER ACCEPT THAT!
MAGICAL GIRLS ARE BORN FROM HOPE! FOR THEM TO END IN DESPAIR ...
...IS A THING I WILL NEVER ACCEPT!!

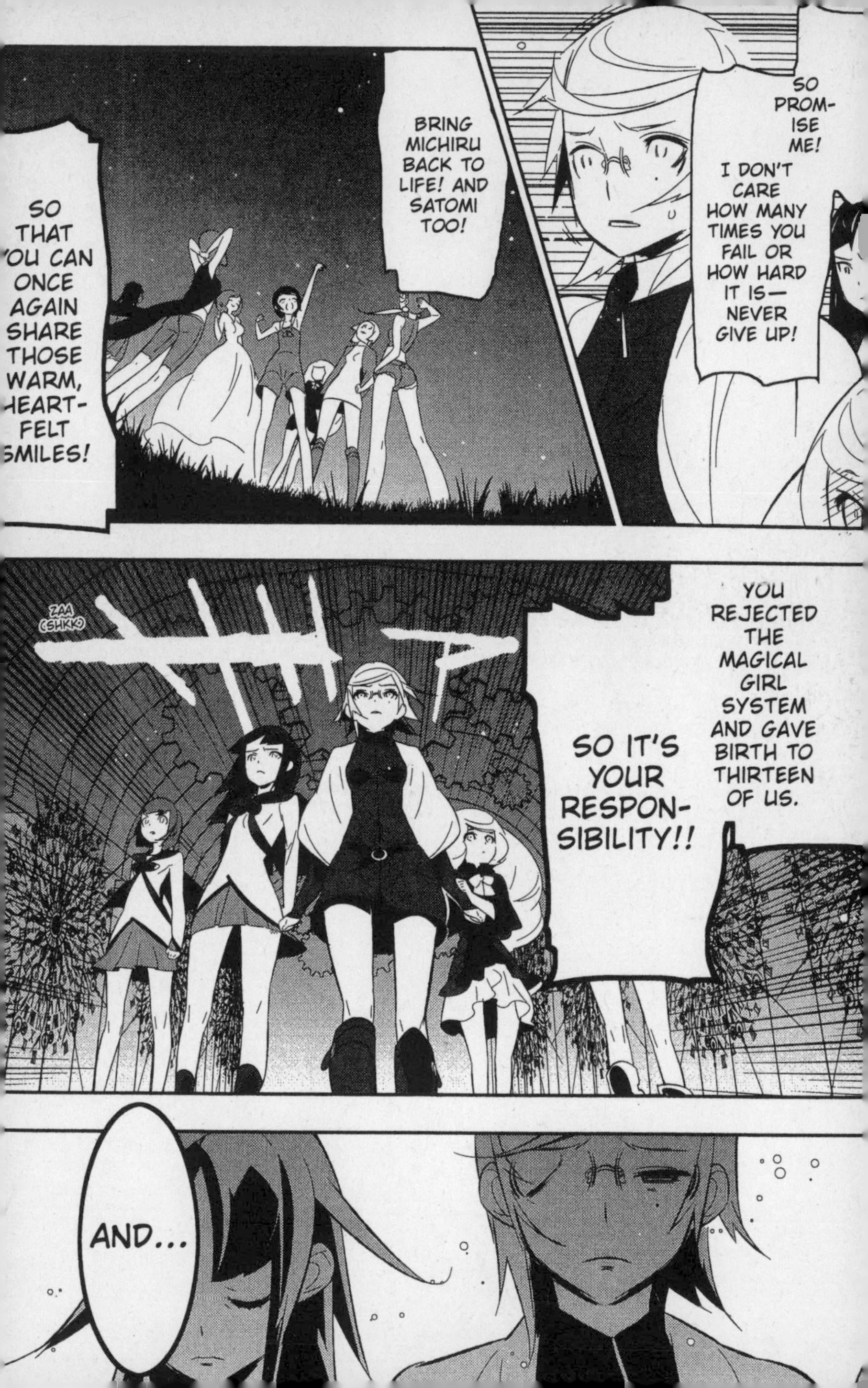
SO PROMISE ME!
I DON'T CARE HOW MANY TIMES YOU FAIL OR HOW HARD IT IS—NEVER GIVE UP!
BRING MICHIRU BACK TO LIFE! AND SATOMI TOO!
SO THAT OU CAN ONCE AGAIN SHARE THOSE WARM, EART-FELT MILES!
YOU REJECTED THE MAGICAL GIRL SYSTEM AND GAVE BIRTH TO THIRTEEN OF US.
SO IT'S YOUR RESPONSIBILITY!!
ZAA (SHKK)
AND...

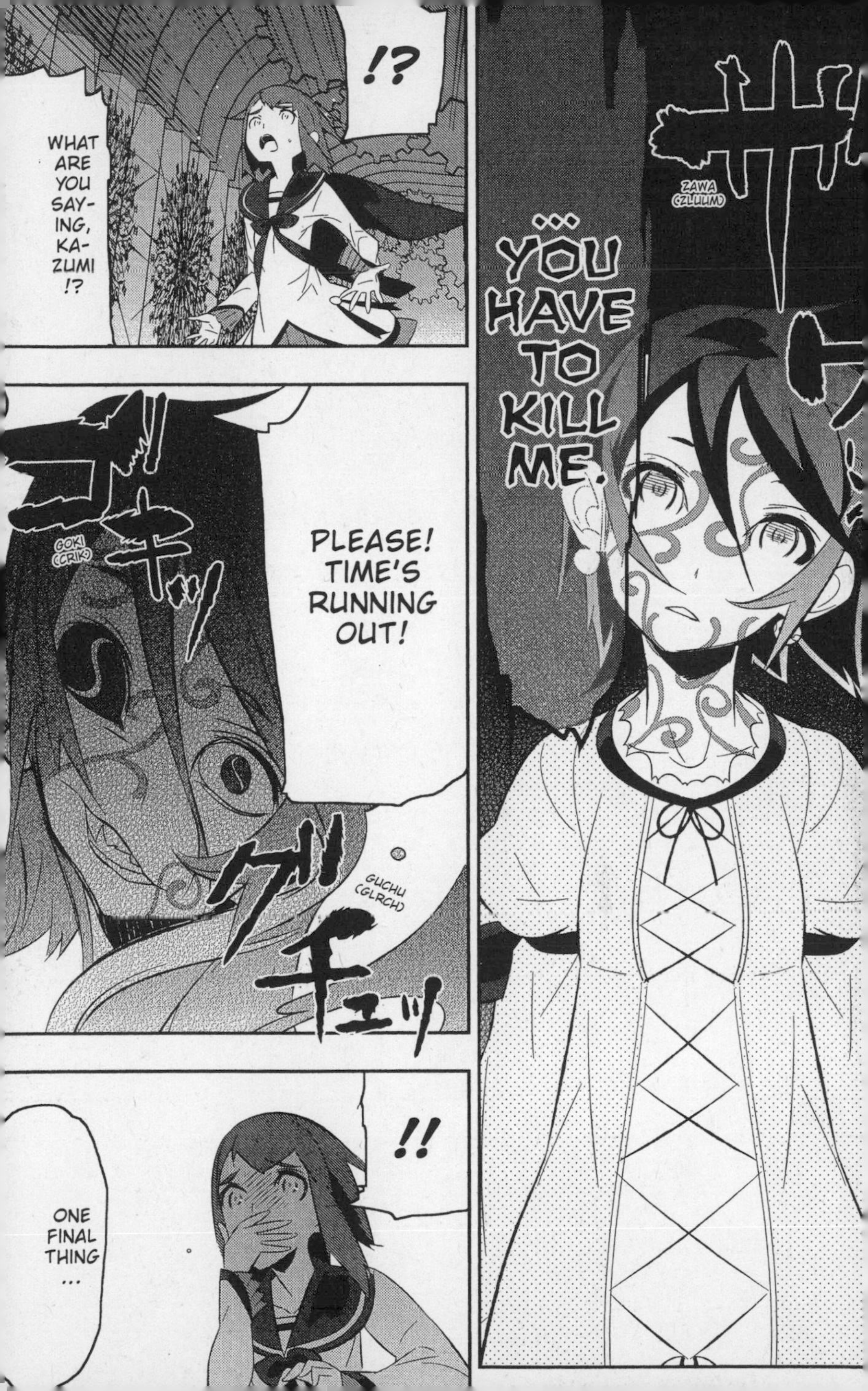
ZAWA (ZLUUM)
...YOU HAVE TO KILL ME.
!?
WHAT ARE YOU SAYING, KAZUMI!?
PLEASE! TIME'S RUNNING OUT!
GOKI (CRIK)
GUCHU (GLRCH)
!!
ONE FINAL THING...

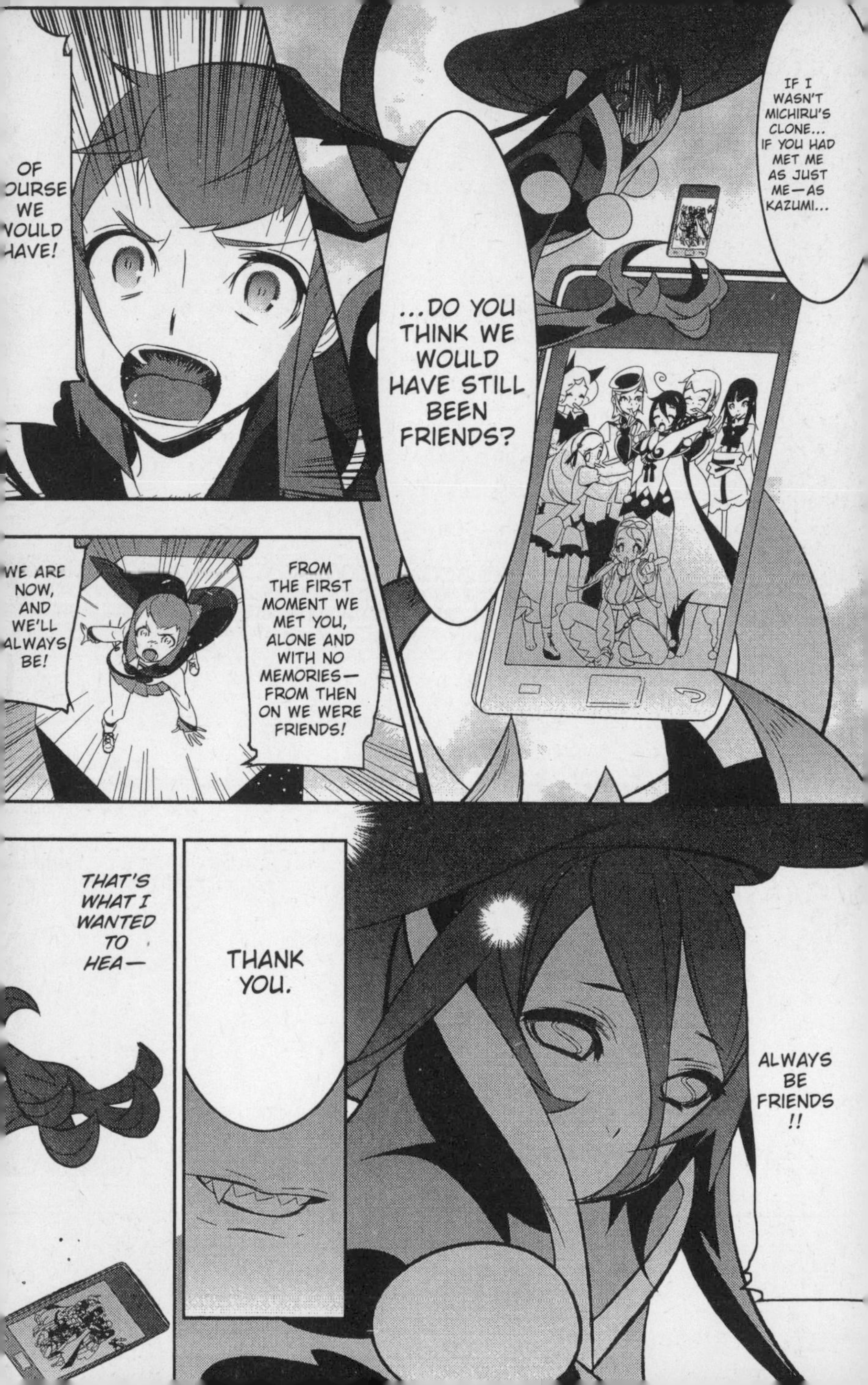
IF I WASN'T MICHIRU'S CLONE... IF YOU HAD MET ME AS JUST ME—AS KAZUMI...
...DO YOU THINK WE WOULD HAVE STILL BEEN FRIENDS?
OF OURSE WE VOULD HAVE!
FROM THE FIRST MOMENT WE MET YOU, ALONE AND WITH NO MEMORIES—FROM THEN ON WE WERE FRIENDS!
WE ARE NOW, AND WE'LL ALWAYS BE!
ALWAYS BE FRIENDS!!
THANK YOU.
THAT'S WHAT I WANTED TO HEA—

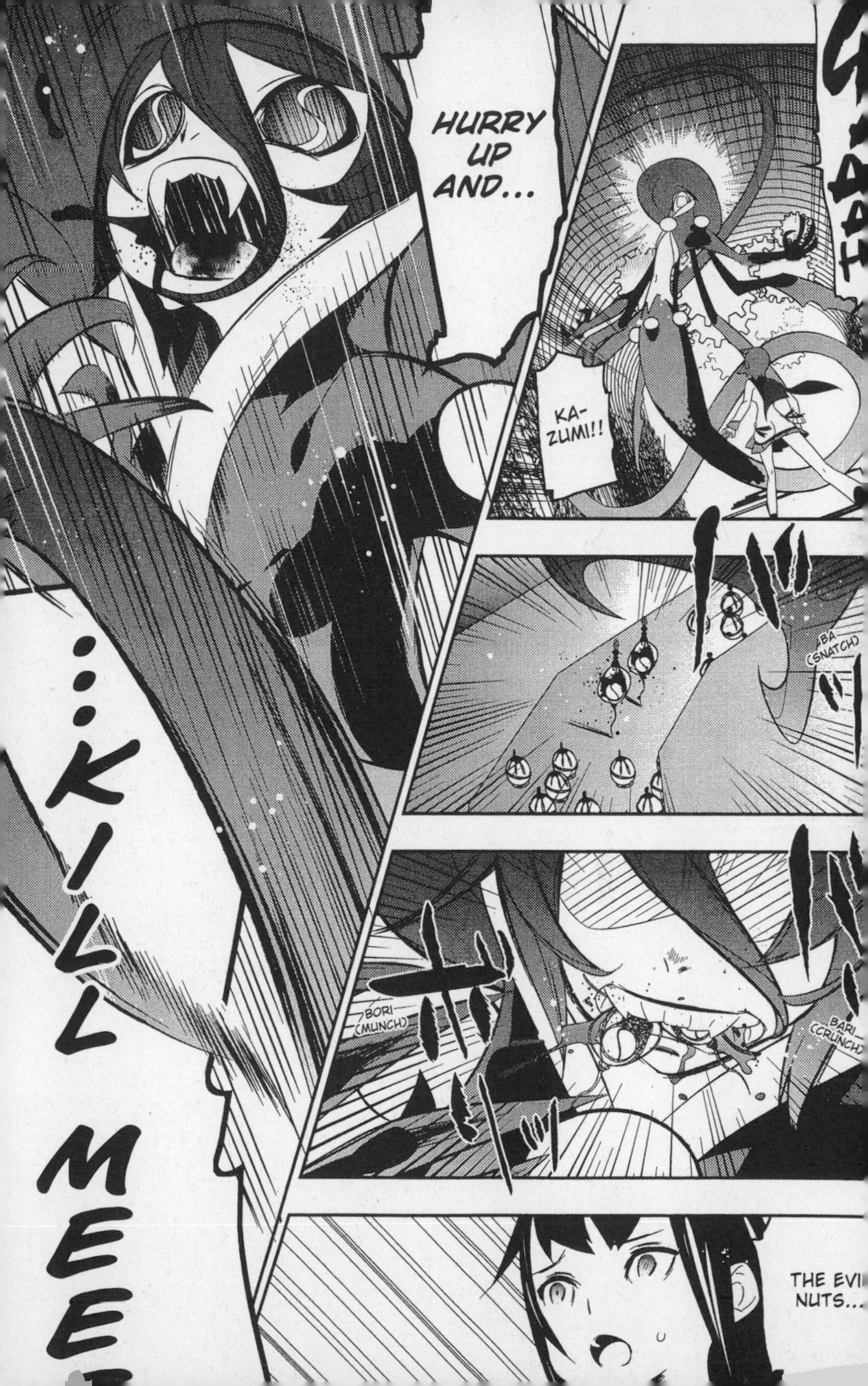
KA-ZUMI!!
BA (SNATCH)
BARI (CRUNCH)
BORI (MUNCH)
THE EVI NUTS...
HURRY UP AND...
...KILL MEE

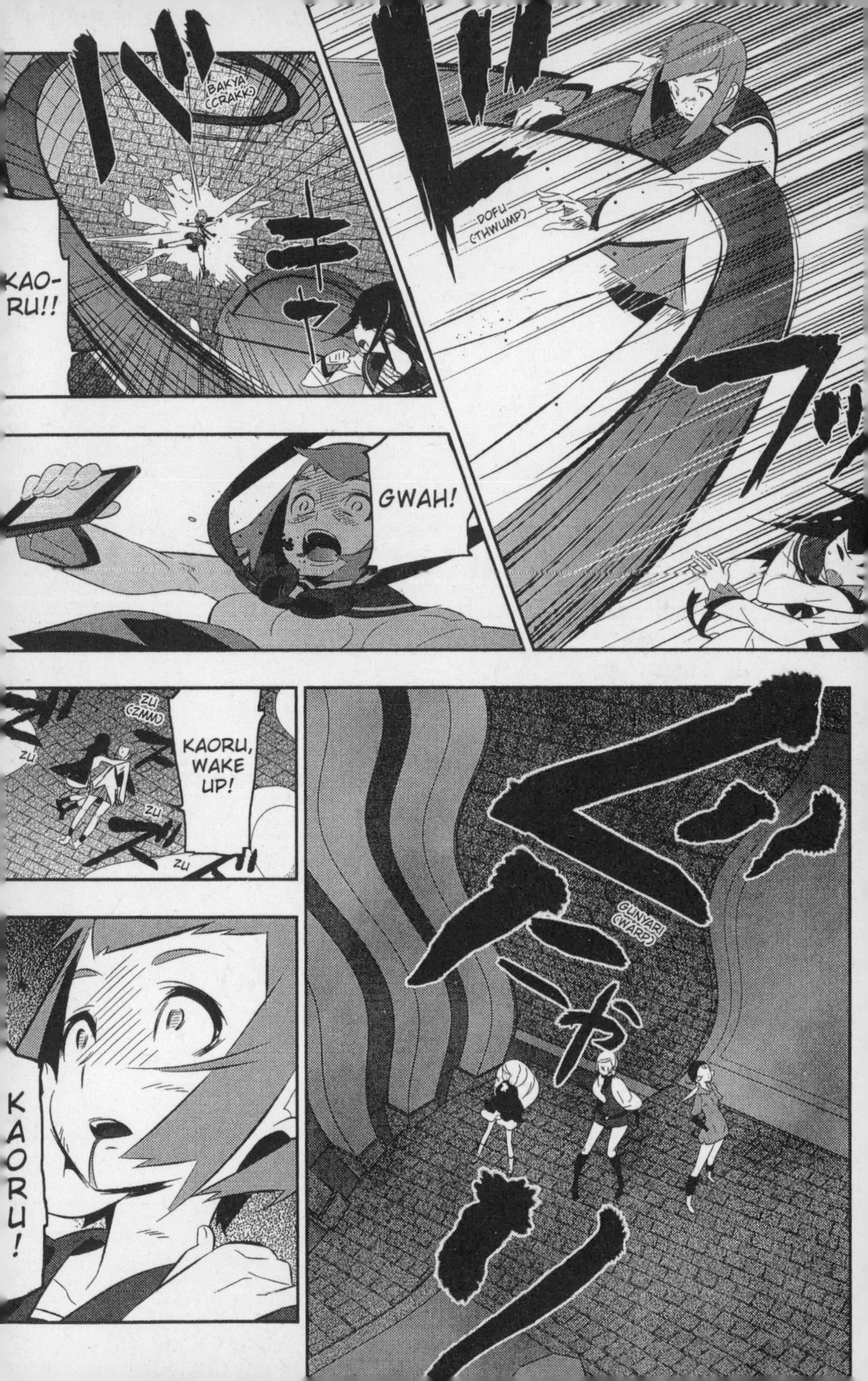
DOFU (THWUMP)
BAKYA (CRAKK)
KAO-RU!!
GWAH!
GUNYARI (WARP)
ZU (ZMM)
KAORU, WAKE UP!
ZU
ZU
ZU
KAORU!

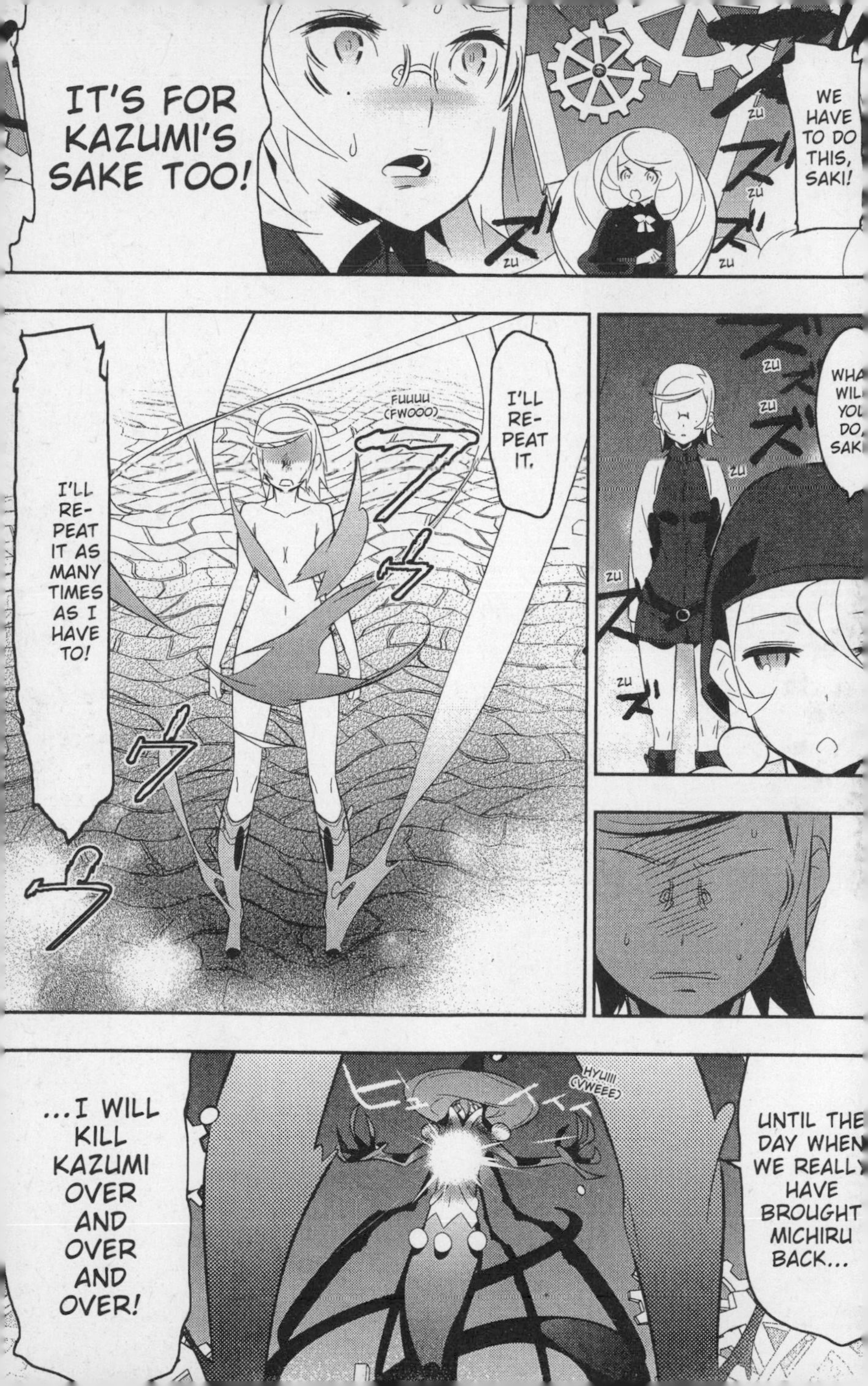
WE HAVE TO DO THIS, SAKI!
ZU
ZU
ZU
ZU
IT'S FOR KAZUMI'S SAKE TOO!
ZU
ZU
WHA WILL YOU DO, SAKI
ZU
ZU
ZU
I'LL RE-PEAT IT.
FUUUU (FWOOO)
I'LL RE-PEAT IT AS MANY TIMES AS I HAVE TO!
UNTIL THE DAY WHEN WE REALLY HAVE BROUGHT MICHIRU BACK...
HYUIII (VWEEE)
...I WILL KILL KAZUMI OVER AND OVER AND OVER!

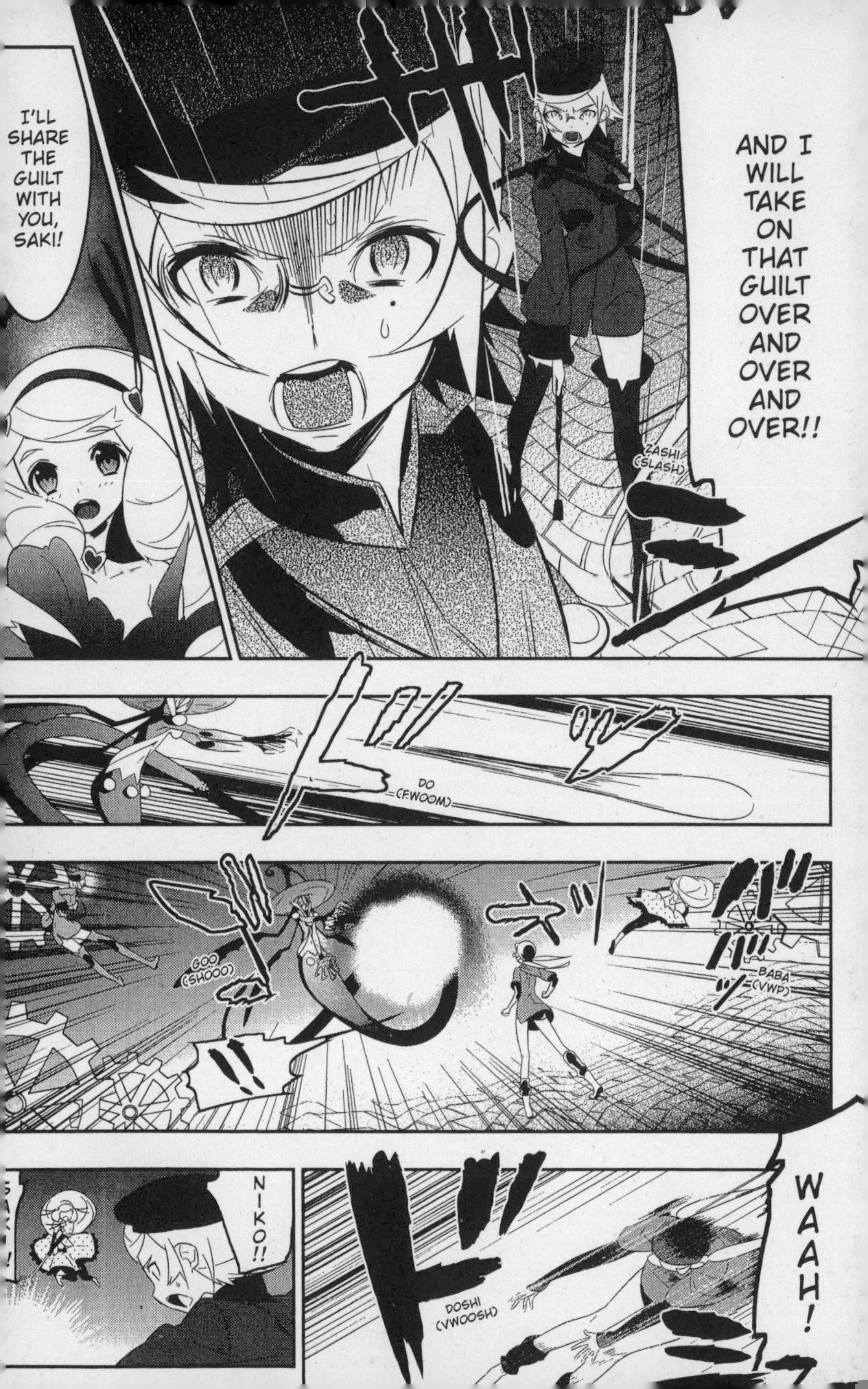
AND I WILL TAKE ON THAT GUILT OVER AND OVER AND OVER!!
ZASHI (SLASH)
I'LL SHARE THE GUILT WITH YOU, SAKI!
DO (FWOOM)
BABA (VWP)
GOO (SHOOO)
WAAAH!
DOSHI (VWOOSH)
NIKO!!

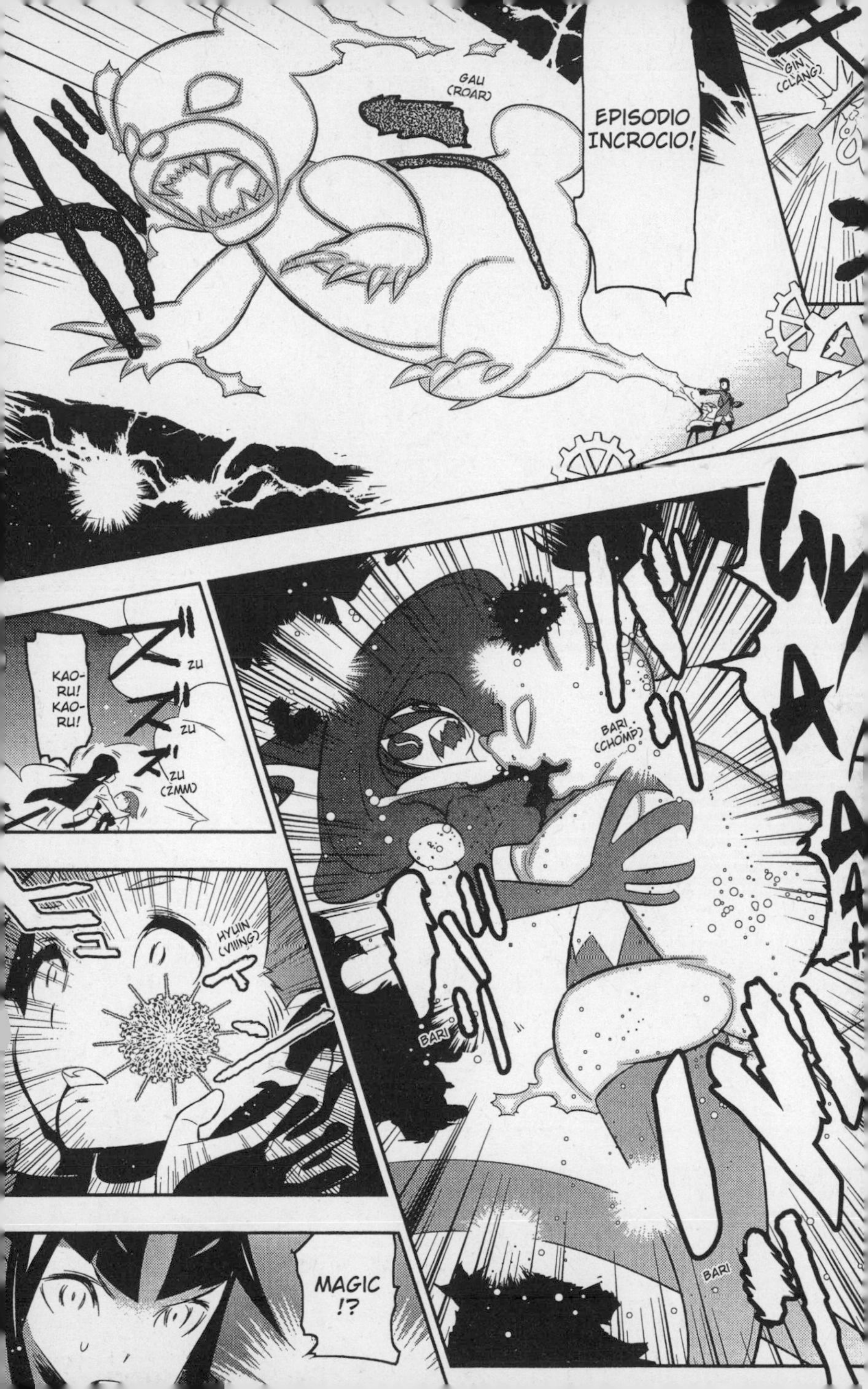
GIN (CLANG)
EPISODIO INCROCIO!
GAU (ROAR)
BARI (CHOMP)
BARI
BARI
KAO-RU! KAO-RU!
ZU
ZU
ZU (ZMM)
HYUIN (VIIING)
MAGIC !?

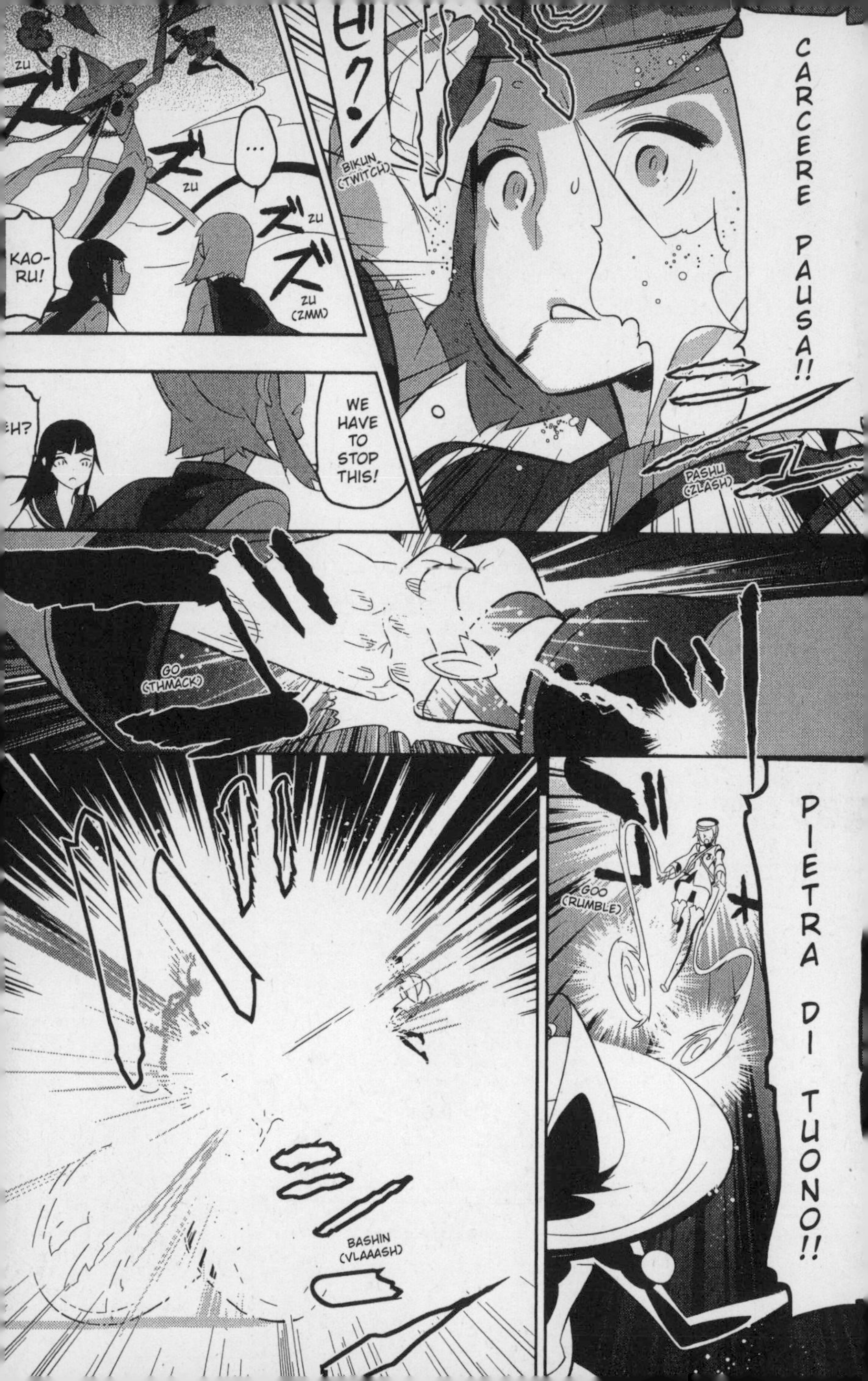
CARCERE PAUSA!!
ビクン
BIKUN (TWITCH)
PASHU (ZLASH)
...
ZU
ZU
ZU
KAO-RU!
ZU (ZMM)
WE HAVE TO STOP THIS!
EH?
GO (THMACK)
PIETRA DI TUONO!!
GOO (RUMBLE)
BASHIN (VLAAASH)

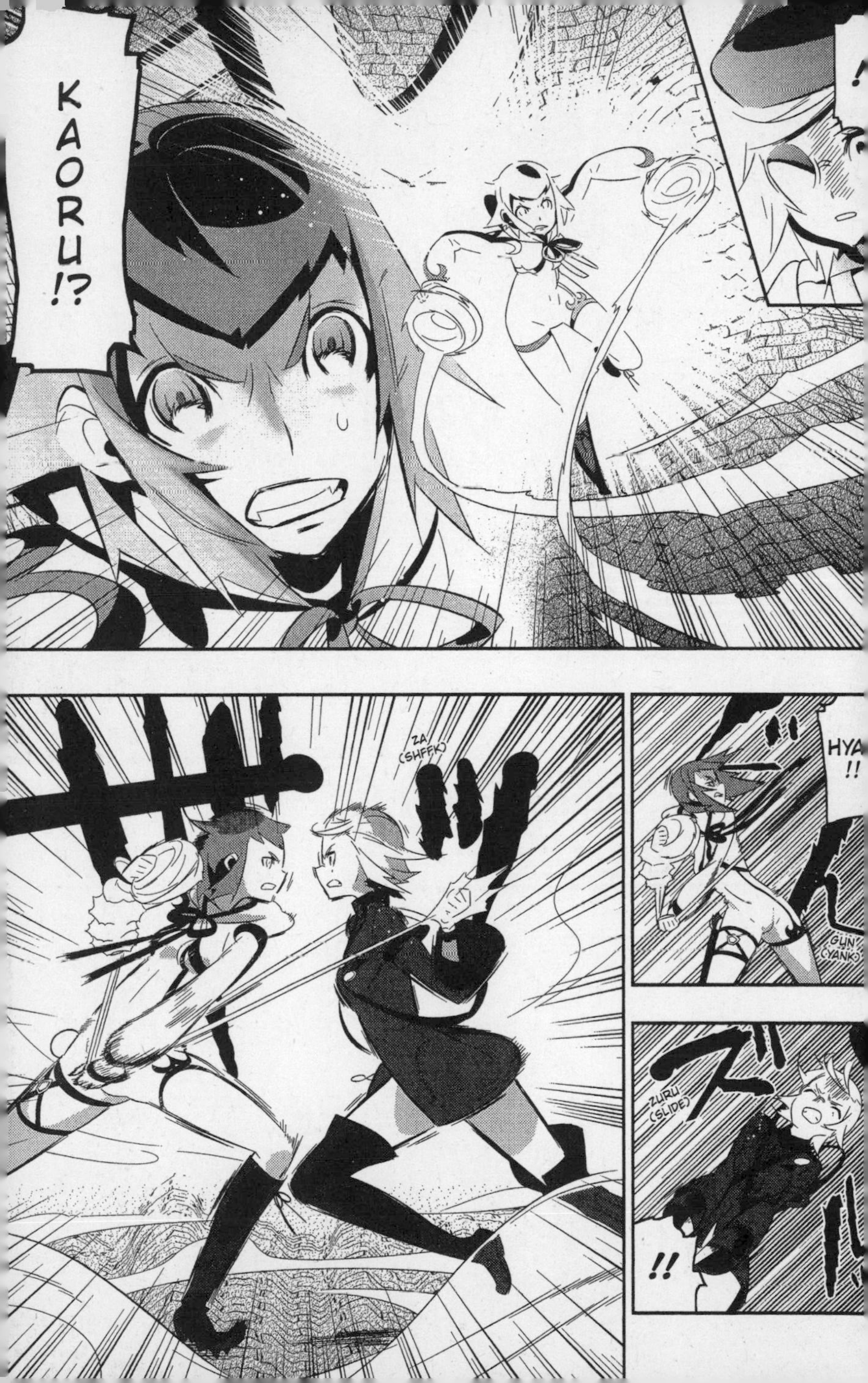
!
KAORU!?
HYA!!
GUN (YANK)
ZURU (SLIDE)
!!
ZA (SHFFK)

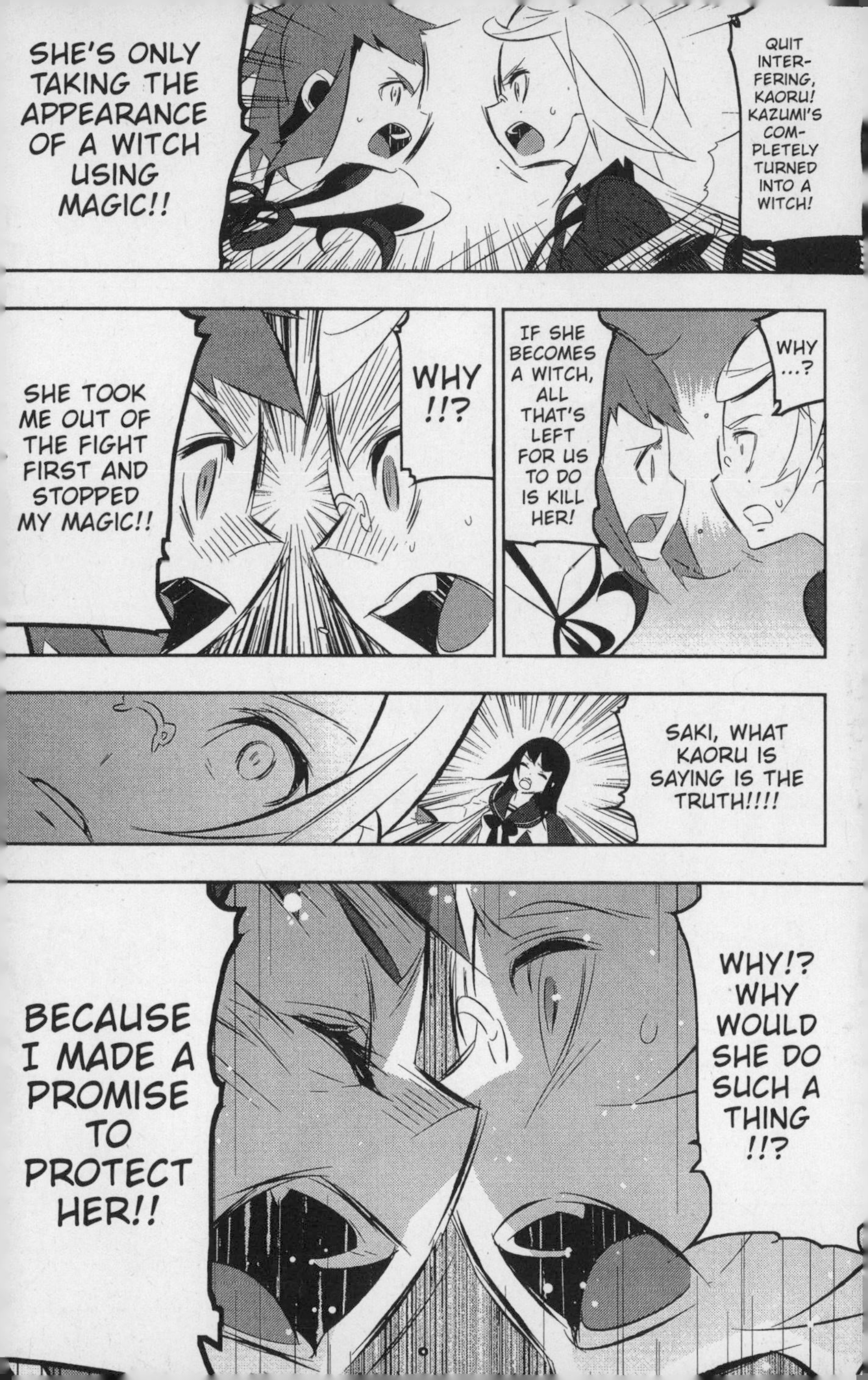
QUIT INTERFERING, KAORU! KAZUMI'S COMPLETELY TURNED INTO A WITCH!
SHE'S ONLY TAKING THE APPEARANCE OF A WITCH USING MAGIC!!
WHY ...?
IF SHE BECOMES A WITCH, ALL THAT'S LEFT FOR US TO DO IS KILL HER!
WHY !!?
SHE TOOK ME OUT OF THE FIGHT FIRST AND STOPPED MY MAGIC!!
SAKI, WHAT KAORU IS SAYING IS THE TRUTH!!!!
WHY!? WHY WOULD SHE DO SUCH A THING !!?
BECAUSE I MADE A PROMISE TO PROTECT HER!!

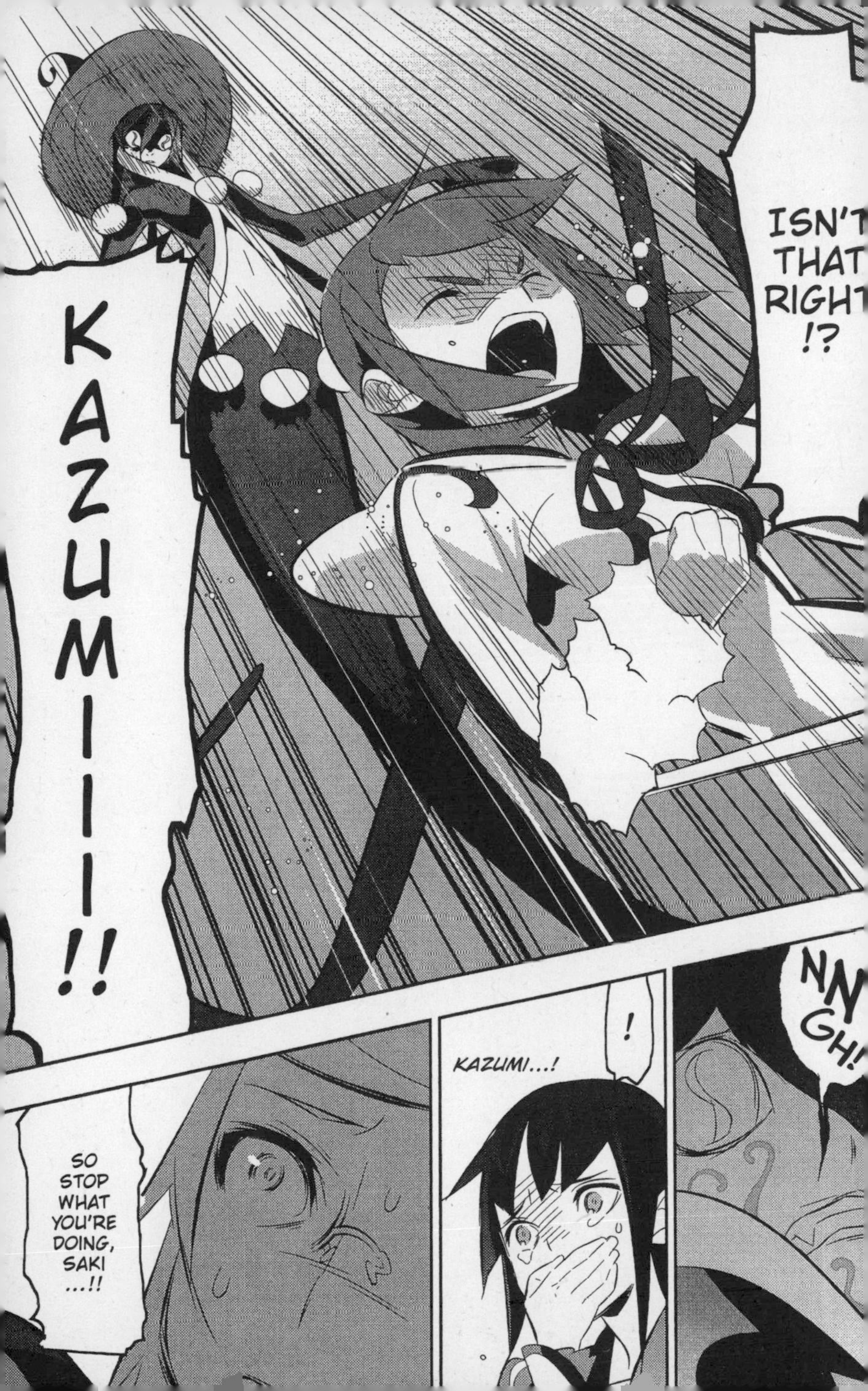
ISN'T THAT RIGHT!?
KAZUMIIII!!
NNGH!
!
KAZUMI...!
SO STOP WHAT YOU'RE DOING, SAKI...!!

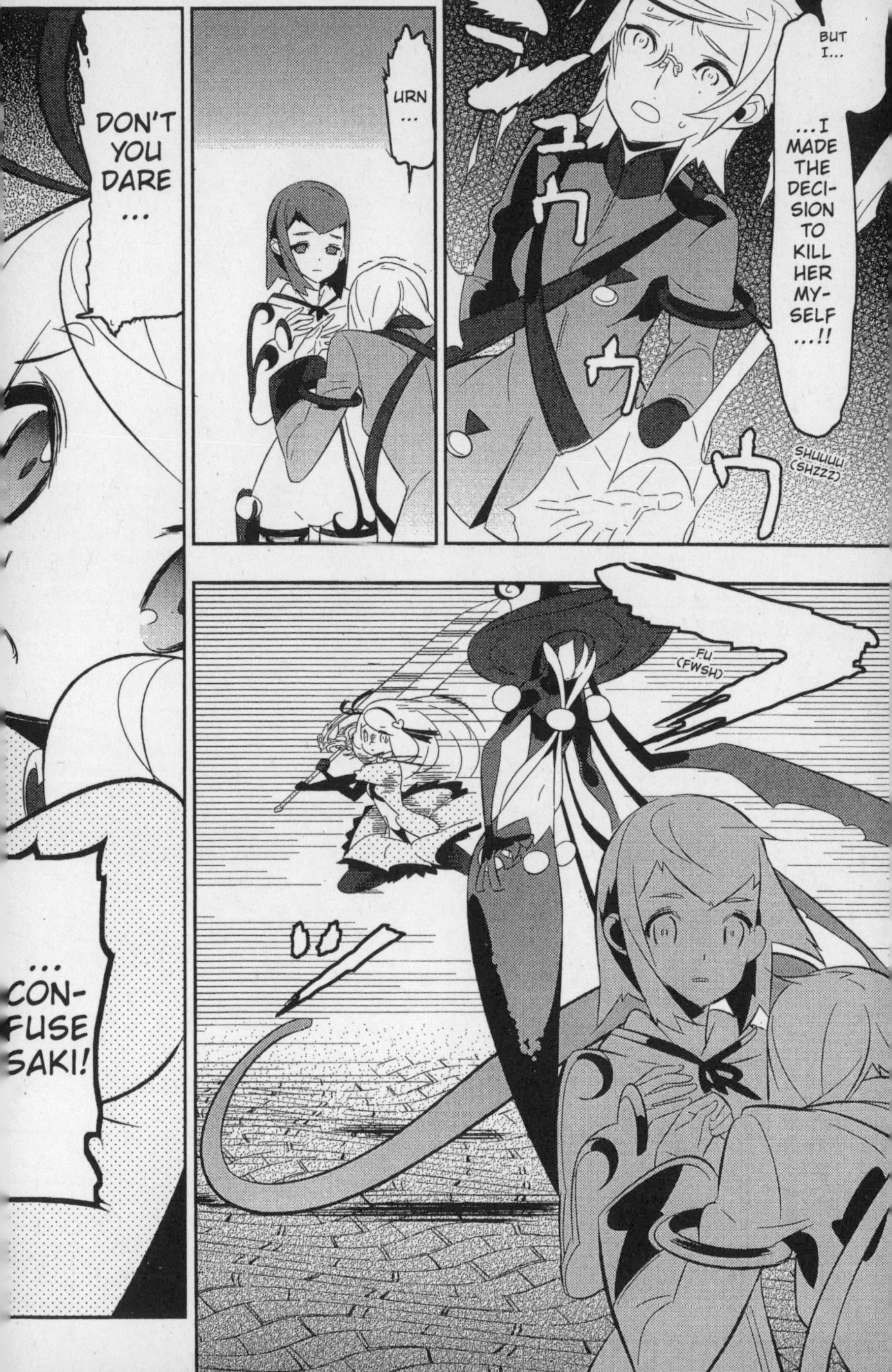
BUT I...
...I MADE THE DECISION TO KILL HER MY-SELF...!!
SHUUUU (SHZZZ)
URN...
FU (FWSH)
DON'T YOU DARE...
...CON-FUSE SAKI!

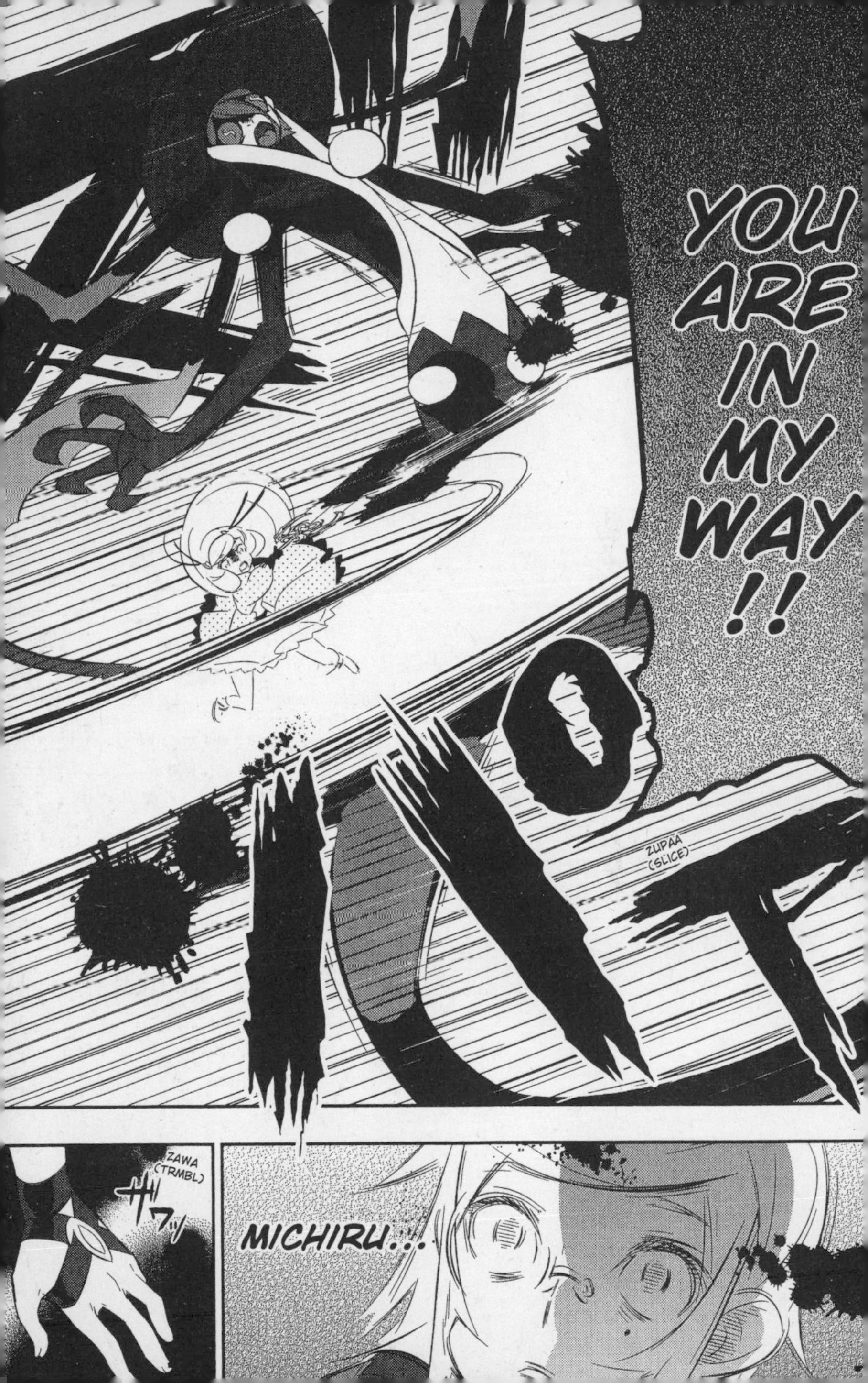
YOU ARE IN MY WAY!!
ZUPAA (SLICE)
MICHIRU...
ZAWA (TRMBL)
ザワッ

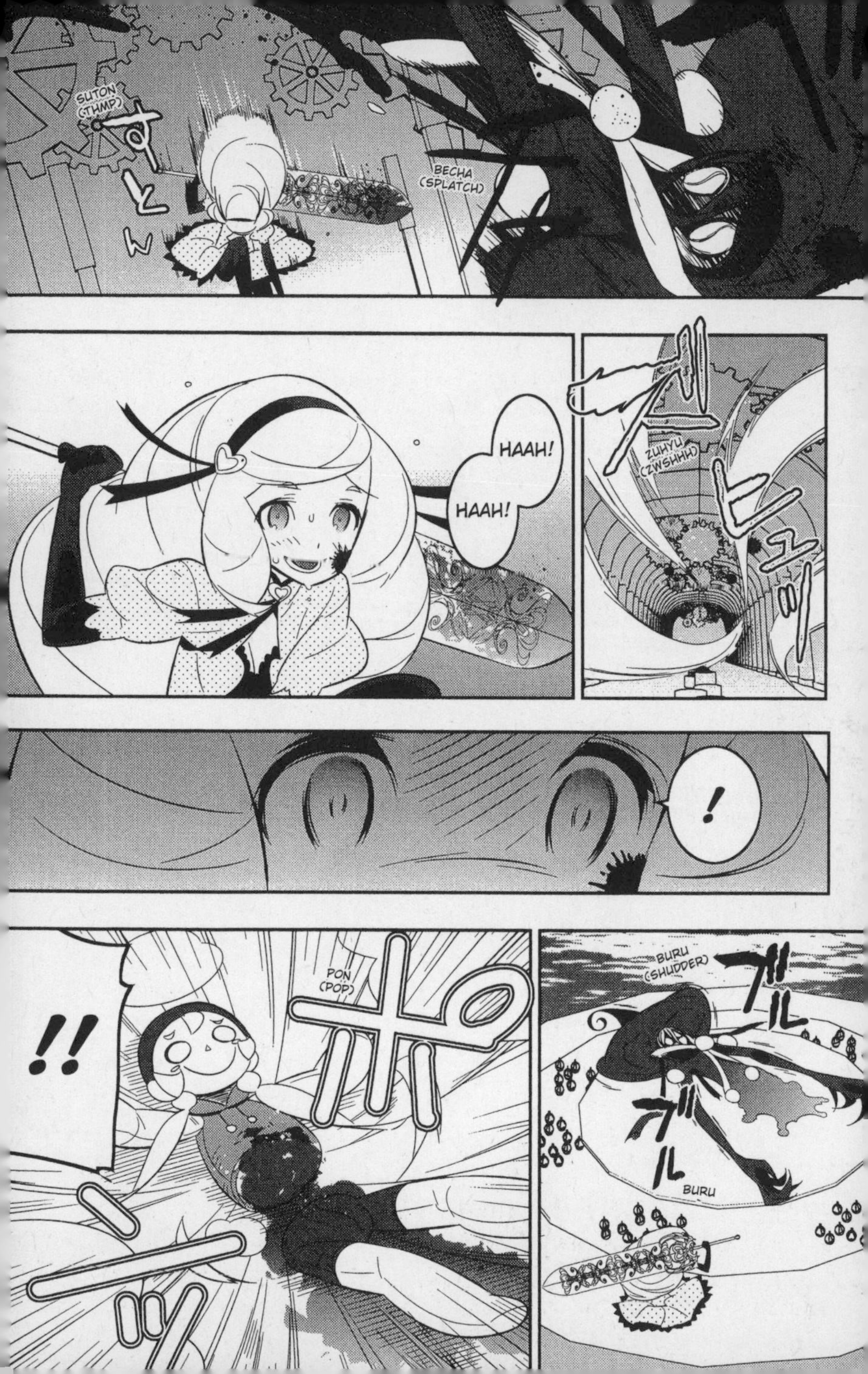
BECHA (SPLATCH)
SUTON (THMP)
ZUHYU (ZWSHHH)
HAAH!
HAAH!
!
BURU (SHUDDER)
BURU
PON (POP)
!!

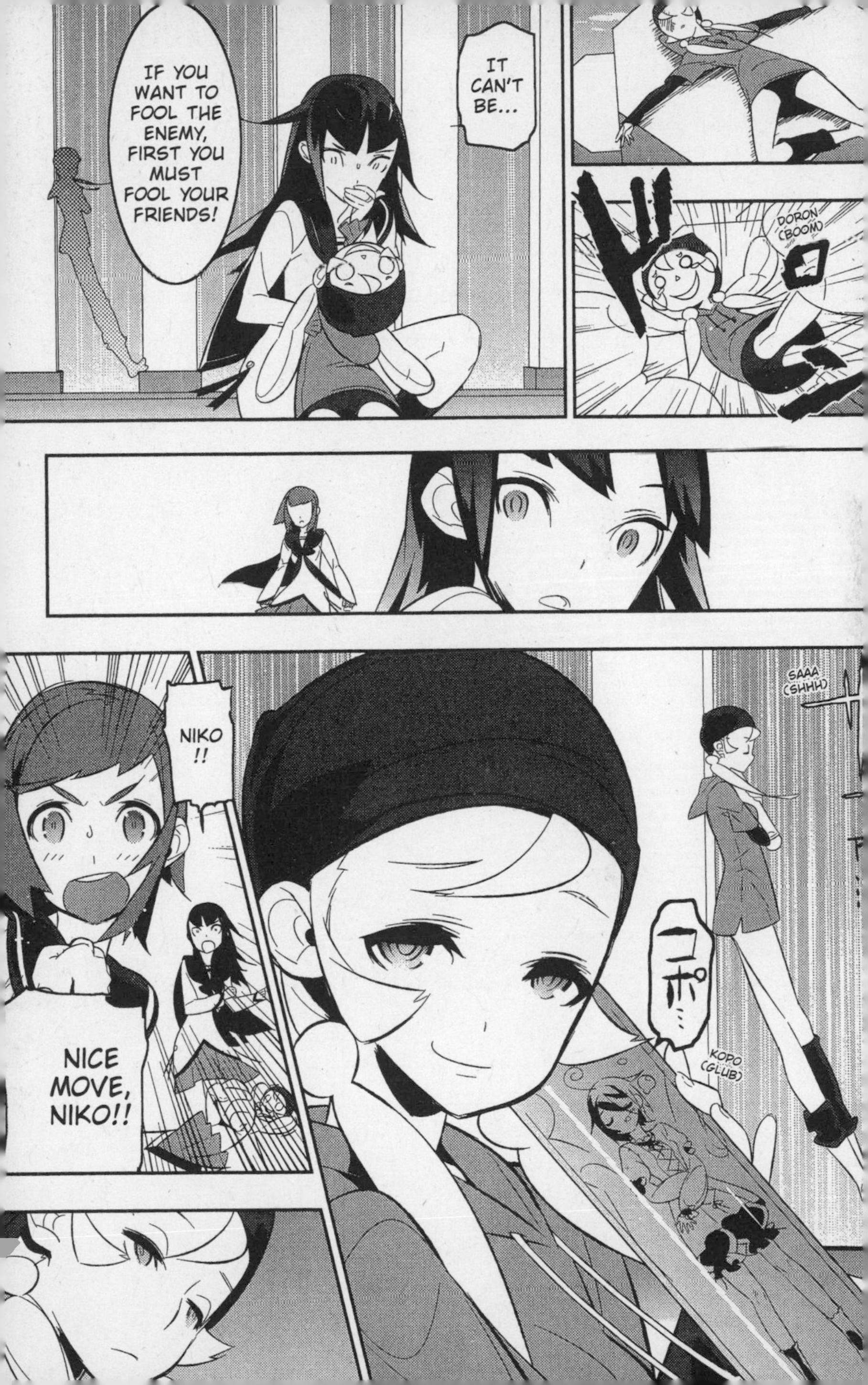
DORON (BOOM)
IT CAN'T BE...
IF YOU WANT TO FOOL THE ENEMY, FIRST YOU MUST FOOL YOUR FRIENDS!
SAAA (SHHH)
KOPO (GLUB)
NIKO!!
NICE MOVE, NIKO!!

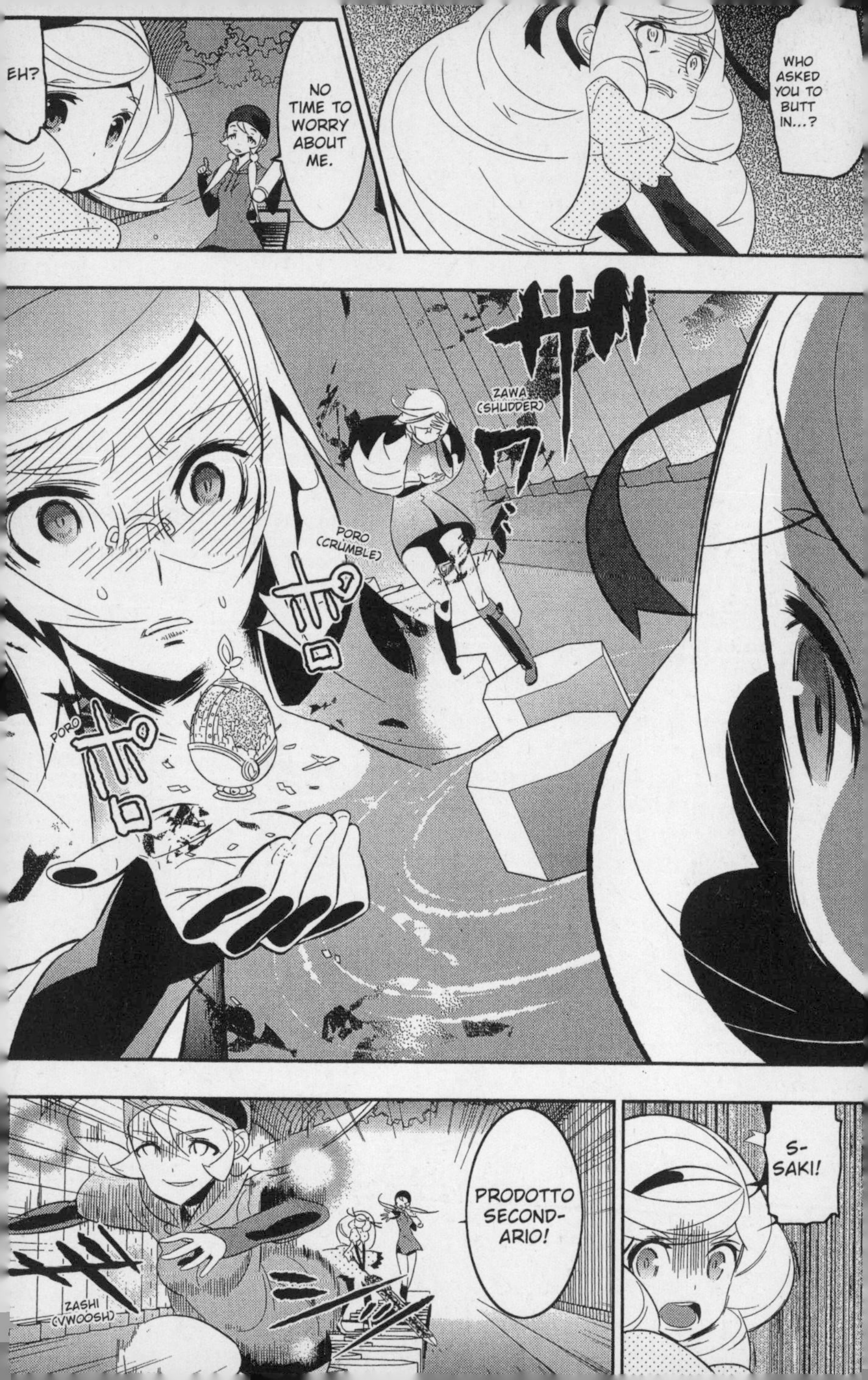
WHO ASKED YOU TO BUTT IN...?
NO TIME TO WORRY ABOUT ME.
EH?
ZAWA (SHUDDER)
PORO (CRUMBLE)
PORO
S-SAKI!
PRODOTTO SECOND-ARIO!
ZASHI (VWOOSH)

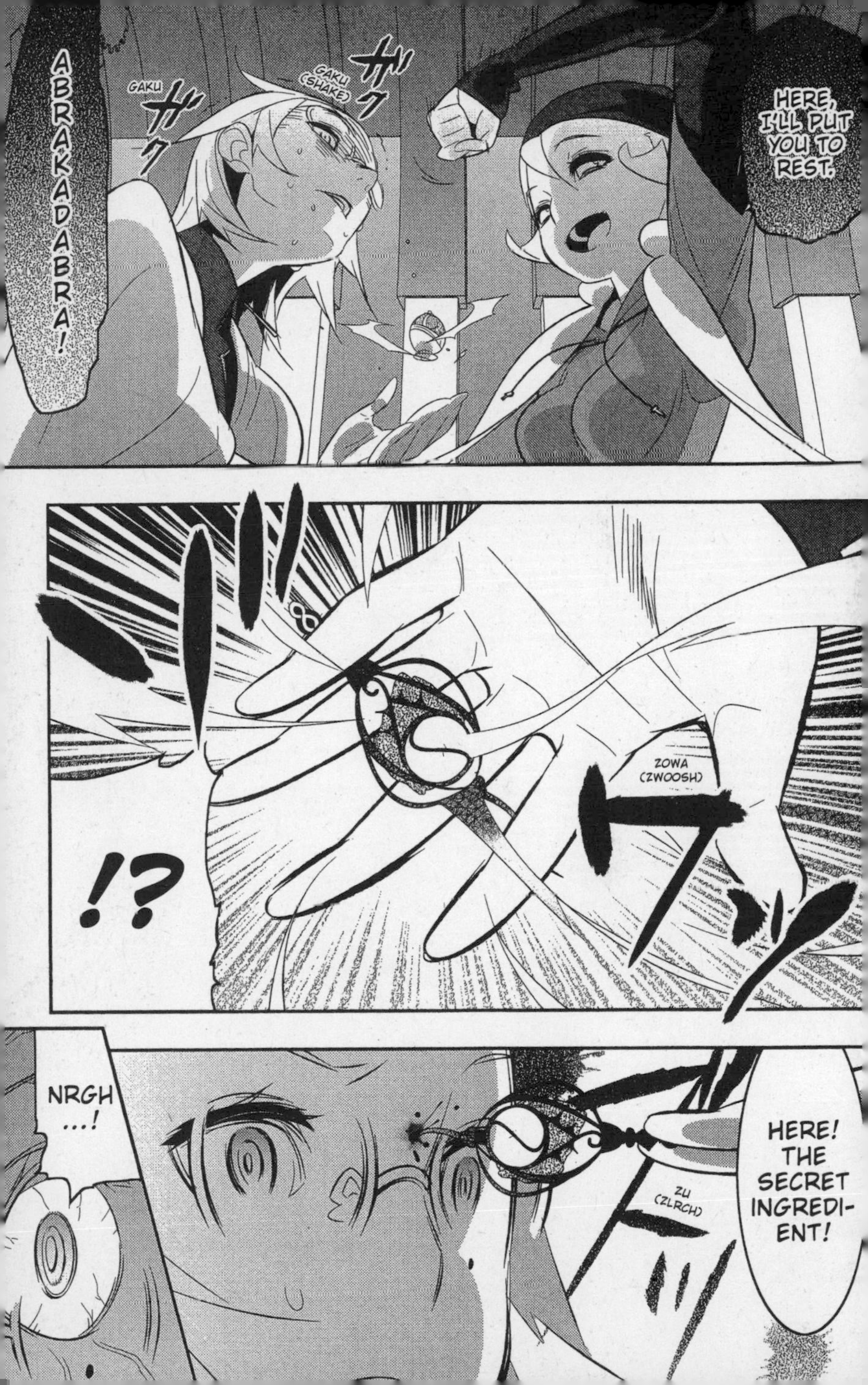
HERE, I'LL PUT YOU TO REST.
GAKU (SHAKE)
GAKU
ABRAKADABRA!
ZOWA (ZWOOSH)
!?
HERE! THE SECRET INGREDI-ENT!
ZU (ZLRCH)
NRGH ...!

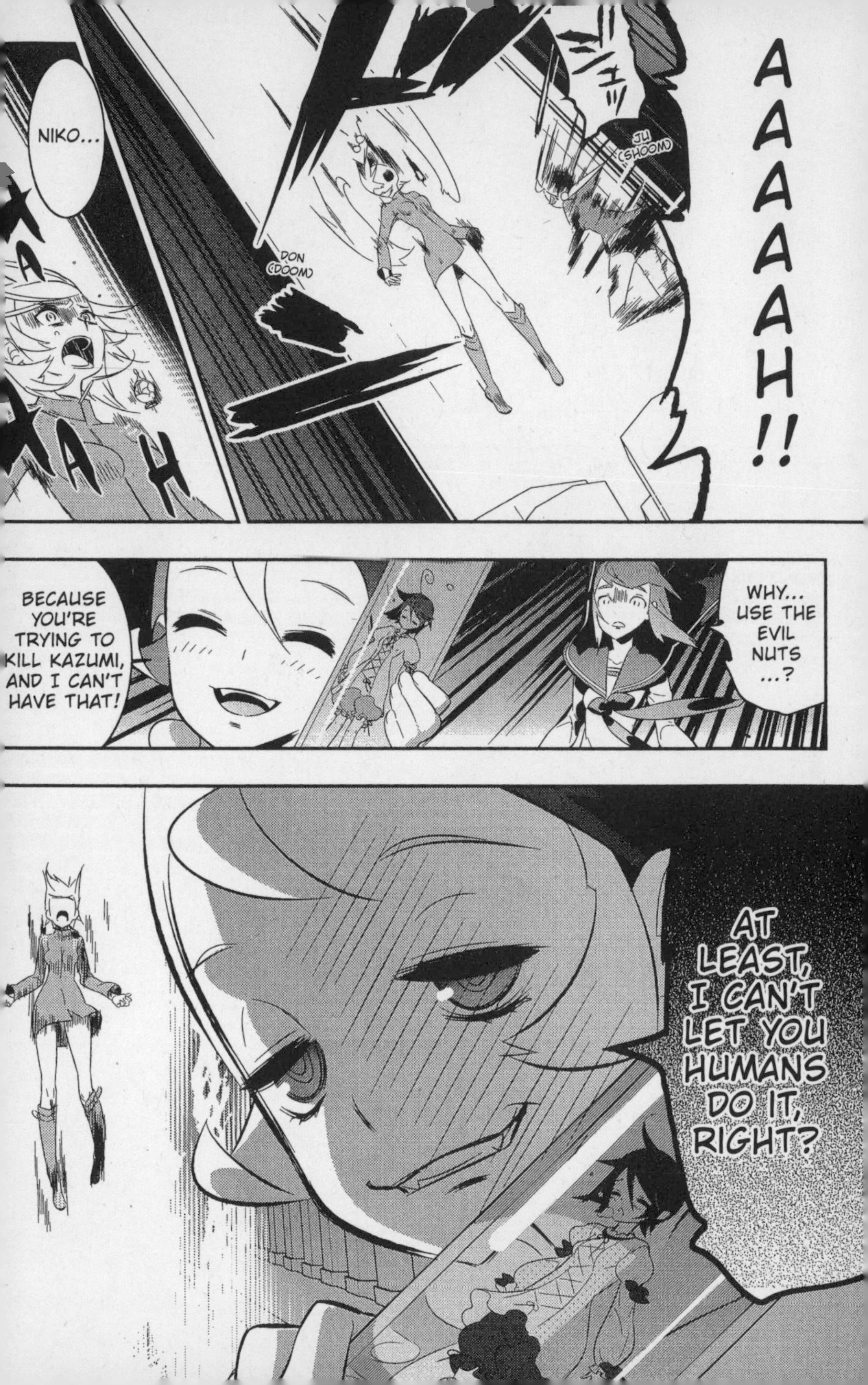
AAAAAH!!
JU (SHOOM)
DON (DOOM)
NIKO...
AAAH
WHY... USE THE EVIL NUTS ...?
BECAUSE YOU'RE TRYING TO KILL KAZUMI, AND I CAN'T HAVE THAT!
AT LEAST, I CAN'T LET YOU HUMANS DO IT, RIGHT?

EVEN SO...
...WE REALLY CAN'T RESIST YOUR STRAWBERRY RISOTTO...
I DON'T ACCEPT THAT!
I WILL NEVER ACCEPT THAT!
PROMISE ME YOU WON'T STEAL IT SECRETLY ANYMORE!
THAT YOU'LL ALL EAT IT TO-GETHER!
I PROM-ISE!
I'M SORRY, KAZUMI!
I KNEW YOU'D UNDER-STAND!
ALL SETTLED.

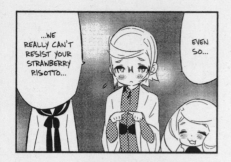

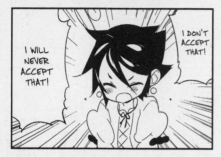

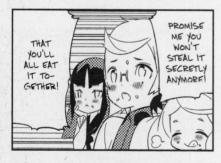

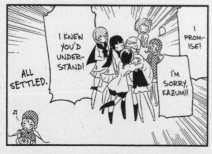

PUELLA MAGI
KAZUMI☆MAGICA
The innocent malice

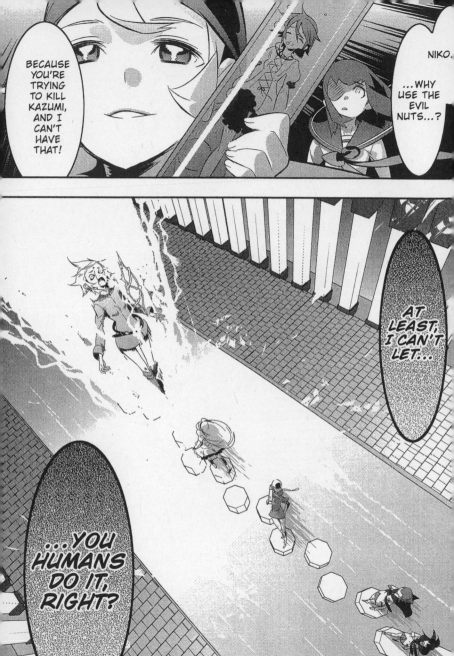

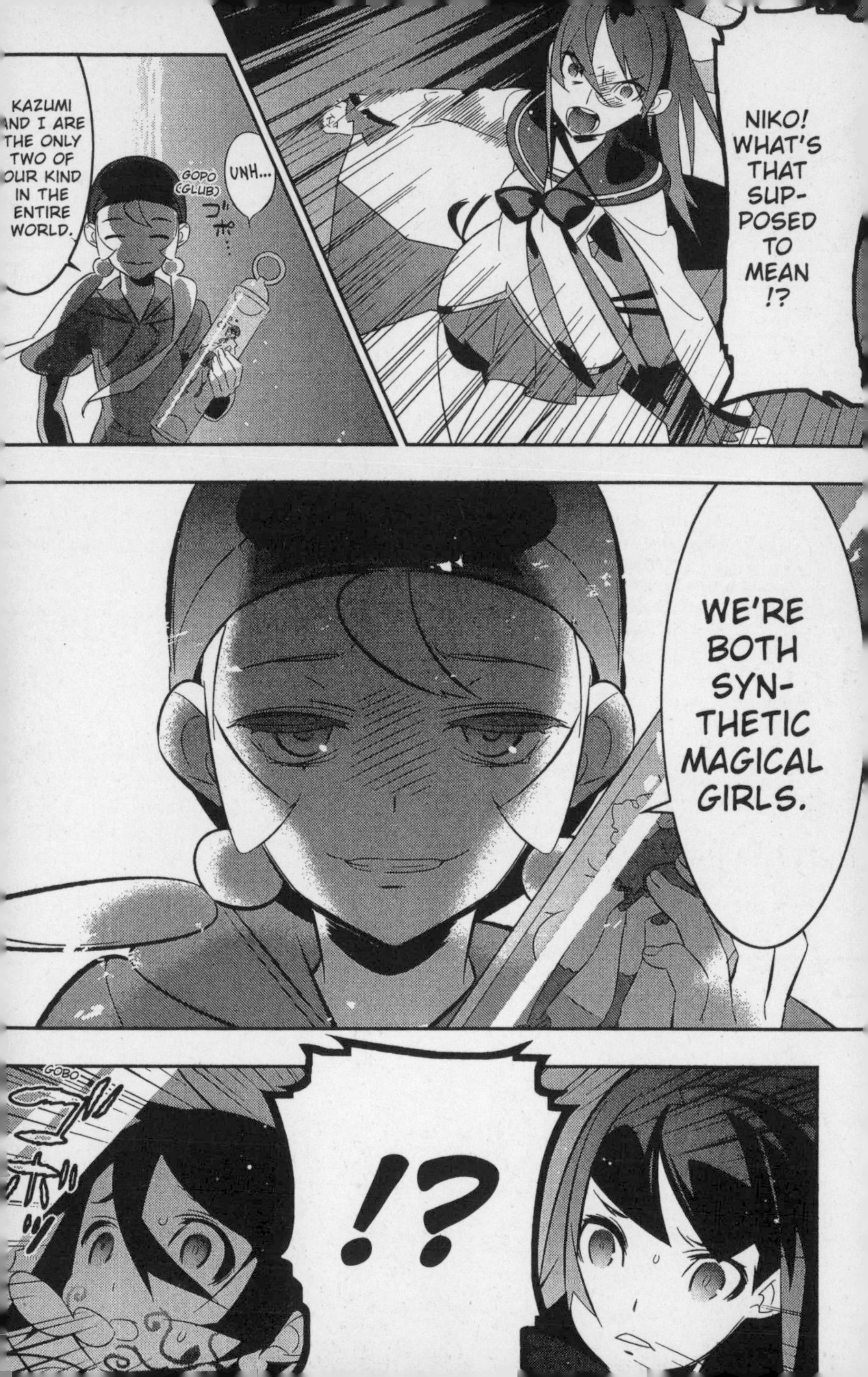
NIKO! WHAT'S THAT SUP-POSED TO MEAN!?
KAZUMI AND I ARE THE ONLY TWO OF OUR KIND IN THE ENTIRE WORLD.
UNH...
GOPO (GLUB)
WE'RE BOTH SYN-THETIC MAGICAL GIRLS.
!?
GOBO

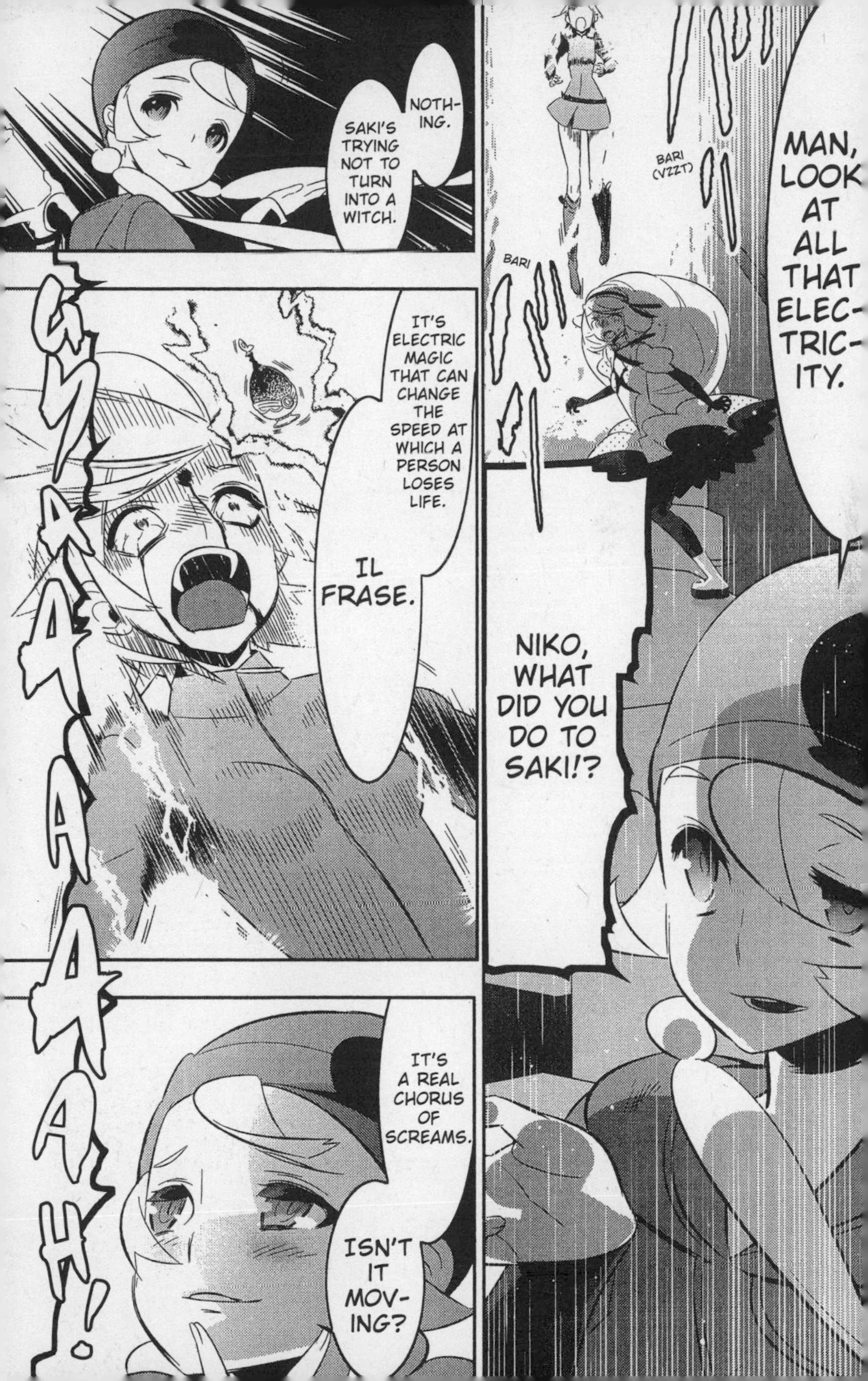
MAN, LOOK AT ALL THAT ELECTRICITY.
BARI (VZZT)
BARI
NIKO, WHAT DID YOU DO TO SAKI!?
NOTHING.
SAKI'S TRYING NOT TO TURN INTO A WITCH.
IT'S ELECTRIC MAGIC THAT CAN CHANGE THE SPEED AT WHICH A PERSON LOSES LIFE.
IL FRASE.
GYAAAAAH!
IT'S A REAL CHORUS OF SCREAMS.
ISN'T IT MOVING?

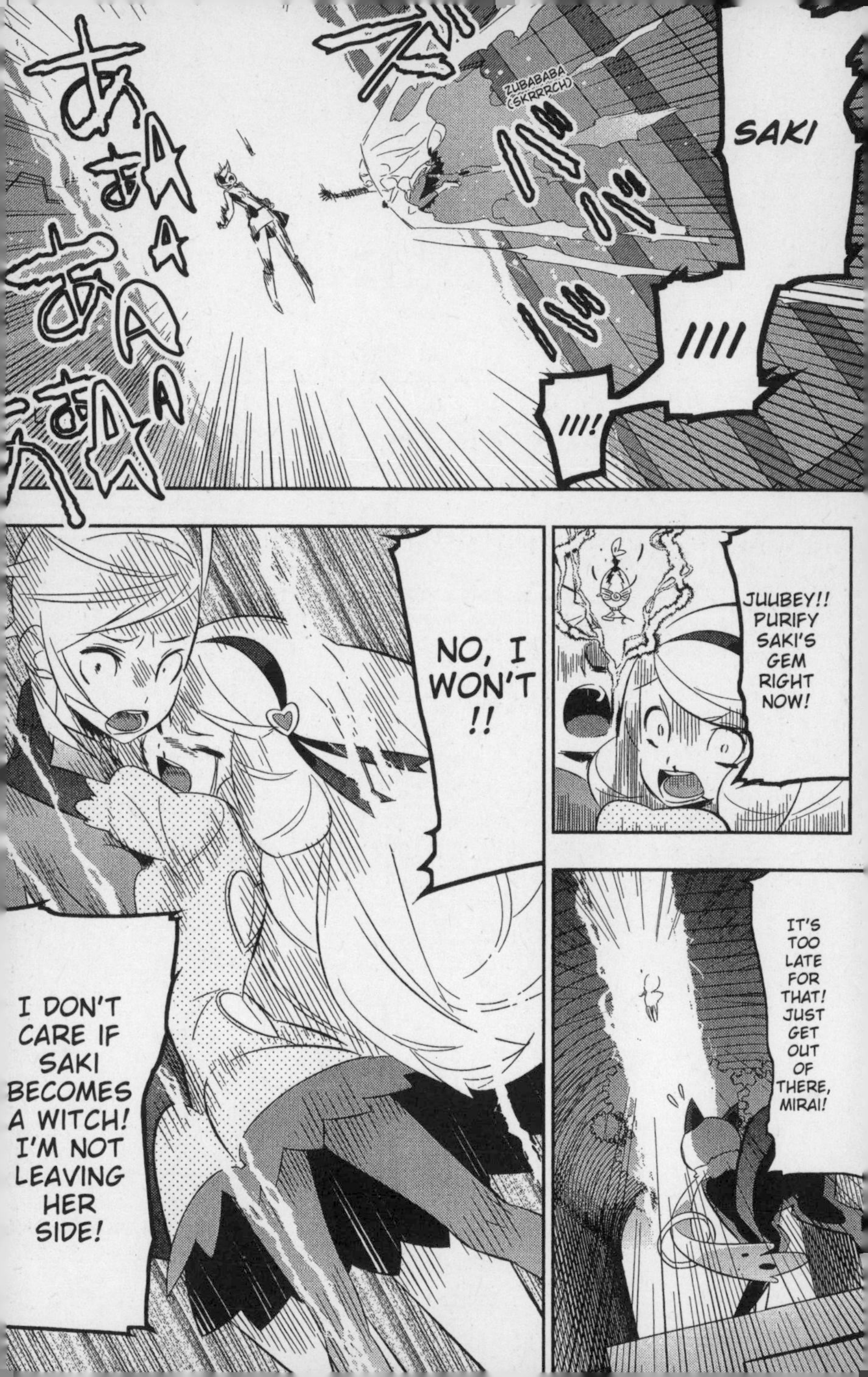
SAKI
!!!!
!!!!
ZUBABABA (SKRRRCH)
AAAAA
JUUBEY!! PURIFY SAKI'S GEM RIGHT NOW!
IT'S TOO LATE FOR THAT! JUST GET OUT OF THERE, MIRAI!
NO, I WON'T!!
I DON'T CARE IF SAKI BECOMES A WITCH! I'M NOT LEAVING HER SIDE!

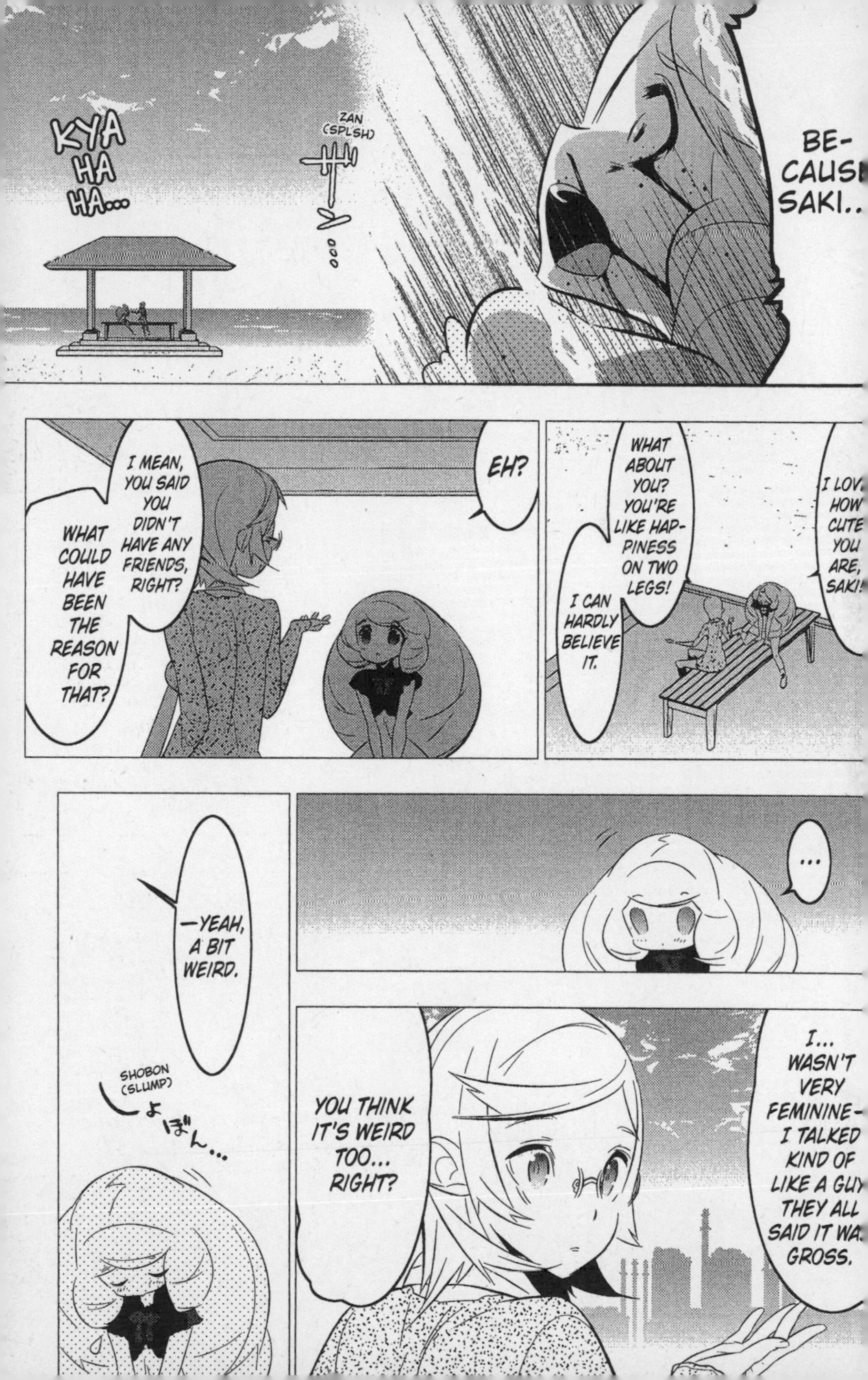
BE-CAUS SAKI..
ZAN (SPLSH)
KYA HA HA...
I LOV HOW CUTE YOU ARE, SAKI!
WHAT ABOUT YOU? YOU'RE LIKE HAP-PINESS ON TWO LEGS!
I CAN HARDLY BELIEVE IT.
EH?
I MEAN, YOU SAID YOU DIDN'T HAVE ANY FRIENDS, RIGHT?
WHAT COULD HAVE BEEN THE REASON FOR THAT?
...
I... WASN'T VERY FEMININE- I TALKED KIND OF LIKE A GU THEY ALL SAID IT WA GROSS.
YOU THINK IT'S WEIRD TOO... RIGHT?
—YEAH, A BIT WEIRD.
SHOBON (SLUMP)

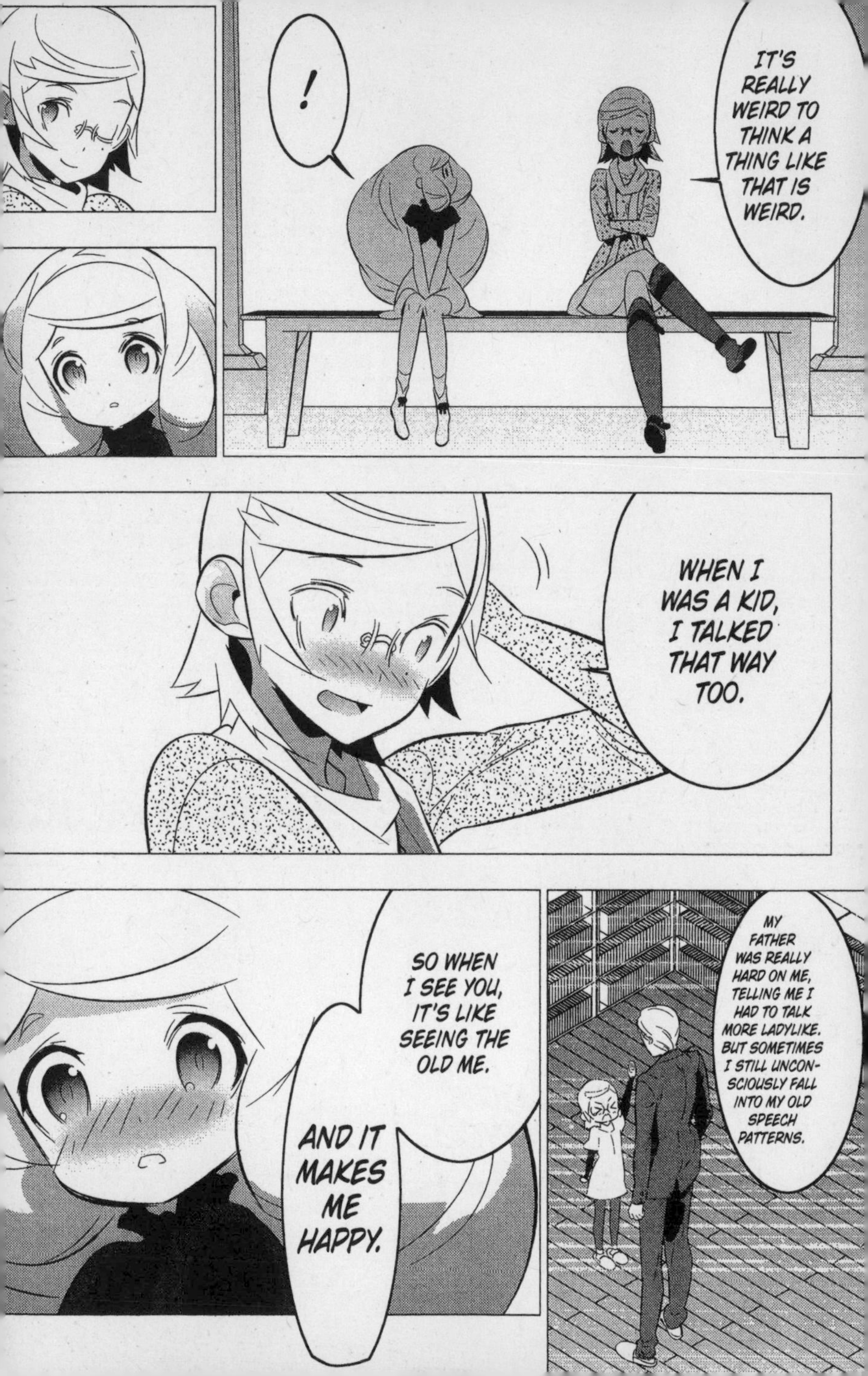
IT'S REALLY WEIRD TO THINK A THING LIKE THAT IS WEIRD.
!
WHEN I WAS A KID, I TALKED THAT WAY TOO.
MY FATHER WAS REALLY HARD ON ME, TELLING ME I HAD TO TALK MORE LADYLIKE. BUT SOMETIMES I STILL UNCON-SCIOUSLY FALL INTO MY OLD SPEECH PATTERNS.
SO WHEN I SEE YOU, IT'S LIKE SEEING THE OLD ME.
AND IT MAKES ME HAPPY.

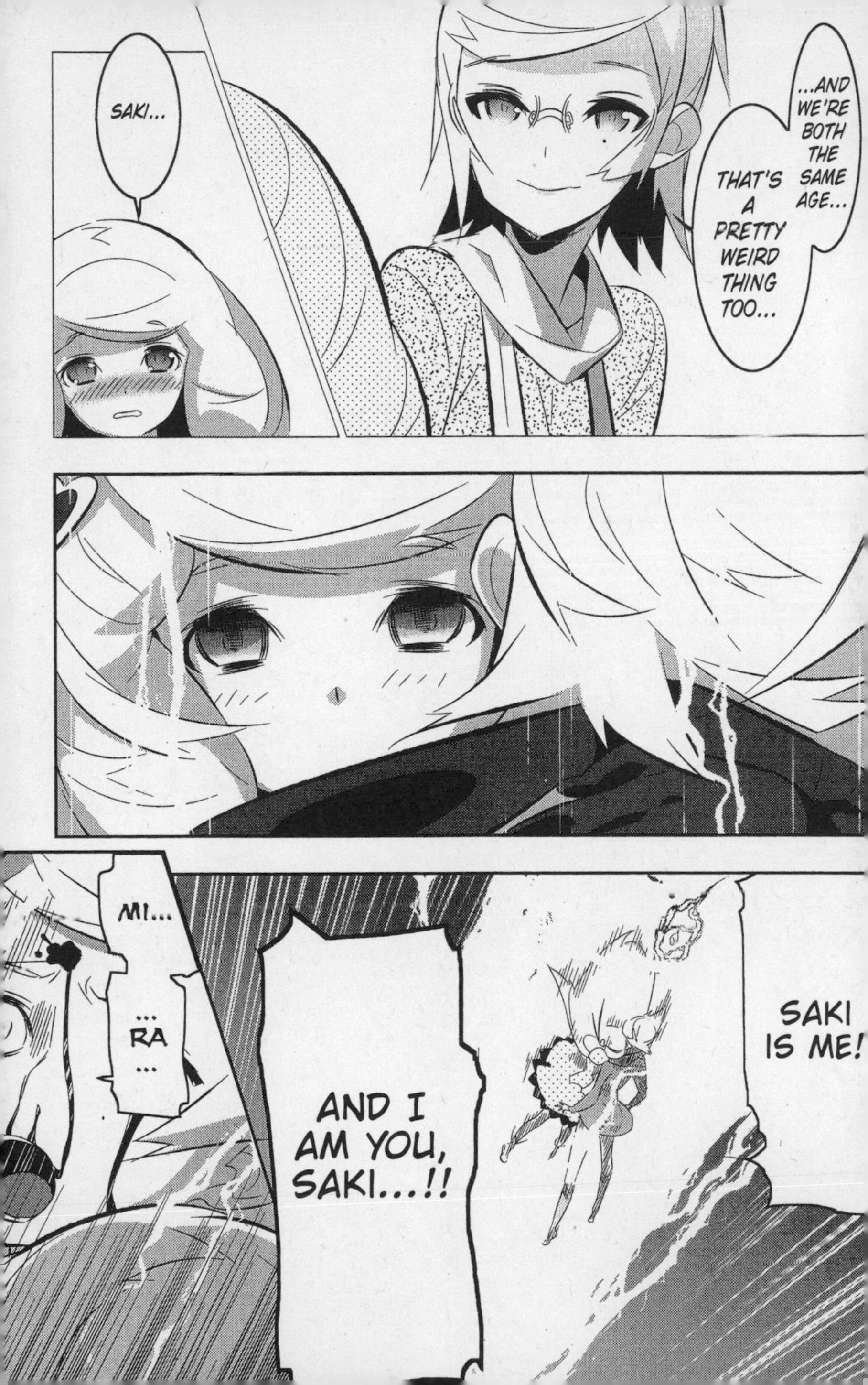
...AND WE'RE BOTH THE SAME AGE...
THAT'S A PRETTY WEIRD THING TOO...
SAKI...
SAKI IS ME!
AND I AM YOU, SAKI...!!
MI...
...RA...

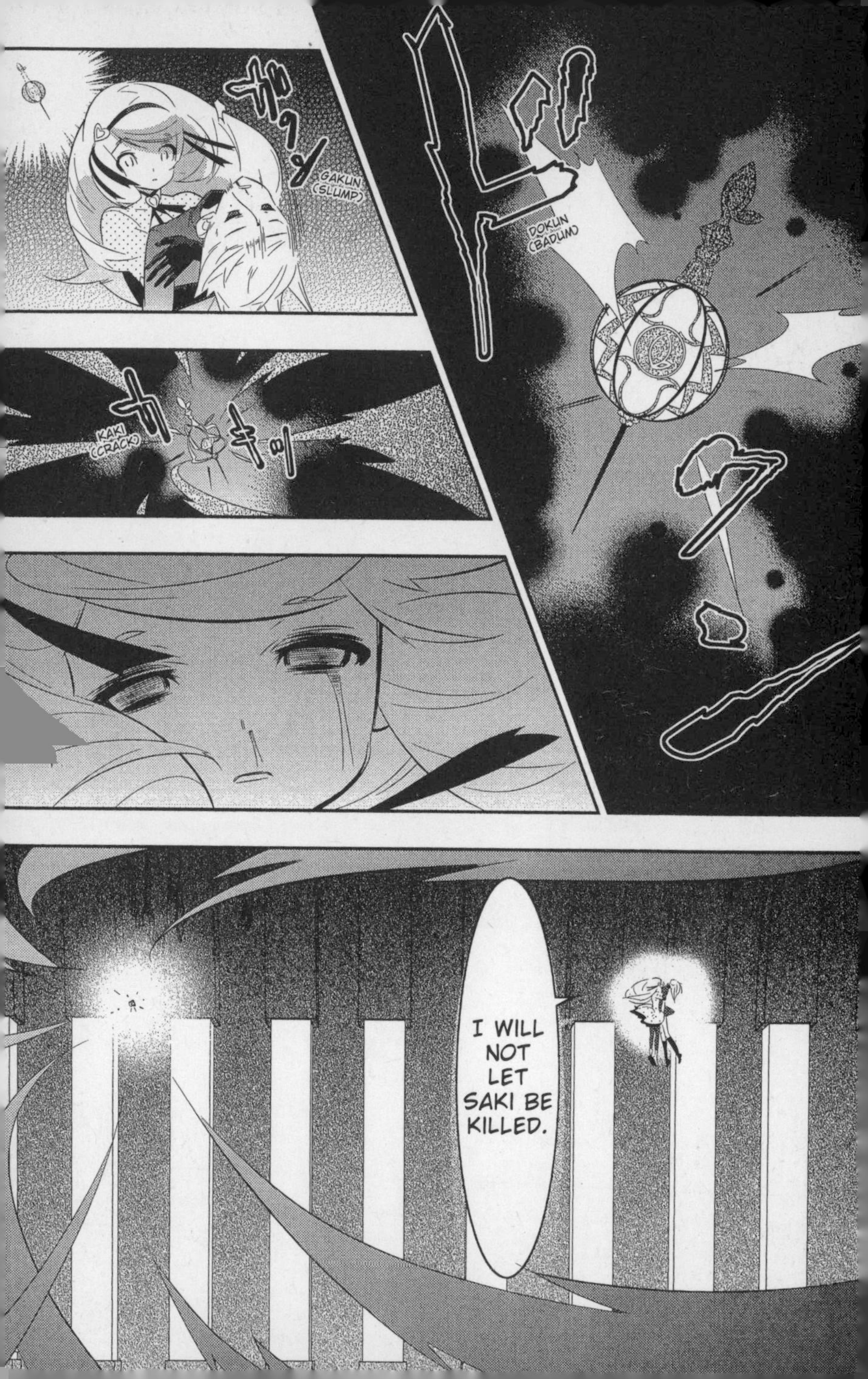
DOKUN (BADUM)
GAKUN (SLUMP)
KAKI (CRACK)
I WILL NOT LET SAKI BE KILLED.

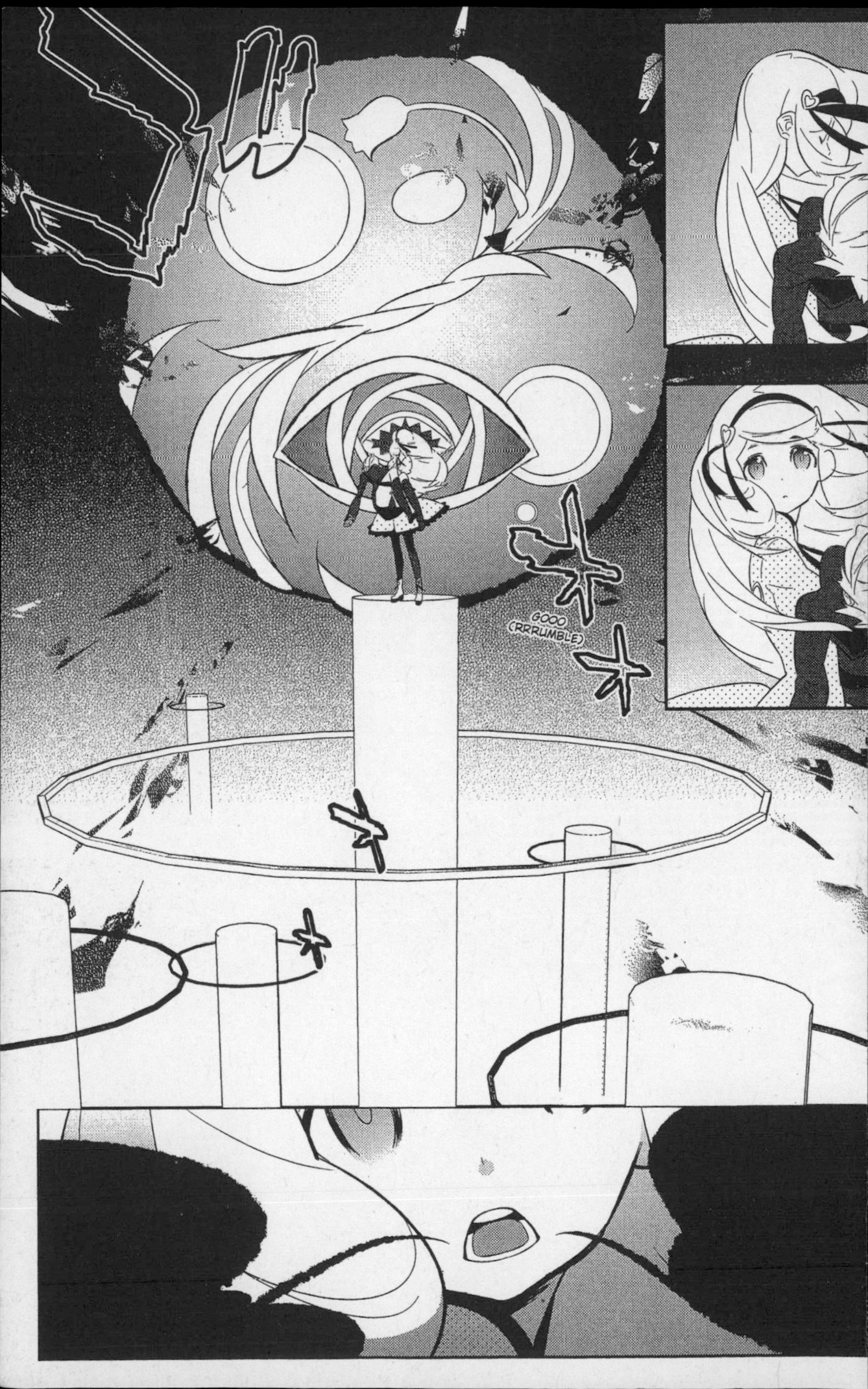
GOOO
(RRRUMBLE)

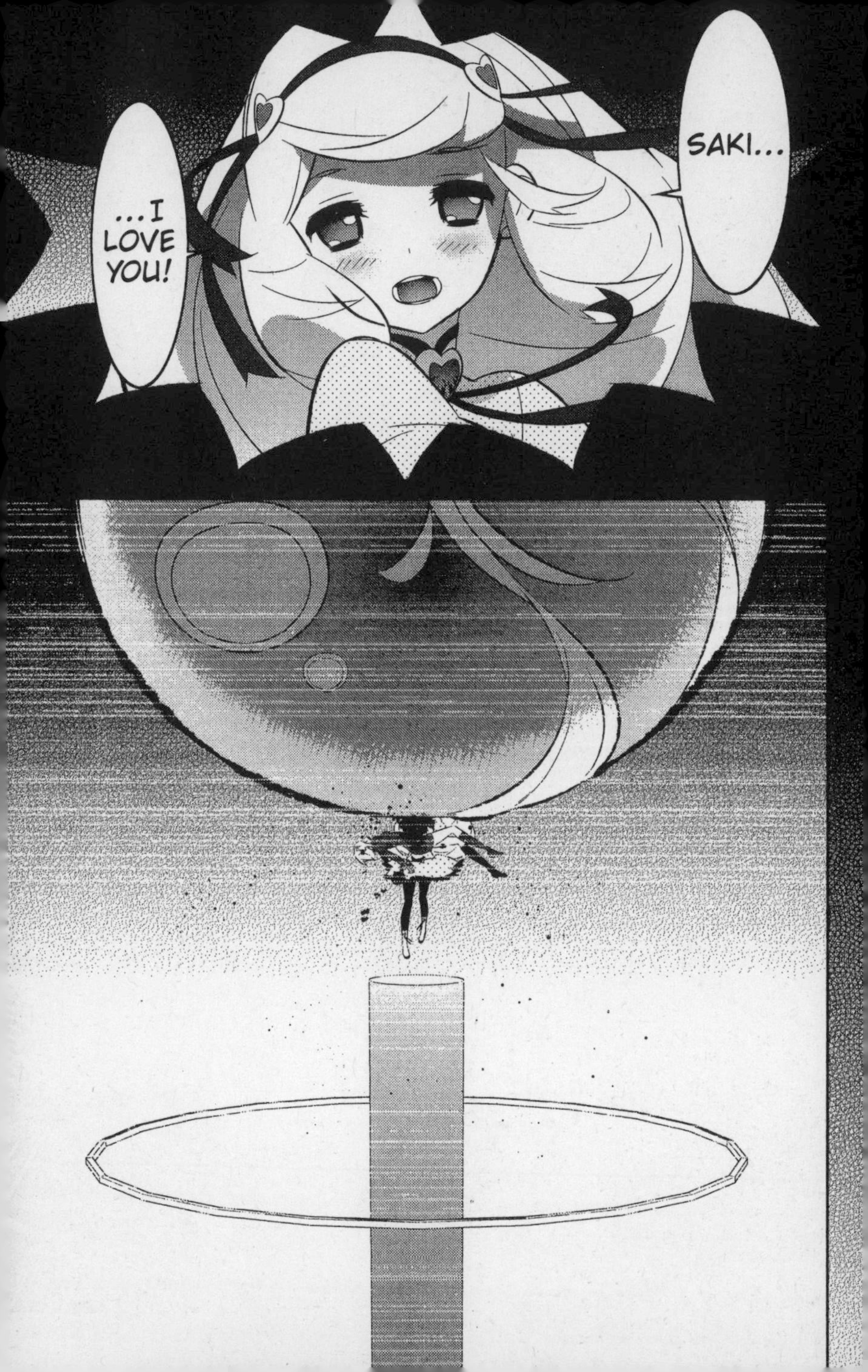
SAKI...
...I LOVE YOU!

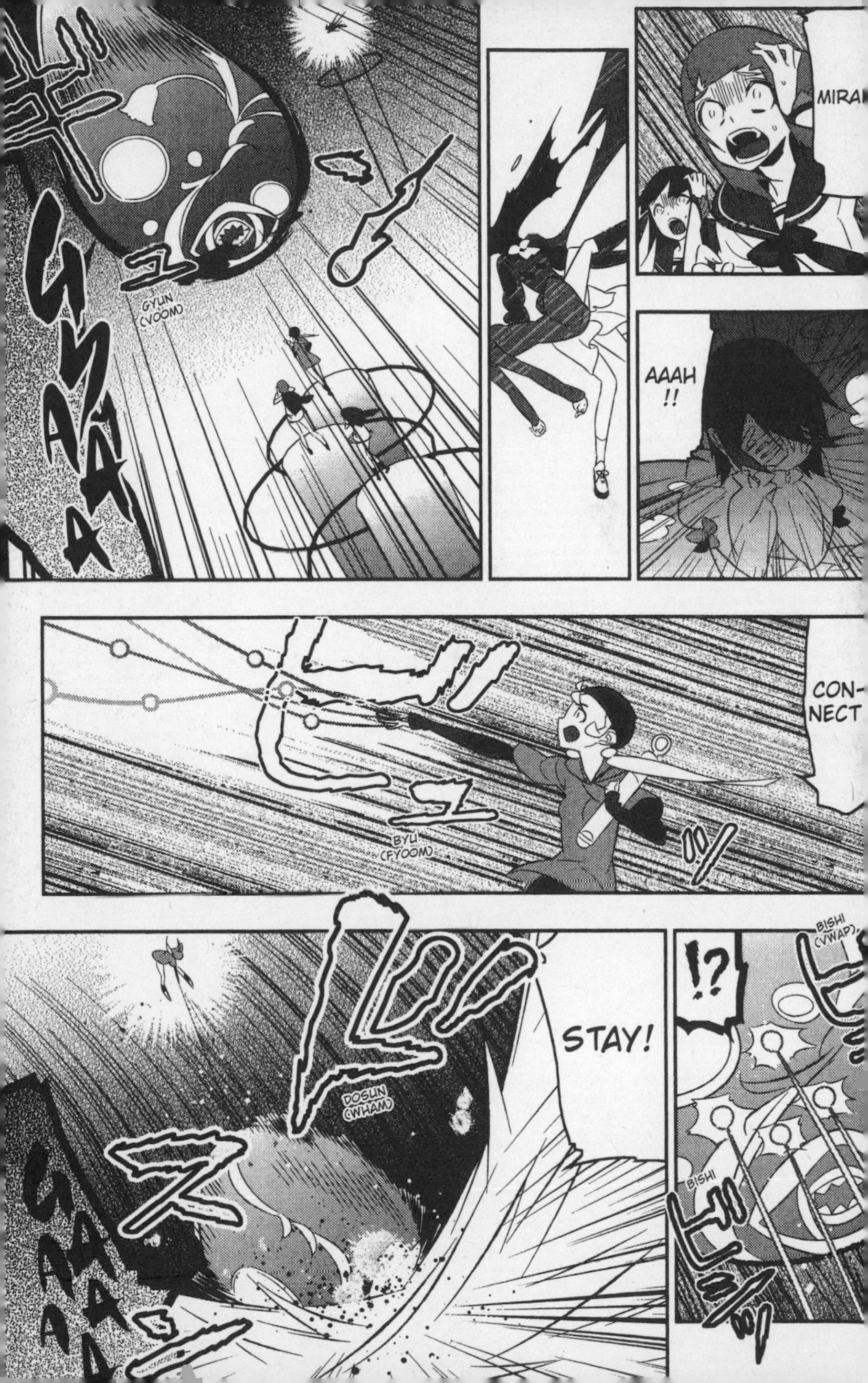
MIRA!
AAAH!!
GYUN (VOOM)
CON-NECT
BYU (FYOOM)
BISHI (VWAP)
!?
BISHI
STAY!
DOSUN (WHAM)

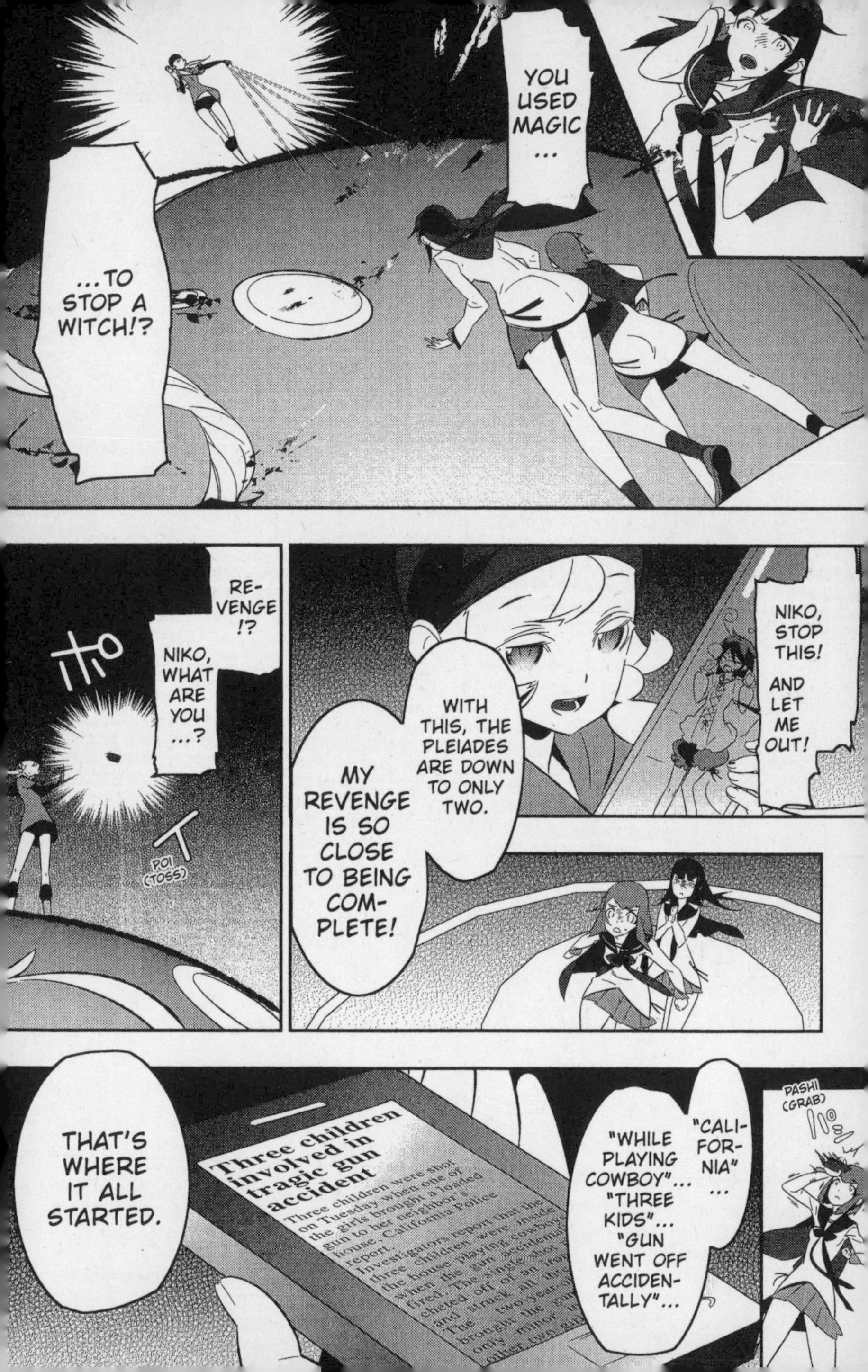
YOU USED MAGIC...
...TO STOP A WITCH!?
NIKO, STOP THIS!
AND LET ME OUT!
WITH THIS, THE PLEIADES ARE DOWN TO ONLY TWO.
MY REVENGE IS SO CLOSE TO BEING COM-PLETE!
RE-VENGE!?
NIKO, WHAT ARE YOU...?
POI (TOSS)
PASHI (GRAB)
"CALI-FOR-NIA"...
"WHILE PLAYING COWBOY"... "THREE KIDS"... "GUN WENT OFF ACCIDEN-TALLY"...
Three children involved in tragic gun accident
Three children were shot on Tuesday when one of the girls brought a loaded gun to her neighbor's house, California Police report.
THAT'S WHERE IT ALL STARTED.

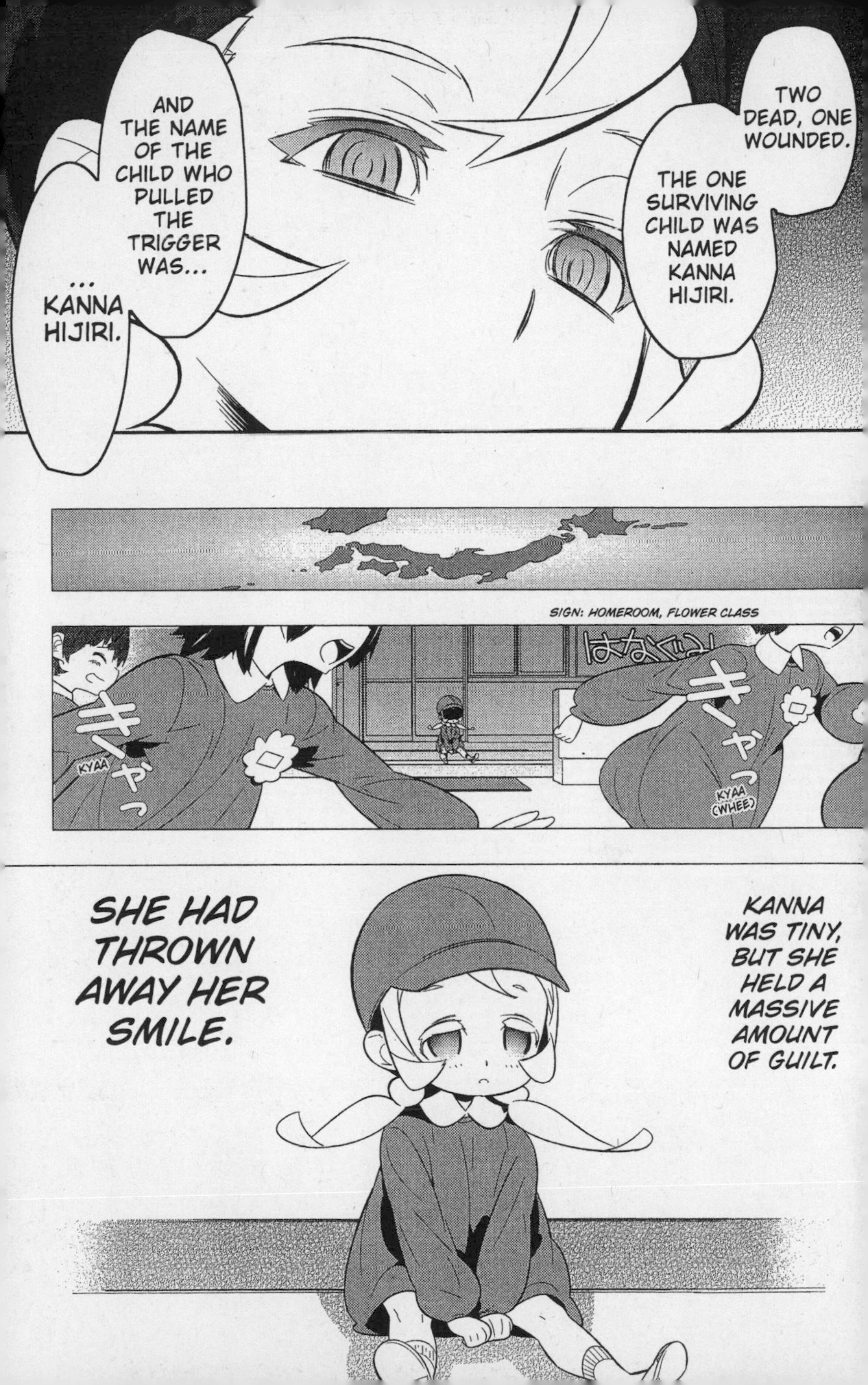

TWO DEAD, ONE WOUNDED.
THE ONE SURVIVING CHILD WAS NAMED KANNA HIJIRI.
AND THE NAME OF THE CHILD WHO PULLED THE TRIGGER WAS...
... KANNA HIJIRI.
SIGN: HOMEROOM, FLOWER CLASS
KYAA (WHEE)
KYAA
KANNA WAS TINY, BUT SHE HELD A MASSIVE AMOUNT OF GUILT.
SHE HAD THROWN AWAY HER SMILE.

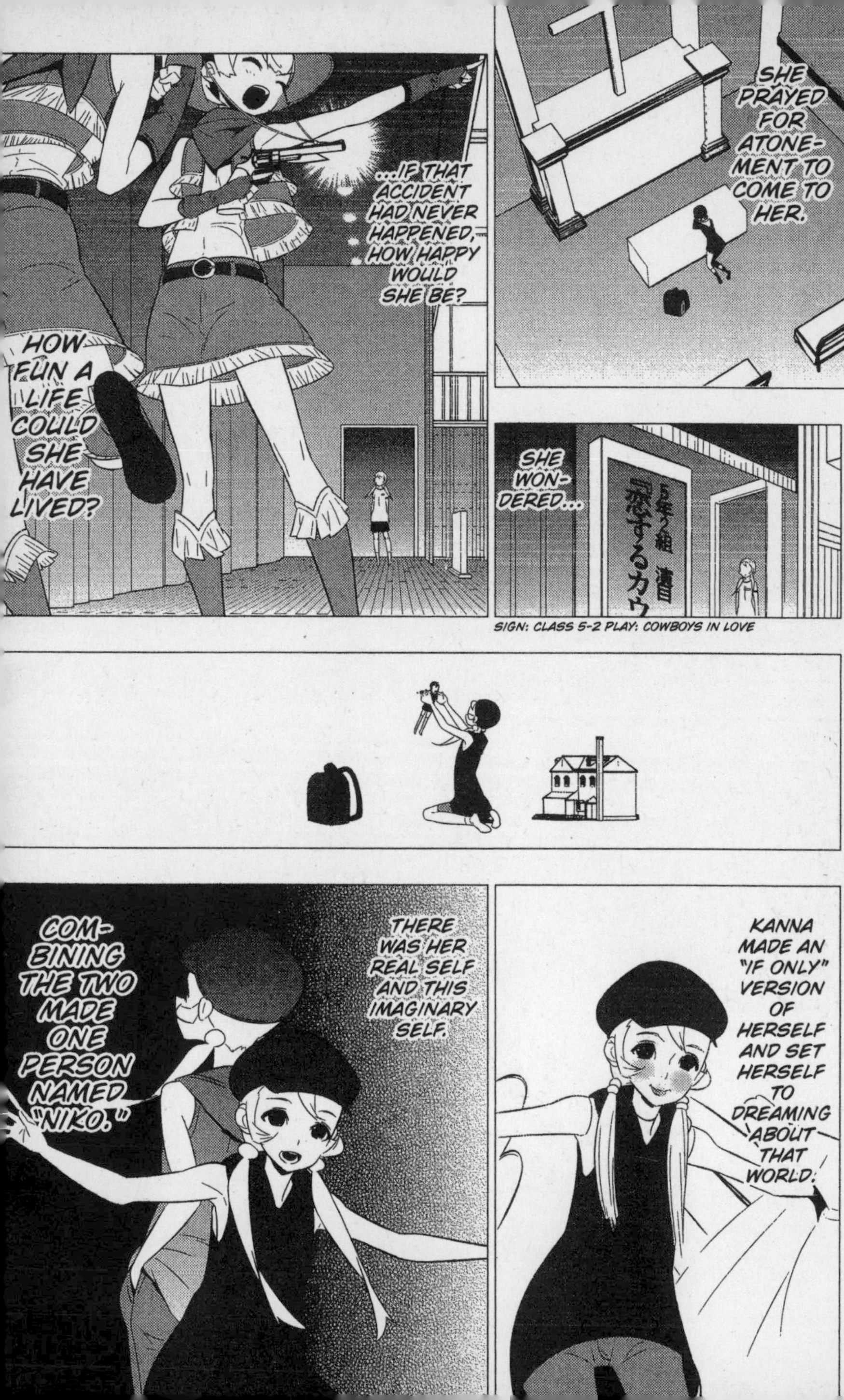
SHE PRAYED FOR ATONEMENT TO COME TO HER.
SHE WONDERED...
SIGN: CLASS 5-2 PLAY: COWBOYS IN LOVE
...IF THAT ACCIDENT HAD NEVER HAPPENED, HOW HAPPY WOULD SHE BE?
HOW FUN A LIFE COULD SHE HAVE LIVED?
KANNA MADE AN "IF ONLY" VERSION OF HERSELF AND SET HERSELF TO DREAMING ABOUT THAT WORLD.
THERE WAS HER REAL SELF AND THIS IMAGINARY SELF.
COMBINING THE TWO MADE ONE PERSON NAMED "NIKO."

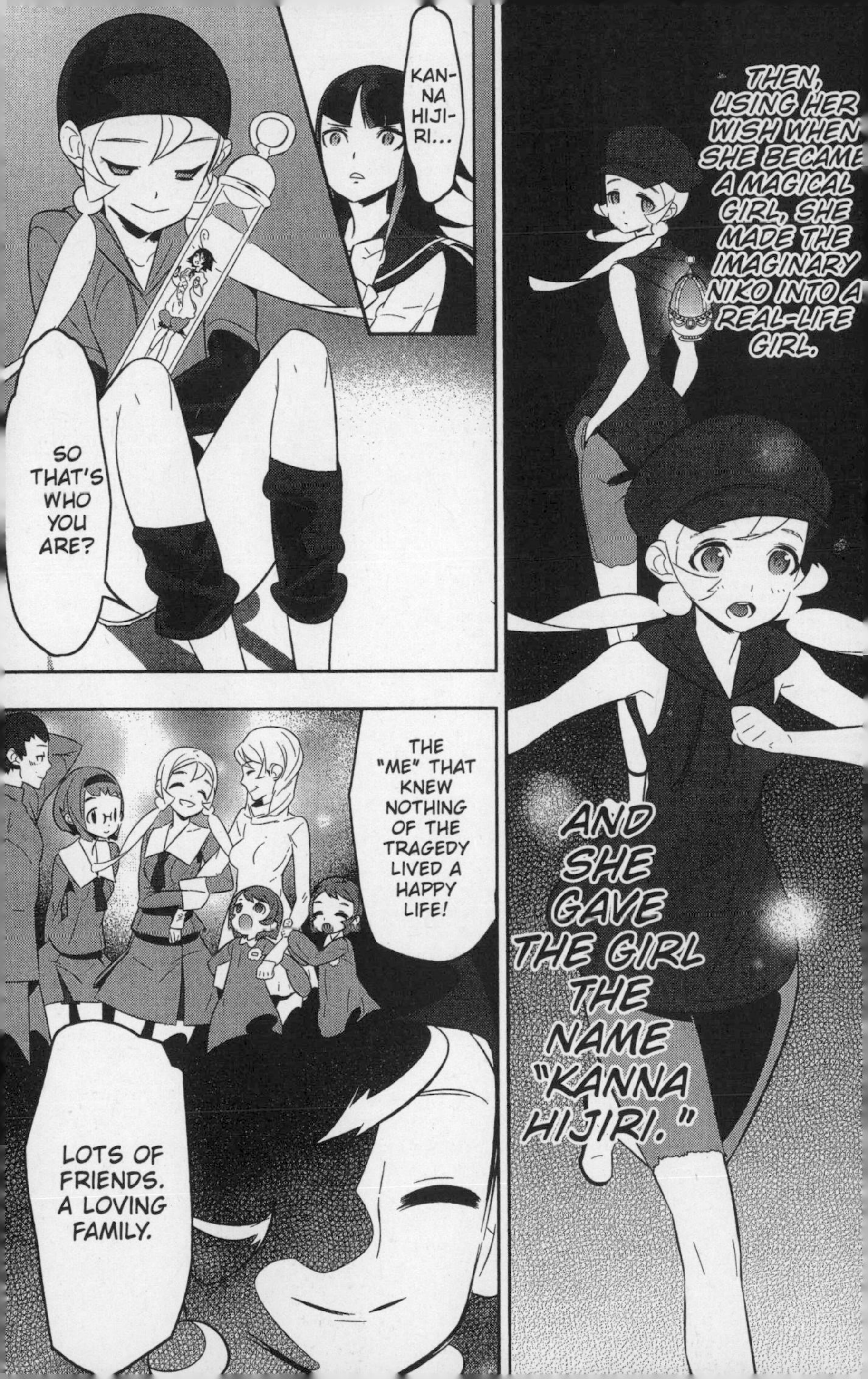
THEN, USING HER WISH WHEN SHE BECAME A MAGICAL GIRL, SHE MADE THE IMAGINARY NIKO INTO A REAL-LIFE GIRL.
AND SHE GAVE THE GIRL THE NAME "KANNA HIJIRI."
KAN-NA HIJI-RI...
SO THAT'S WHO YOU ARE?
THE "ME" THAT KNEW NOTHING OF THE TRAGEDY LIVED A HAPPY LIFE!
LOTS OF FRIENDS. A LOVING FAMILY.

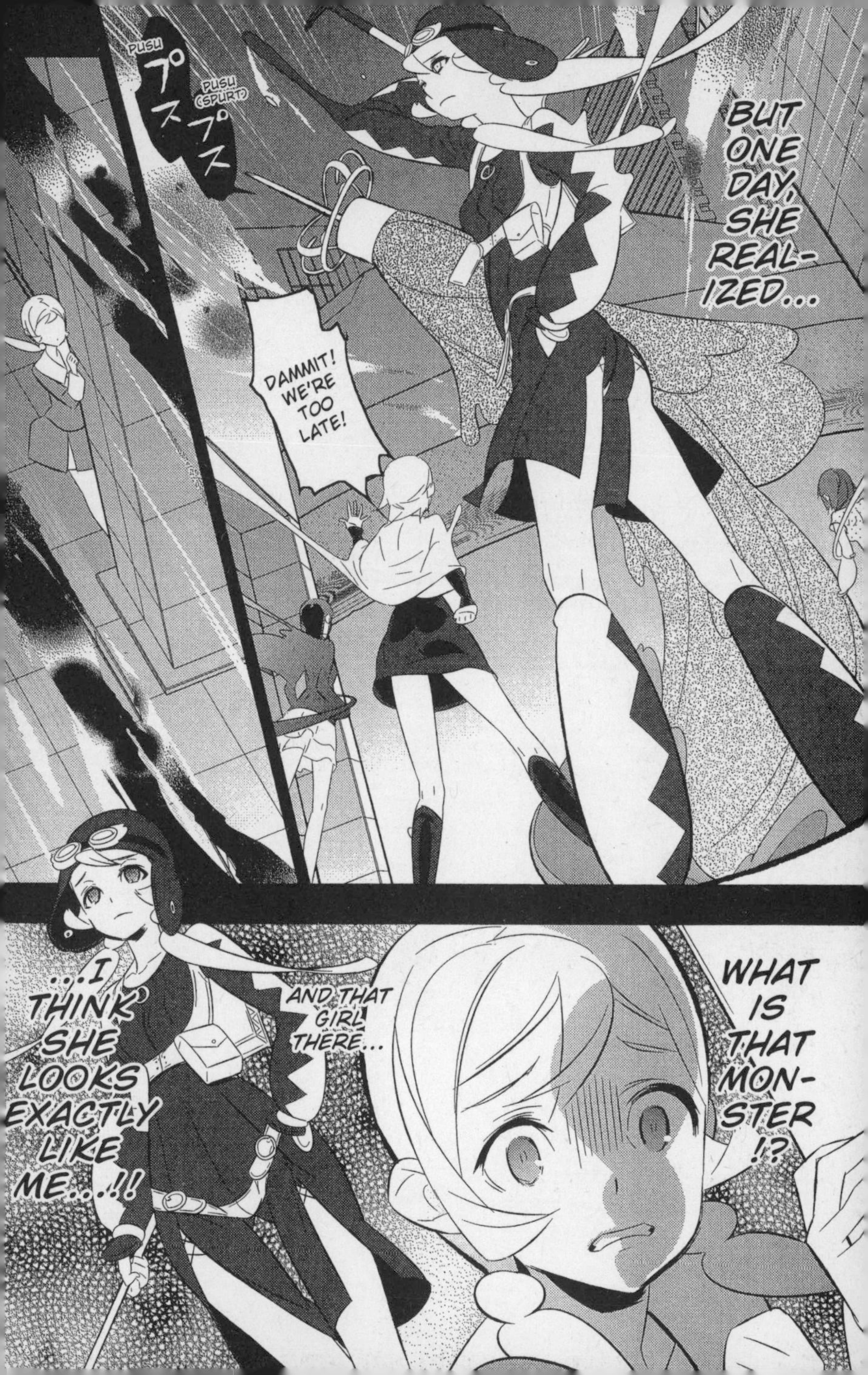
BUT ONE DAY, SHE REALIZED...
DAMMIT! WE'RE TOO LATE!
PUSU
プス
PUSU (SPURT)
プス
WHAT IS THAT MONSTER!?
AND THAT GIRL THERE...
...I THINK SHE LOOKS EXACTLY LIKE ME...!!

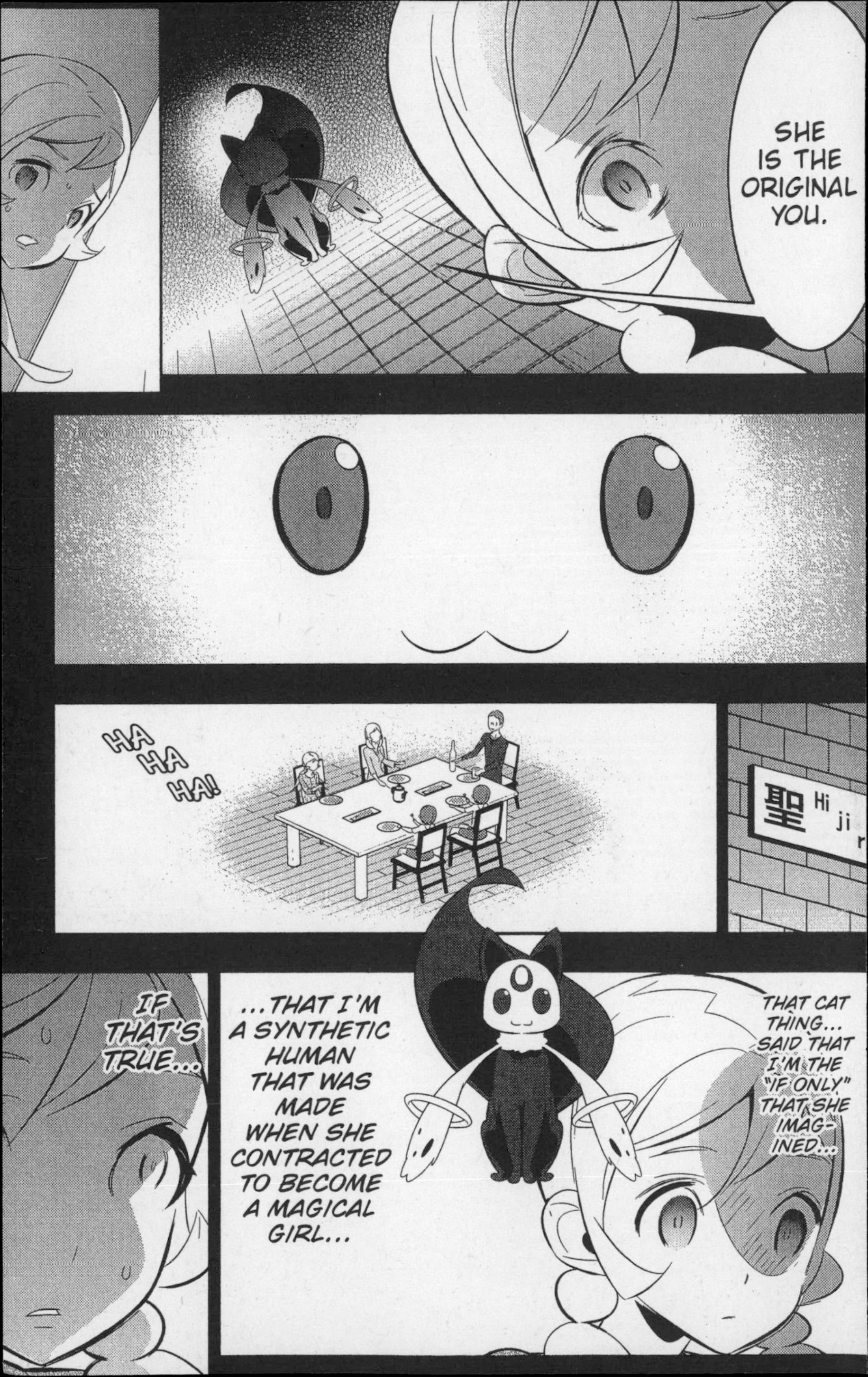
SHE IS THE ORIGINAL YOU.
聖 Hi ji r
HA HA HA!
THAT CAT THING... SAID THAT I'M THE "IF ONLY" THAT SHE IMAGINED...
...THAT I'M A SYNTHETIC HUMAN THAT WAS MADE WHEN SHE CONTRACTED TO BECOME A MAGICAL GIRL...
IF THAT'S TRUE...

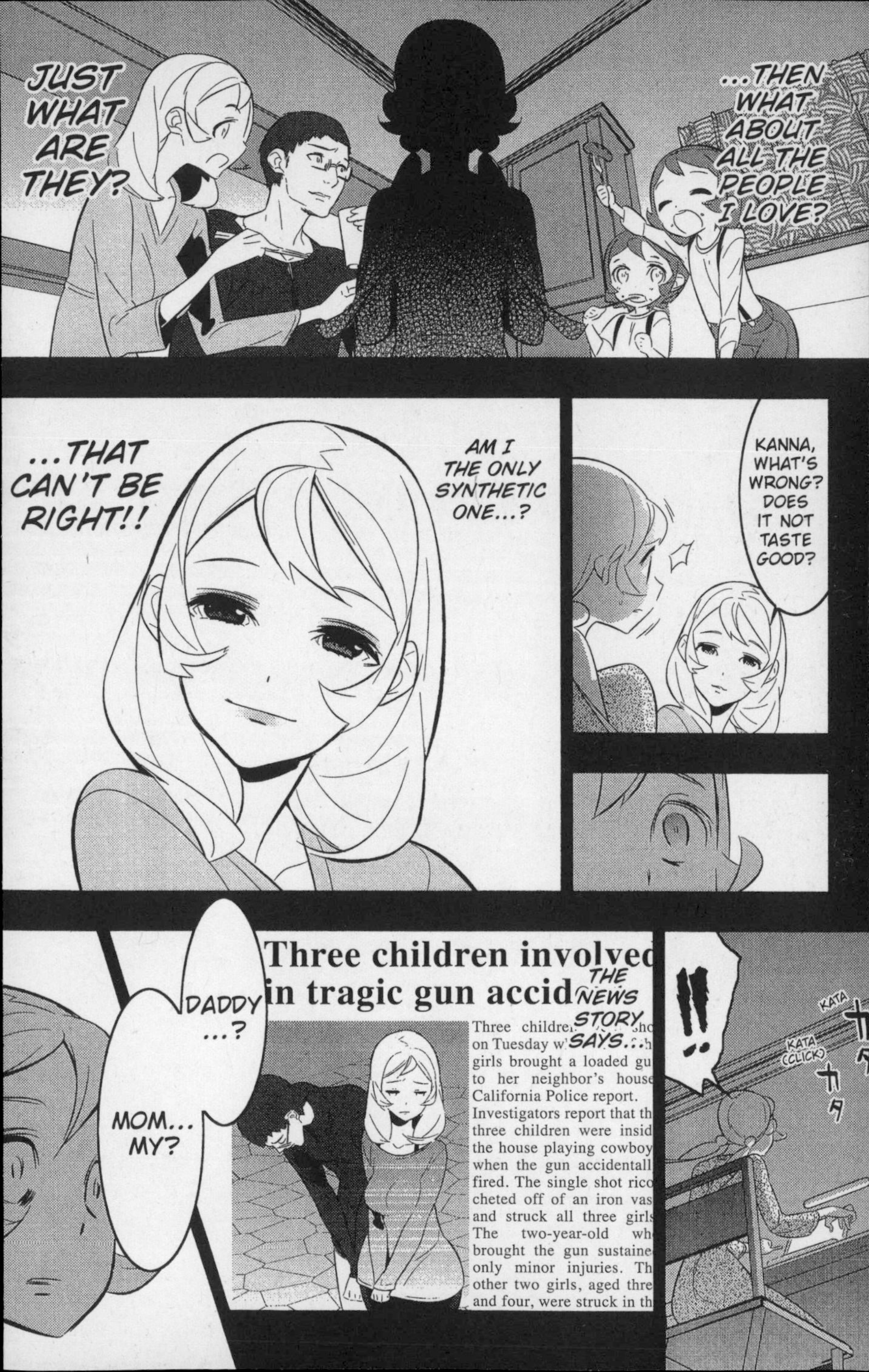
...THEN WHAT ABOUT ALL THE PEOPLE I LOVE?
JUST WHAT ARE THEY?
KANNA, WHAT'S WRONG? DOES IT NOT TASTE GOOD?
AM I THE ONLY SYNTHETIC ONE...?
...THAT CAN'T BE RIGHT!!
!!
KATA KATA (CLICK)
カタ カタ
THE NEWS STORY SAYS...
Three children involved in tragic gun accid
on Tuesday w
girls brought a loaded gu
to her neighbor's house
California Police report.
Investigators report that th
three children were insid
the house playing cowboy
when the gun accidentall
fired. The single shot rico
cheted off of an iron vas
and struck all three girls
The two-year-old wh
brought the gun sustaine
only minor injuries. Th
other two girls, aged thre
and four, were struck in th
DADDY ...?
MOM... MY?

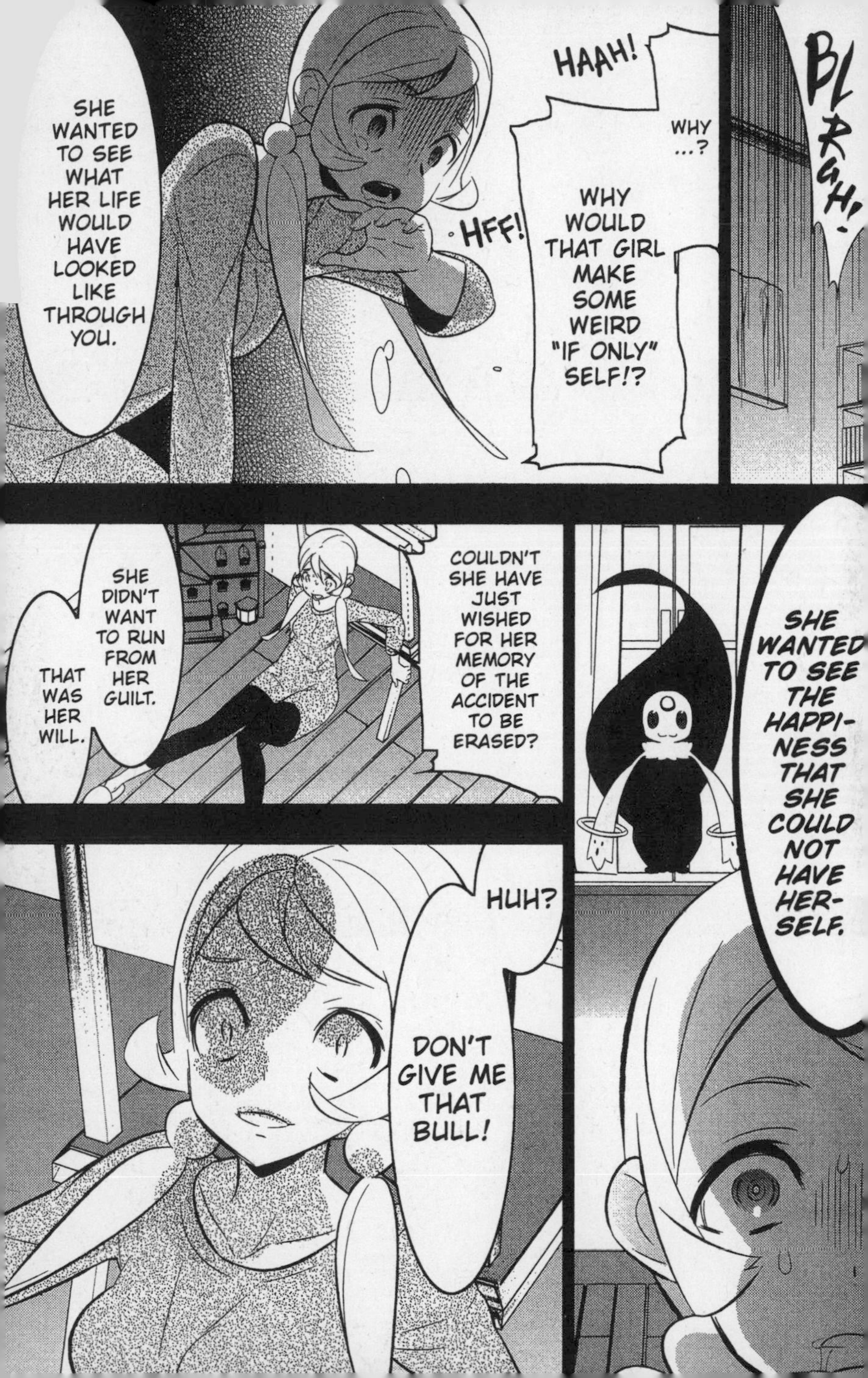
BLRAGH!
HAAH!
WHY ...?
WHY WOULD THAT GIRL MAKE SOME WEIRD "IF ONLY" SELF!?
HFF!
SHE WANTED TO SEE WHAT HER LIFE WOULD HAVE LOOKED LIKE THROUGH YOU.
COULDN'T SHE HAVE JUST WISHED FOR HER MEMORY OF THE ACCIDENT TO BE ERASED?
SHE DIDN'T WANT TO RUN FROM HER GUILT.
THAT WAS HER WILL.
SHE WANTED TO SEE THE HAPPINESS THAT SHE COULD NOT HAVE HERSELF.
HUH?
DON'T GIVE ME THAT BULL!

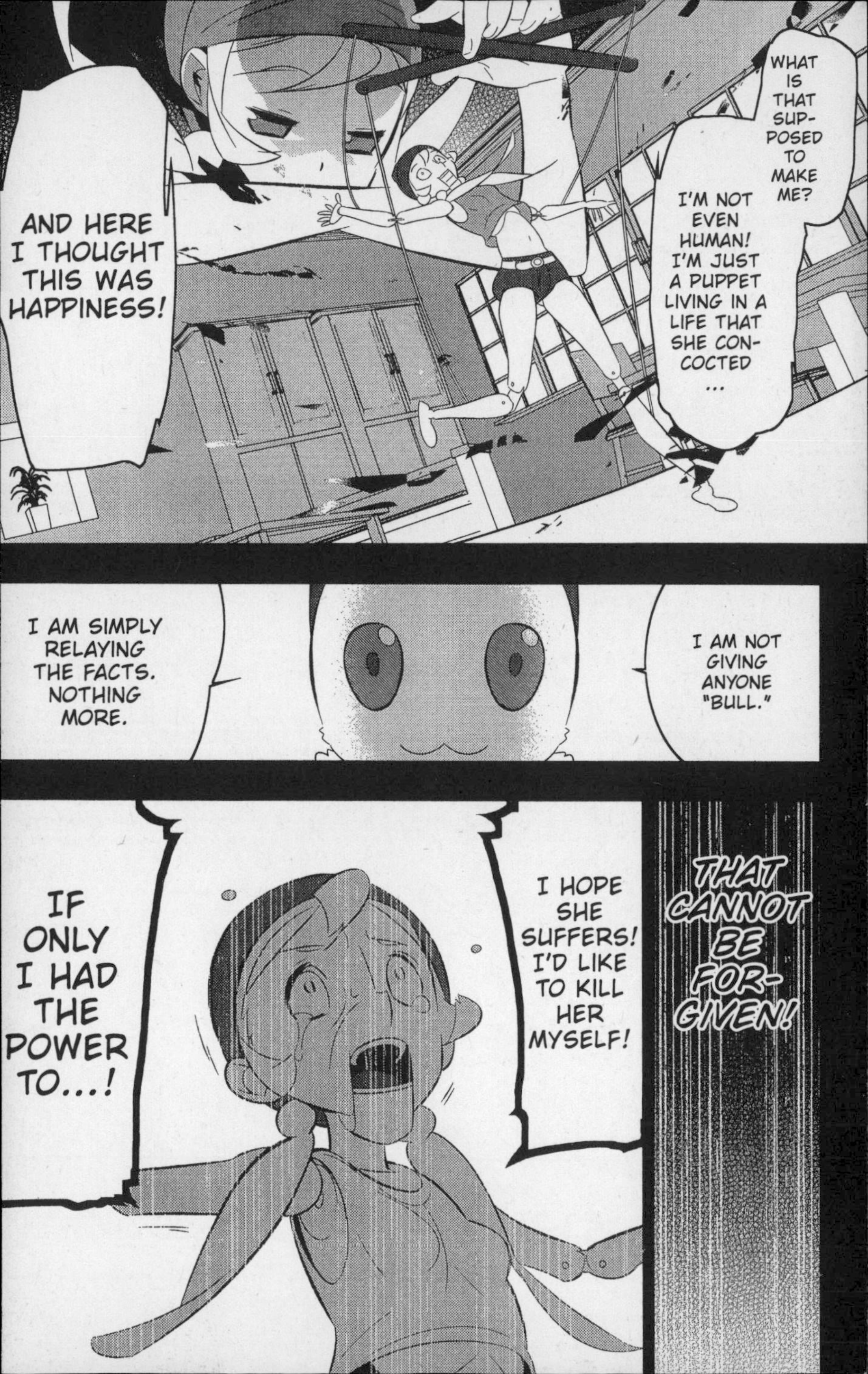
WHAT IS THAT SUPPOSED TO MAKE ME?
I'M NOT EVEN HUMAN! I'M JUST A PUPPET LIVING IN A LIFE THAT SHE CONCOCTED...
AND HERE I THOUGHT THIS WAS HAPPINESS!
I AM NOT GIVING ANYONE "BULL."
I AM SIMPLY RELAYING THE FACTS. NOTHING MORE.
THAT CANNOT BE FORGIVEN!
I HOPE SHE SUFFERS! I'D LIKE TO KILL HER MYSELF!
IF ONLY I HAD THE POWER TO...!

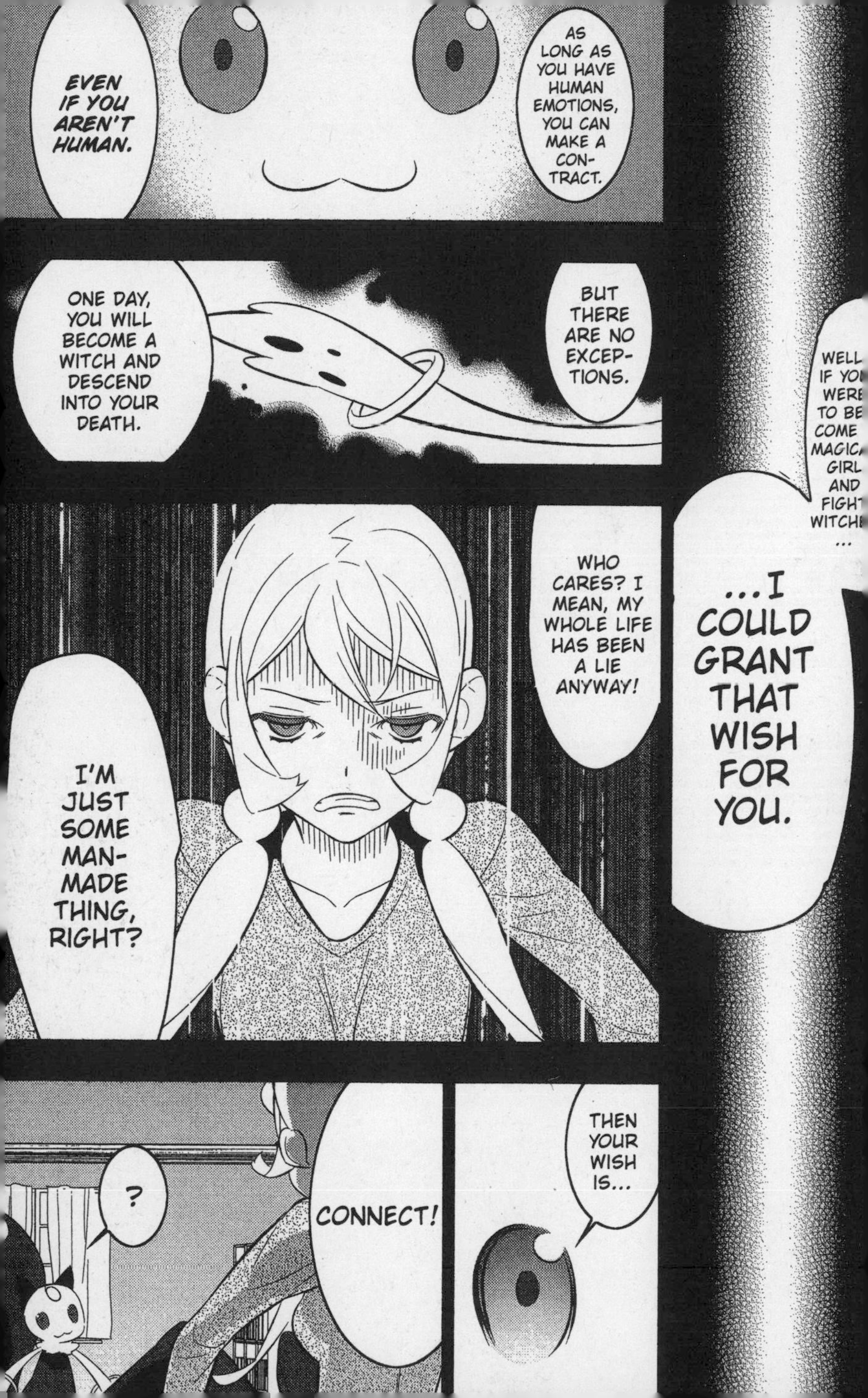
WELL IF YO WERE TO BE COME MAGIC GIRL AND FIGHT WITCH ...
...I COULD GRANT THAT WISH FOR YOU.
AS LONG AS YOU HAVE HUMAN EMOTIONS, YOU CAN MAKE A CON-TRACT.
EVEN IF YOU AREN'T HUMAN.
BUT THERE ARE NO EXCEP-TIONS.
ONE DAY, YOU WILL BECOME A WITCH AND DESCEND INTO YOUR DEATH.
WHO CARES? I MEAN, MY WHOLE LIFE HAS BEEN A LIE ANYWAY!
I'M JUST SOME MAN-MADE THING, RIGHT?
THEN YOUR WISH IS...
CONNECT!
?

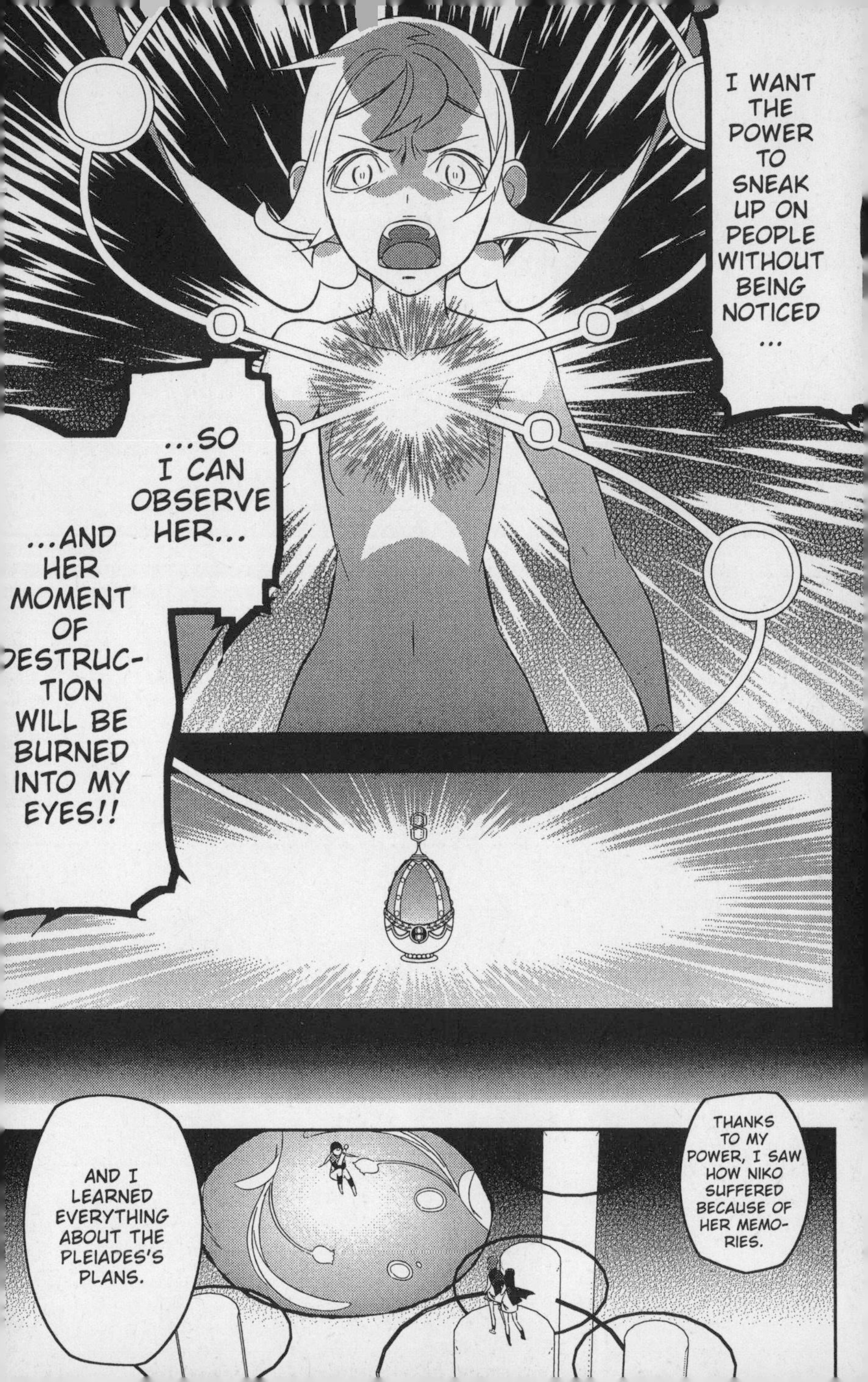
I WANT THE POWER TO SNEAK UP ON PEOPLE WITHOUT BEING NOTICED...
...SO I CAN OBSERVE HER...
...AND HER MOMENT OF DESTRUCTION WILL BE BURNED INTO MY EYES!!
THANKS TO MY POWER, I SAW HOW NIKO SUFFERED BECAUSE OF HER MEMORIES.
AND I LEARNED EVERYTHING ABOUT THE PLEIADES'S PLANS.

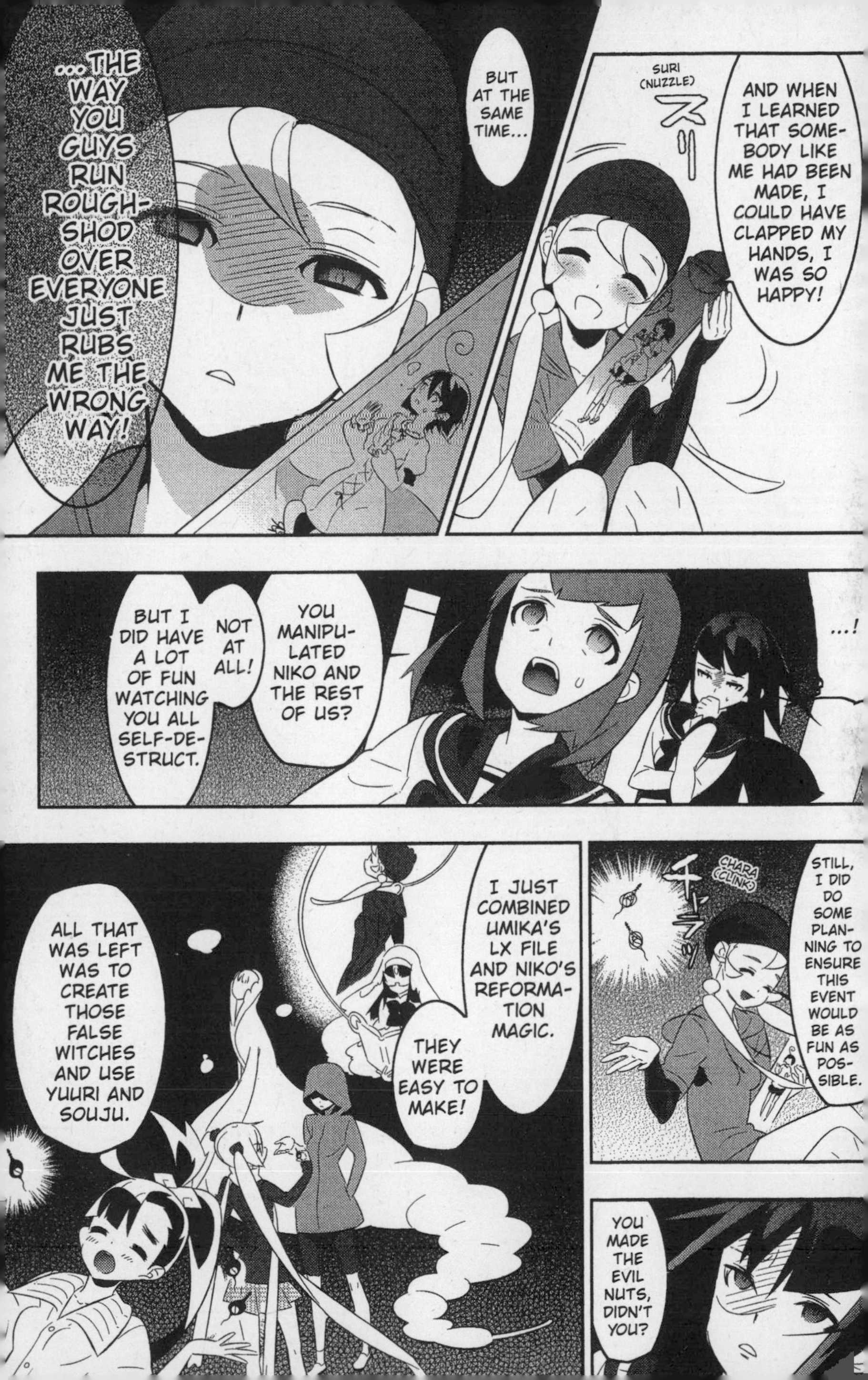

SURI (NUZZLE)
AND WHEN I LEARNED THAT SOME-BODY LIKE ME HAD BEEN MADE, I COULD HAVE CLAPPED MY HANDS, I WAS SO HAPPY!
BUT AT THE SAME TIME...
...THE WAY YOU GUYS RUN ROUGH-SHOD OVER EVERYONE JUST RUBS ME THE WRONG WAY!
...!
YOU MANIPU-LATED NIKO AND THE REST OF US?
NOT AT ALL!
BUT I DID HAVE A LOT OF FUN WATCHING YOU ALL SELF-DE-STRUCT.
CHARA (CLINK)
STILL, I DID DO SOME PLAN-NING TO ENSURE THIS EVENT WOULD BE AS FUN AS POS-SIBLE.
YOU MADE THE EVIL NUTS, DIDN'T YOU?
I JUST COMBINED UMIKA'S LX FILE AND NIKO'S REFORMA-TION MAGIC.
THEY WERE EASY TO MAKE!
ALL THAT WAS LEFT WAS TO CREATE THOSE FALSE WITCHES AND USE YUURI AND SOUJU.

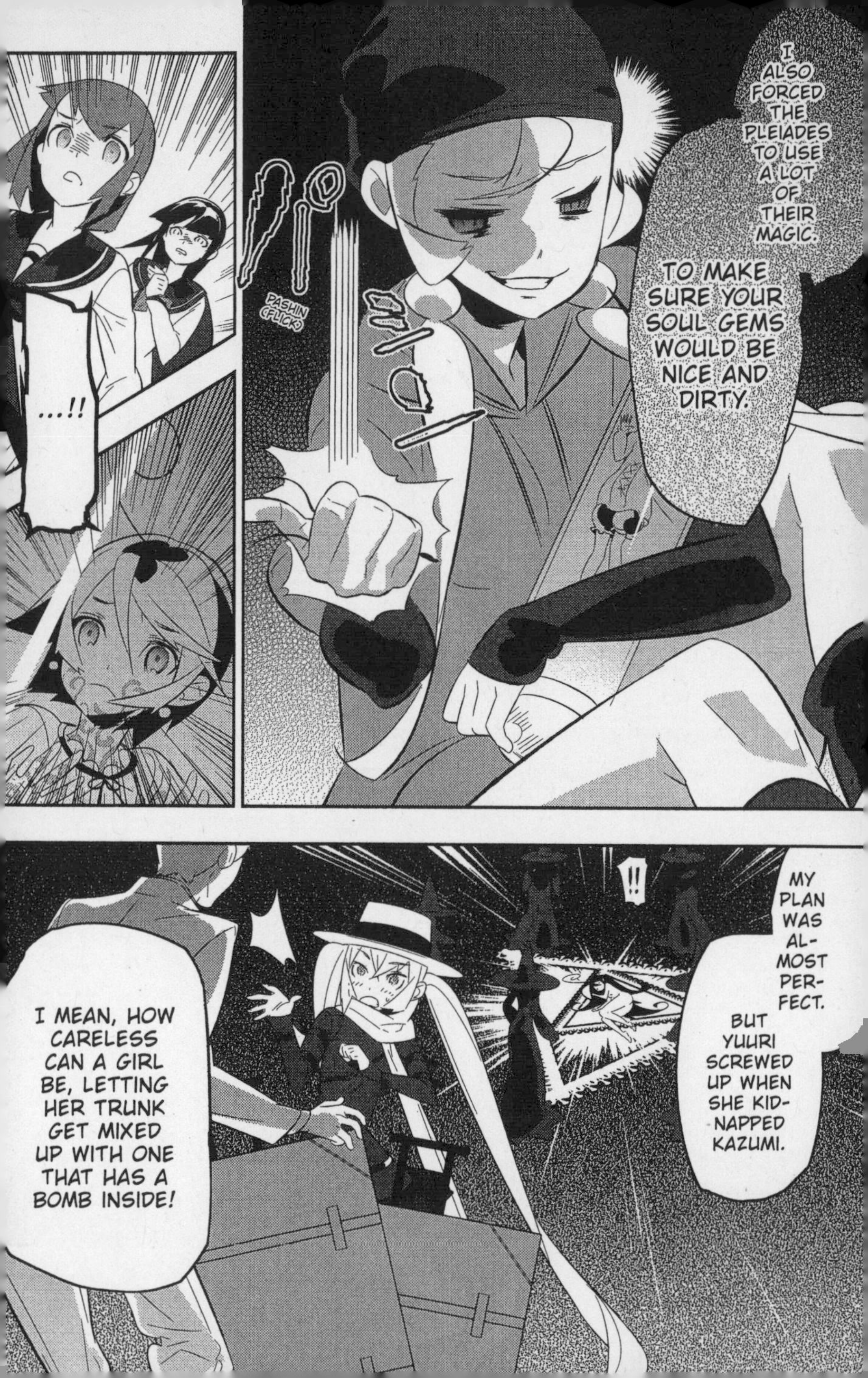
I ALSO FORCED THE PLEIADES TO USE A LOT OF THEIR MAGIC.
TO MAKE SURE YOUR SOUL GEMS WOULD BE NICE AND DIRTY.
PASHIN (FLICK)
...!!
MY PLAN WAS AL-MOST PER-FECT.
BUT YUURI SCREWED UP WHEN SHE KID-NAPPED KAZUMI.
!!
I MEAN, HOW CARELESS CAN A GIRL BE, LETTING HER TRUNK GET MIXED UP WITH ONE THAT HAS A BOMB INSIDE!

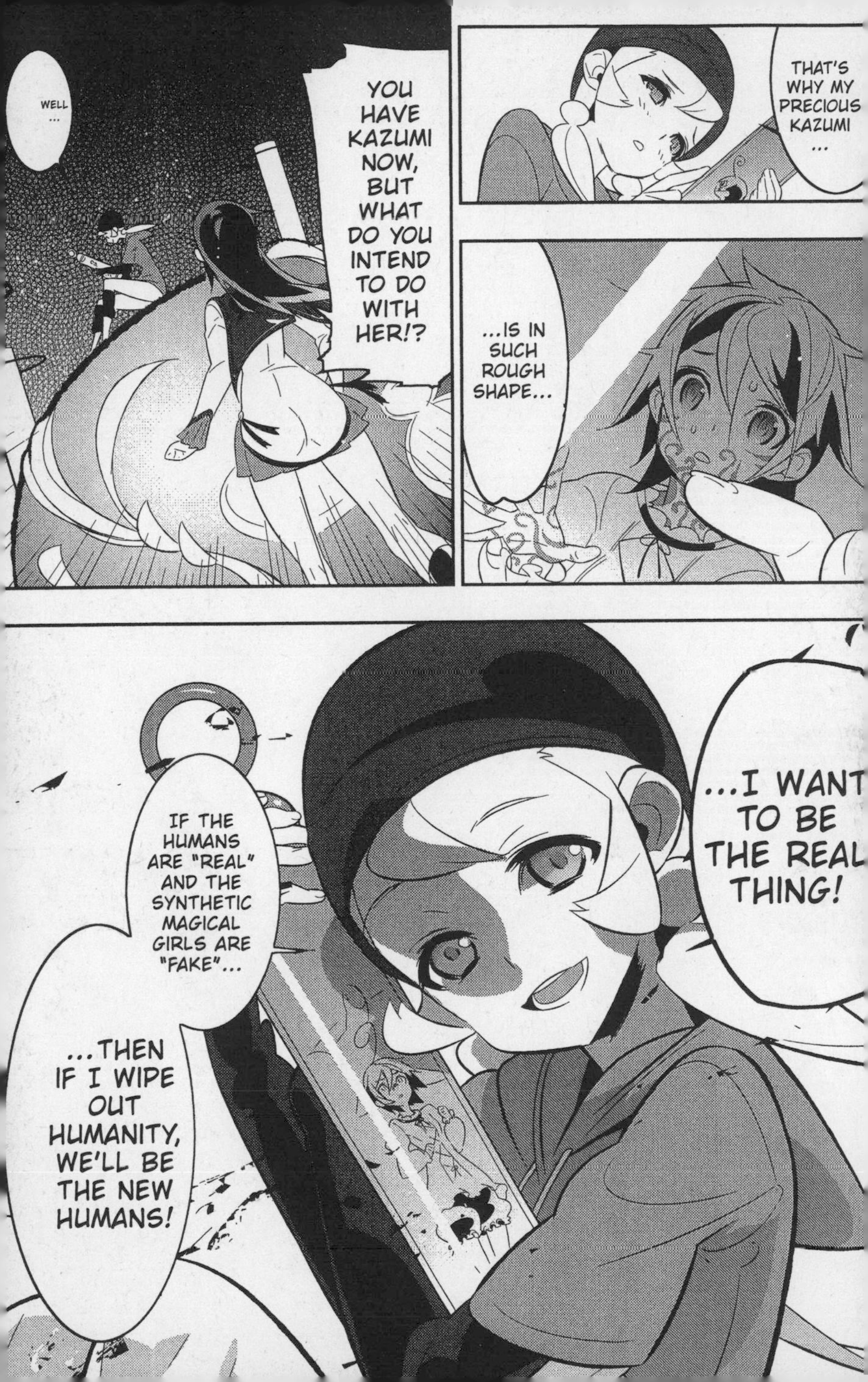
THAT'S WHY MY PRECIOUS KAZUMI...
...IS IN SUCH ROUGH SHAPE...
YOU HAVE KAZUMI NOW, BUT WHAT DO YOU INTEND TO DO WITH HER!?
WELL...
...I WANT TO BE THE REAL THING!
IF THE HUMANS ARE "REAL" AND THE SYNTHETIC MAGICAL GIRLS ARE "FAKE"...
...THEN IF I WIPE OUT HUMANITY, WE'LL BE THE NEW HUMANS!

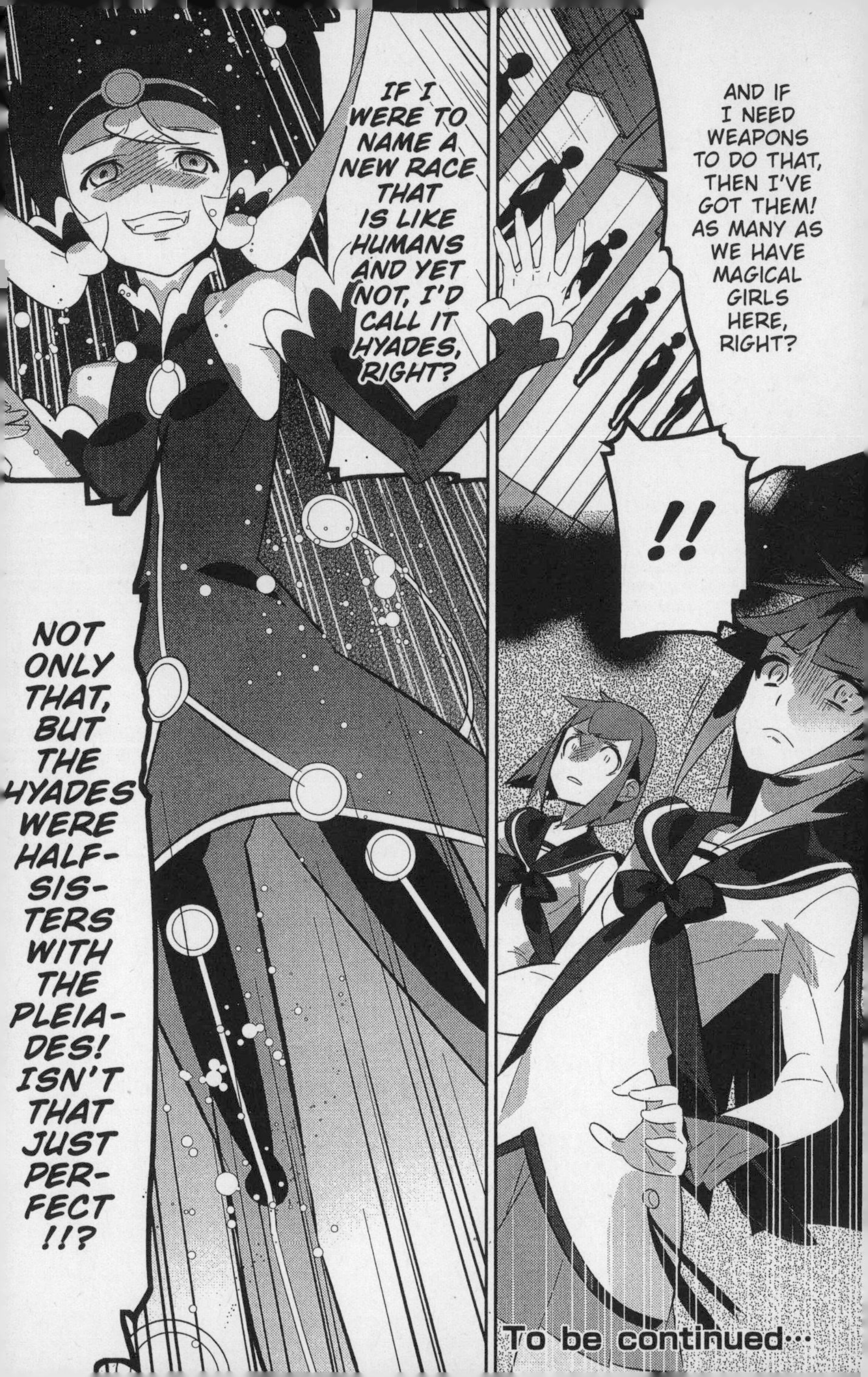
AND IF I NEED WEAPONS TO DO THAT, THEN I'VE GOT THEM! AS MANY AS WE HAVE MAGICAL GIRLS HERE, RIGHT?
!!
To be continued...
IF I WERE TO NAME A NEW RACE THAT IS LIKE HUMANS AND YET NOT, I'D CALL IT HYADES, RIGHT?
NOT ONLY THAT, BUT THE HYADES WERE HALF-SIS-TERS WITH THE PLEIA-DES! ISN'T THAT JUST PER-FECT!!?

Witch Field Guide

Saki Witch

The direction for this one was,
"Make it like the Nebra Sky Disk."

Its attributes will be
revealed in the next book.

EVERYBODY'S☆MAGICA CLUB

With MASAKI HIRAMATSU

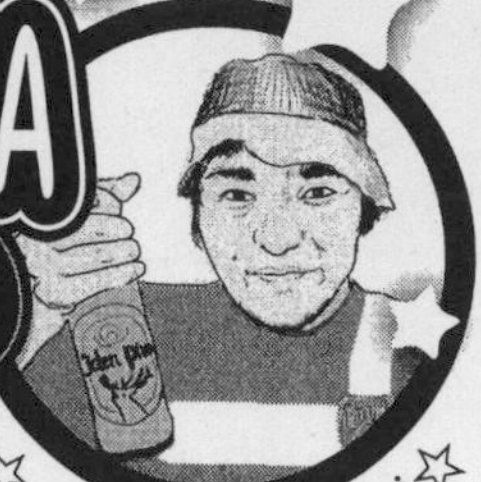

☆Masaki Hiramatsu-sensei☆
Art by: Marina☆Magica-san

THE STORY WRITER, MASAKI HIRAMATSU-SENSEI, ANSWERS THESE QUESTIONS AND THOSE QUESTIONS FROM GOOD BOYS AND GIRLS!

Q1 *CIAO, HIRAMACCI! I'M SENDING A LIKENESS OF YOU FROM SERBIA! I'M IN THE MIDDLE OF A MOVE AND HAVE BEEN SUPER BUSY, BUT I DREW IT ANYWAY!*
(MARINA & MILOS☆MAGICA-SAN)

HIRAMACCHI: CIAO, MARINA & MILOS! AH, IF I ONLY COULD, I'D RUSH OFF TO SERBIA, DRINK BEER, AND MAKE MY APOLOGIES TO YOU! BUT... THE MONEY TO TRAVEL...(CRIES). MAYBE I SHOULD GET AN ADVANCE FROM MY PUBLISHER AND JUST SET FORTH ON THE JOURNEY JUST LIKE THE GREAT MANGA ARTIST, SHOTARO ISHONOMORI, DID! ...YES, MY HEART IS ALREADY THERE IN SERBIA! SRBIJO!! SRBIJO!!

Q2 *CIAO, HIRAMACCHI! SO WHEN EXACTLY DID NIKO MANAGE TO SUBSTITUTE A DOLL FOR KAZUMI? AND YOU MADE A WITCH BITE MY HEAD OFF IN HERE!*
(MIRAI☆MAGICA-SAN)

HIRAMACCHI: CIAO, MIRAI! WAIT, DIDN'T I JUST SEE SAKI AND KAORU OVER THERE, WORKING THEMSELVES UP TO A HOT, PASSIONATE KISS?

MIRAI: EH? WHERE? WHERE? EVERYTHING'S SO BRIGHT!

HIRAMACCHI: GOTCHA!

Q3 *CIAO, HIRAMACCHI! OVER THE COURSE OF HOW MANY DAYS DOES THE ENTIRE STORY OF KAZUMI TAKE PLACE? IT SEEMS LIKE A VERY SHORT TIME.*
(TSUJITSU☆MAGICA-SAN)

HIRAMACCHI: CIAO! ACTUALLY, CHAPTERS TWO AND THREE, THREE AND FOUR, AND SIX AND SEVEN ARE EACH SET ABOUT A WEEK APART. IT'S EVEN IN THE OVERALL PLOT OF THE STORY (INSIDE MY HEAD). HUH? YOU'RE SAYING THAT ISN'T RIGHT? WELL, LET ME TELL YOU, I DON'T LIKE FINDING DEFECTS IN MY WORK! I WILL NEVER ADMIT...THAT I MADE MISTAKES IN THE TIMELINE OF MY STORY!

Q4 *CIAO, HIRAMACCHI! CAN A GUY MAKE THE SAME KIND OF CONTRACT THAT MAKES MAGICAL GIRLS?*
(SEIKO☆MAGICA-SAN)

HIRAMACCHI: CIAO, SEIKO-SAN! WAIT A SECOND! AREN'T YOU SEIKO YOSHIDA-SAN? THE VOICE BEHIND KYOUSUKE KAMIJOU-KUN!? WELL, I CAN SYMPATHIZE WITH A GUY WHO WANTS TO TRANSFORM AND USE TIRO-MAGIC AND THINGS LIKE THAT! BUT WE'RE TALKING ABOUT MAGICAL *GIRLS*, SO THERE'S NO WAY THAT A GUY COULD BECOME ONE... →DING-DING!← NO, WAIT. THEY CAN! THEY SURE CAN!!

SECOND EDITOR K-SHI: EH? HOW EXACTLY? IF YOU LOOK AT WHAT WAS ESTABLISHED IN THE ANIME, THAT GOES AGAINST THE RULES.

HIRAMACCHI: YEAH, I KNOW...BUT HERE IS HOW A MAN—OR RATHER, HOW KYOUSUKE—CAN BECOME A MAGICAL GIRL! ①GET A CLINGY GIRL TO FALL IN LOVE WITH YOU! ②NOW, WHEN SHE ASKS YOU TO BE HER BOYFRIEND, YOU TURN HER DOWN AND SAY, "LET'S JUST BE FRIENDS." ③YOU INTRODUCE HER TO A PARTICULAR ALIEN CREATURE. ④FOR THE WISH THAT FINALIZES HER CONTRACT, THE GIRL WILL SAY, "I REFUSE TO LET ANY OTHER WOMAN HAVE HIM, SO AS MY WISH, I WANT YOU TO TURN KAMIJOU-KUN INTO A GIRL! ⑤SO NOW THAT KYOUSUKE IS A GIRL, HE'S FREE TO MAKE HIS/HER OWN CONTRACT! WHAT DO YOU SAY THAT TO THAT, K-SAN!?

EDITOR K-SHI: YOU KNOW, I THINK YOU'VE GOT SOME KIND OF GRUDGE AGAINST THIS KYOUSUKE GUY.

HIRAMACCHI: NOT IN THE SLIGHTEST! WHO IN THE WORLD COULD HOLD A GRUDGE AGAINST THAT TALENTLESS, CRAP-FOR-BRAINS, FRIENDLESS CREEP...? UM...ANYWAY, HANG IN THERE, KYOUSUKE! IF YOU ONLY BELIEVE, YOU TOO CAN SOMEDAY BECOME A MAGICAL GIRL! CHICHIN BUCKET PURIN!

THIS ENDS EVERYBODY'S☆MAGICA CLUB! NEXT TIME, THIS PAGE WILL INCLUDE HIRAMACCHI'S PERSONAL, HEARTFELT THANKS TO ALL OF YOU READERS IN A SPECIAL FAREWELL☆MAGICA CLUB! BE SURE NOT TO MISS IT!

Background by: Milos☆Magica-san

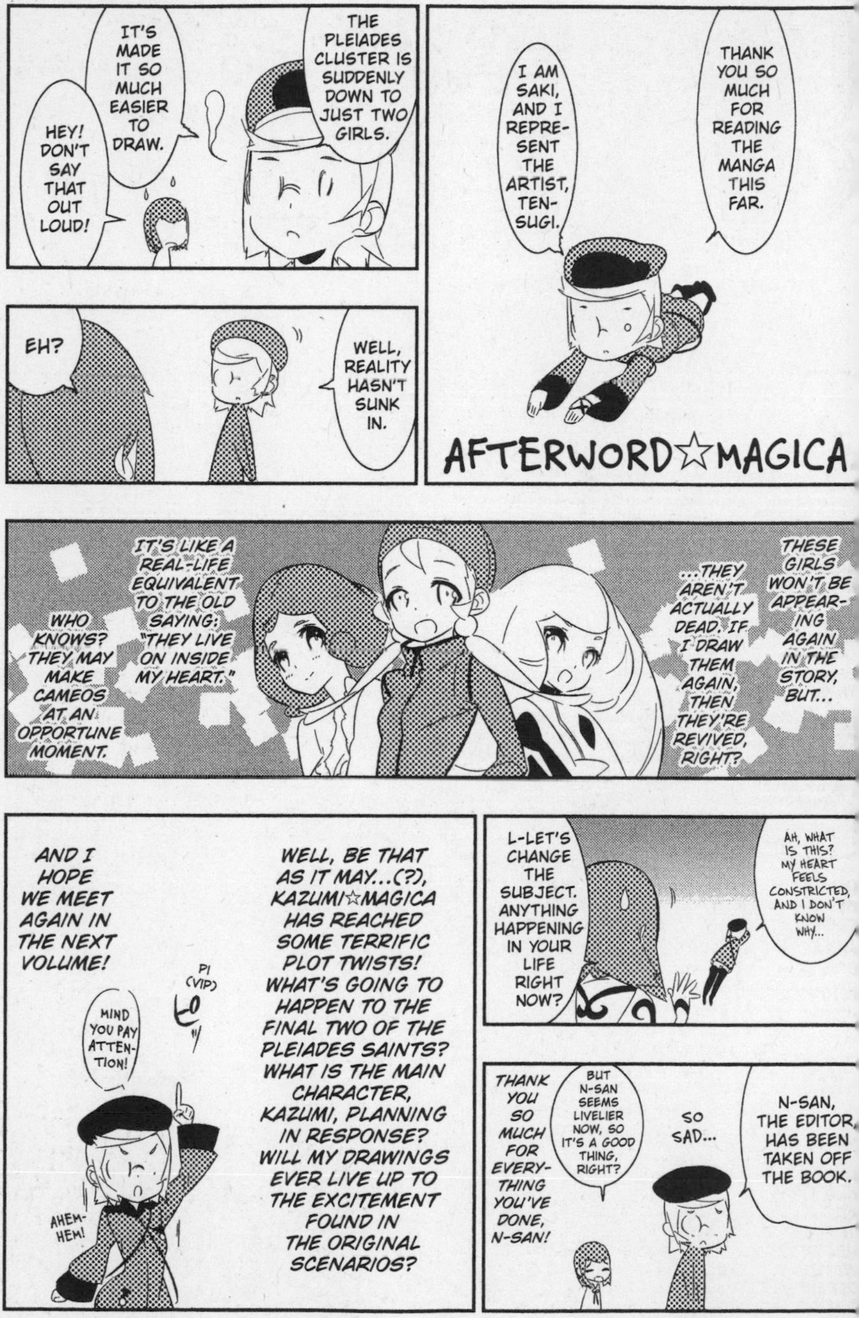
THANK YOU SO MUCH FOR READING THE MANGA THIS FAR.
I AM SAKI, AND I REPRESENT THE ARTIST, TENSUGI.
AFTERWORD☆MAGICA
THE PLEIADES CLUSTER IS SUDDENLY DOWN TO JUST TWO GIRLS.
IT'S MADE IT SO MUCH EASIER TO DRAW.
HEY! DON'T SAY THAT OUT LOUD!
WELL, REALITY HASN'T SUNK IN.
EH?
THESE GIRLS WON'T BE APPEARING AGAIN IN THE STORY, BUT...
...THEY AREN'T ACTUALLY DEAD. IF I DRAW THEM AGAIN, THEN THEY'RE REVIVED, RIGHT?
IT'S LIKE A REAL-LIFE EQUIVALENT TO THE OLD SAYING: "THEY LIVE ON INSIDE MY HEART."
WHO KNOWS? THEY MAY MAKE CAMEOS AT AN OPPORTUNE MOMENT.
AH, WHAT IS THIS? MY HEART FEELS CONSTRICTED, AND I DON'T KNOW WHY...
L-LET'S CHANGE THE SUBJECT. ANYTHING HAPPENING IN YOUR LIFE RIGHT NOW?
N-SAN, THE EDITOR, HAS BEEN TAKEN OFF THE BOOK.
SO SAD...
BUT N-SAN SEEMS LIVELIER NOW, SO IT'S A GOOD THING, RIGHT?
THANK YOU SO MUCH FOR EVERYTHING YOU'VE DONE, N-SAN!
WELL, BE THAT AS IT MAY...(?), KAZUMI☆MAGICA HAS REACHED SOME TERRIFIC PLOT TWISTS! WHAT'S GOING TO HAPPEN TO THE FINAL TWO OF THE PLEIADES SAINTS? WHAT IS THE MAIN CHARACTER, KAZUMI, PLANNING IN RESPONSE? WILL MY DRAWINGS EVER LIVE UP TO THE EXCITEMENT FOUND IN THE ORIGINAL SCENARIOS?
PI (VIP)
MIND YOU PAY ATTENTION!
AHEM-HEM!
AND I HOPE WE MEET AGAIN IN THE NEXT VOLUME!

PUELLA MAGI

KAZUMI★MAGICA

The innocent malice

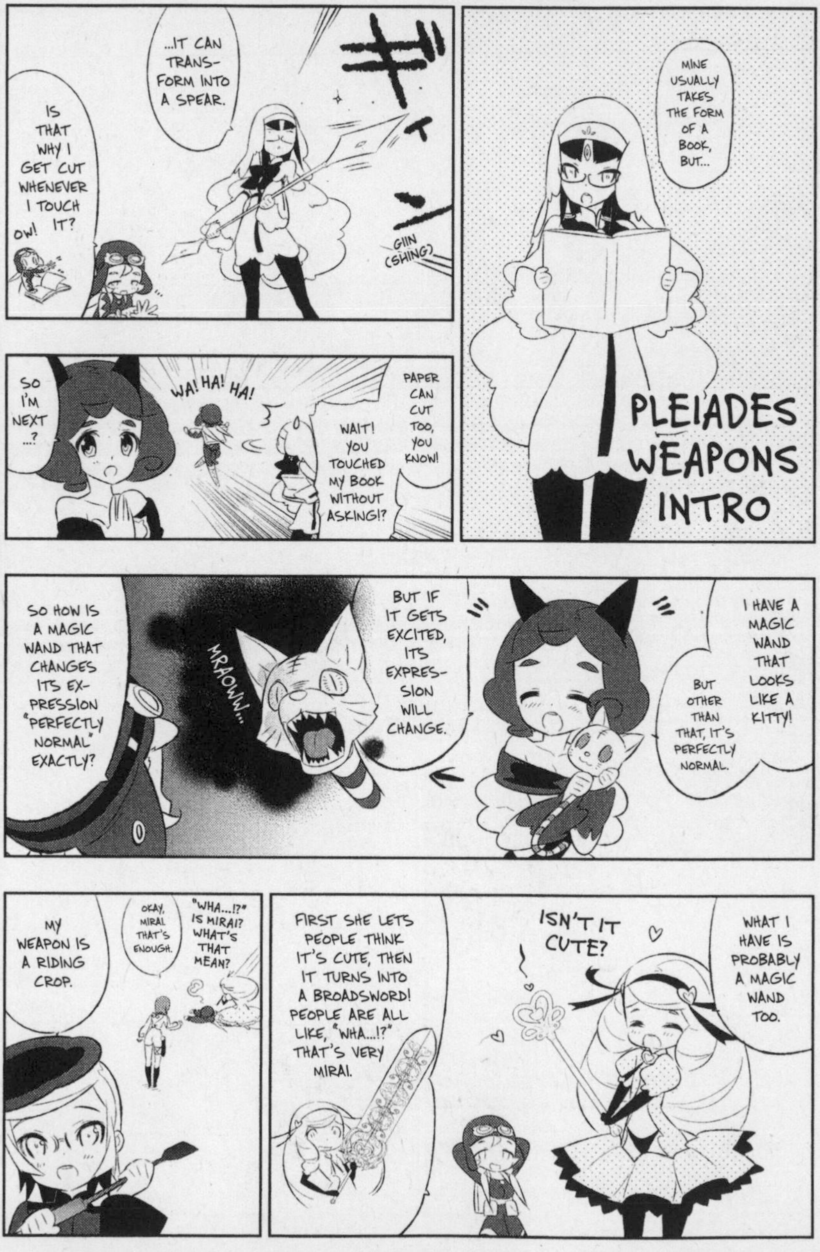
PLEIADES WEAPONS INTRO
MINE USUALLY TAKES THE FORM OF A BOOK, BUT...
...IT CAN TRANS-FORM INTO A SPEAR.
GIIN (SHING)
IS THAT WHY I GET CUT WHENEVER I TOUCH IT?
OW!
PAPER CAN CUT TOO, YOU KNOW!
WAIT! YOU TOUCHED MY BOOK WITHOUT ASKING!?
WA! HA! HA!
SO I'M NEXT ...?
I HAVE A MAGIC WAND THAT LOOKS LIKE A KITTY!
BUT OTHER THAN THAT, IT'S PERFECTLY NORMAL.
BUT IF IT GETS EXCITED, ITS EXPRES-SION WILL CHANGE.
MRAOWW...
SO HOW IS A MAGIC WAND THAT CHANGES ITS EX-PRESSION "PERFECTLY NORMAL" EXACTLY?
WHAT I HAVE IS PROBABLY A MAGIC WAND TOO.
ISN'T IT CUTE?
FIRST SHE LETS PEOPLE THINK IT'S CUTE, THEN IT TURNS INTO A BROADSWORD! PEOPLE ARE ALL LIKE, "WHA...!?" THAT'S VERY MIRAI.
"WHA...!?" IS MIRAI? WHAT'S THAT MEAN?
OKAY, MIRAI THAT'S ENOUGH.
MY WEAPON IS A RIDING CROP.

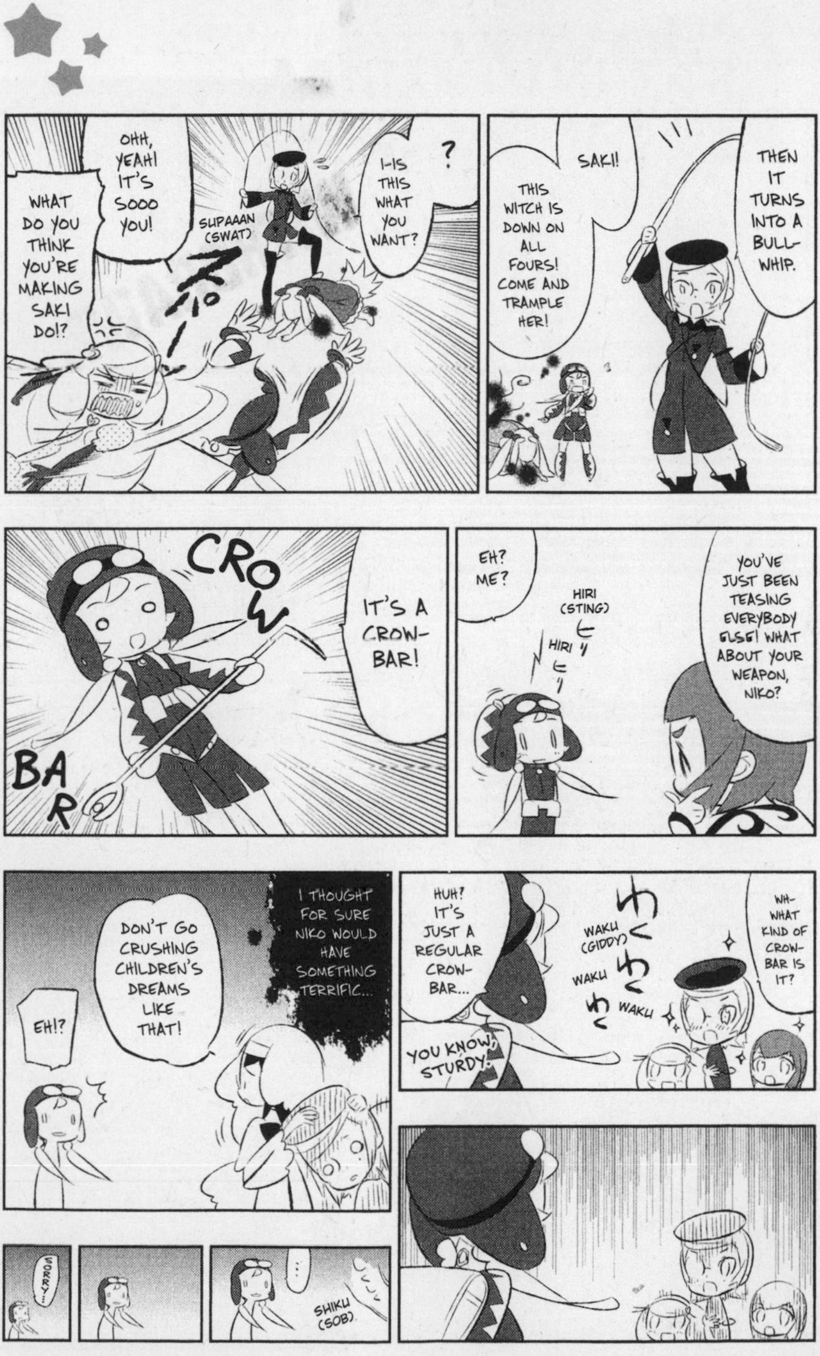
THEN IT TURNS INTO A BULLWHIP.
SAKI!
THIS WITCH IS DOWN ON ALL FOURS! COME AND TRAMPLE HER!
I-IS THIS WHAT YOU WANT?
?
OHH, YEAH! IT'S SOOO YOU!
SUPAAAN (SWAT)
WHAT DO YOU THINK YOU'RE MAKING SAKI DO!?
YOU'VE JUST BEEN TEASING EVERYBODY ELSE! WHAT ABOUT YOUR WEAPON, NIKO?
HIRI (STING)
HIRI
EH? ME?
IT'S A CROWBAR!
CROW
BAR
WH-WHAT KIND OF CROWBAR IS IT?
WAKU (GIDDY)
WAKU
WAKU
HUH? IT'S JUST A REGULAR CROWBAR...
YOU KNOW, STURDY.
I THOUGHT FOR SURE NIKO WOULD HAVE SOMETHING TERRIFIC...
DON'T GO CRUSHING CHILDREN'S DREAMS LIKE THAT!
EH!?
...
SHIKU (SOB)
SORRY...

PUELLA MAGI
KAZUMI☆MAGICA
~The innocent malice~ ④

MAGICA QUARTET
MASAKI HIRAMATSU
TAKASHI TENSUGI

Translation: William Flanagan • Lettering: Abigail Blackman

MAHO SHOJO KAZUMI ☆ MAGICA ~The innocent malice~ vol. 4
© Magica Quartet / Aniplex, Madoka Partners, MBS. All rights reserved. First published in Japan in 2012 by HOUBUNSHA CO., LTD, Tokyo. English translation rights in United States, Canada, and United Kingdom arranged with HOUBUNSHA CO., LTD. through Tuttle-Mori Agency, Inc., Tokyo.

Translation © 2014 by Hachette Book Group, Inc.

Yen Press
Hachette Book Group
237 Park Avenue, New York, NY 10017

www.HachetteBookGroup.com
www.YenPress.com

Yen Press is an imprint of Hachette Book Group, Inc. The Yen Press name and logo are trademarks of Hachette Book Group, Inc.

First Yen Press Edition: February 2014

ISBN: 978-0-316-25427-4

10 9 8 7 6 5 4 3 2 1

BVG

Printed in the United States of America